HOPKINS VARIATIONS

Standing round a Waterfall

BY THE GATE OF THE SACRED
Woodcut by Robert F. McGovern

HOPKINS VARIATIONS

Standing round a Waterfall

JOAQUIN KUHN

AND

JOSEPH J. FEENEY, S.J.

EDITORS

SAINT JOSEPH'S UNIVERSITY PRESS

PHILADELPHIA

AND

FORDHAM UNIVERSITY PRESS

NEW YORK

Copyright © 2002 by Saint Joseph's University Press.

All rights reserved.

No part of this book may be used or reproduced in any manner whatsoever
without written permission.

LIBRARY OF CONGRESS CATALOGING-IN-PUBLICATION DATA

Kuhn, Joaquin, and Feeney, Joseph J., S.J.
Hopkins Variations: Standing round a Waterfall
p. cm.
Includes bibliographical references.
ISBN 0-916101-39-8
1. Hopkins, Gerard Manley, 1844-1889—Criticism and
interpretation. 2. Hopkins, Gerard Manley, 1844-1889—
Appreciation. I. Kuhn, Joaquin. II. Feeney, Joseph J.
PR4803.H44 Z6496 2002
821'.8--dc21
2002004170

Co-published by:

SAINT JOSEPH'S UNIVERSITY PRESS
5600 City Avenue
Philadelphia, Pennsylvania 19131-1395
www.sju.edu/sjupress/

AND

FORDHAM UNIVERSITY PRESS
Canisius Hall, University Box L
Bronx, New York 10458-5172
www.fordham.edu/fordhampress/

Members of the Association of Jesuit University Presses

The rainbow shines, but only in the thought
Of him that looks. Yet not in that alone,
For who makes rainbows by invention?
And many standing round a waterfall
See one bow each, yet not the same to all,
But each a hand's breadth further than the next.
The sun on falling waters writes the text
Which yet is in the eye or in the thought.

'It was a hard thing to undo this knot'
Wales, August 1864

FOR

NORMAN H. MACKENZIE

CONTENTS

PHYSICAL RESPONSES

INTELLECTUAL RESPONSES

PILGRIMAGE TO A TEXT

DRAMATIZING THE TEXT

PERSONAL RESPONSES

GODLY RESPONSES

Drawn in by Hopkins

ON IMAGES AND BEGINNINGS

Music and a waterfall: the book's title-images are vivid and acute. The waterfall—from Hopkins' early poem "'It was a hard thing'"—begets a third image, a rainbow made by the sun hitting the spray. Such images well fit Gerard Hopkins who so deeply prized beauty in art and nature. A fourth image also fits: the people watching the rainbow—the "many standing round a waterfall" who "see one bow each, yet not the same to all"—reflect Hopkins' interest in the multiple perspectives of human perception. These four images—music, waterfall, rainbow, watchers—together epitomize this book of fifty-five reader-responses to Hopkins. His poetry here is both waterfall and rainbow, and the readers are at once an orchestra playing variations on a shared melody yet also fifty-five individuals each seeing the rainbow from a different perspective.

Hopkins Variations began as a twenty-fifth-anniversary volume of *The Hopkins Quarterly*, a journal devoted to the poet and his circle. To celebrate the anniversary, we, the co-editors, asked twenty-nine Hopkins scholars from eight countries to write highly personal essays on either "How I Came to Be a Hopkins Scholar" or "Why Hopkins Matters to Me." The writers' enthusiasm was palpable, and the volume won praise because the essays were so personal, so human, so lively. Struck by its success, Joaquin Kuhn and I then planned a longer, more varied tribute to Hopkins from even broader perspectives. Our invitations were well received, many of the original essays were revised, and *Hopkins Variations* now offers fifty-five responses from poets, actors, translators, scholars, graduate students, a composer, a novelist, a philosopher, a theologian, and an artist. These women and men write from thirteen countries on three continents (Australia might count as a fourth), and they see Hopkins as healer, wordlover, birdlover, musician, truthteller, poetic influence, naturalist, dream-figure, creative theologian, friend, Jesuit, dialoguist with the Jewish midrash, religious teacher, swimmer, carousel-rider, articulator of self, teacher of feminism, and hope-giver for Communism-laden Poles. But above all they see him as a wordloving, worldloving poet grand in sound, language, form, rhythm, and image, with a density hard as granite and a delicacy soft as the spray of a waterfall.

Joseph J. Feeney, S.J.
Philadelphia

When he was nineteen, Hopkins wrote an extended entry on "horn" in words that cannily foreshadow just about everything that he was ever to write, and just about everything that others were to write about him. "The various lights under which a horn may be looked at have given rise to a vast number of words in language." This is only the third entry in the published form of his journals, and he has already touched the nerve of what will preoccupy him as poet, philologist, human, philosopher, priest, through his short life, and what will preoccupy his readers and interpreters for the indeterminable future in generating on their own, about Hopkins, "a vast number of words in language." The interplay between word and object, as well as between mind and word, is nonprejudicially, perhaps even wryly, commented on. Hopkins is here penetratingly attentive to reality as he perceives it, yet he does not put a real material object to the front in this passage. There is no actual, singular horn, although the sentence suggests it. The horn is in the mind. Nor is the word "horn" alone, for at least thirty-nine real or fanciful cognates flow by the reader's eyes as in a Joycean stream. The effect of play and display is impressionistic, a succession of soundalikes which evoke a succession of lookalikes. Yet the tentativeness of the relations and relationships does not force a conclusion or even a meaning. Hopkins follows the opening sentence with what can be taken as an attempt cumulatively to delineate an archetype, but without hard hope of success. "It may be regarded as a projection, a climax, a badge of strength, power or vigour, a tapering body, a spiral, a wavy object, a bow, a vessel to hold withal or to drink from, a smooth hard material not brittle, stony, metallic or wooden, something sprouting up, something to thrust or push with, a sign of honour or pride, an instrument of music, etc." A modern reader will doubtless add phallic and microbiological and even galactic associations to the primitive shape, curve, spiral of "horn" and to the wordsounds which succeed each other in a shimmering sequence of "various lights."

One can substitute for "a horn" in the original sentence "a windhover," "a shipwreck," "a starlight night" and so forth, and acknowledge that one may be talking about the poem itself, in which the various lights are the figures, tropes, sounds, meter, rhythm, syntax, grammar which in combination constitute the poem. Hopkins' poems will bear such stress. Or, complementarily, the "various lights" may be the minds of the illimitable throng of readers of the poem. When a poem subsists on its own through aesthetic coherence—instresses its own inscape—it becomes like an object in the landscape of its home language, recognizably natural to a variety of people who will necessarily read it in various ways, as it passes into the layers of its language. Like some folk tunes, it will seem to be naturally there. If "inscape" means anything, it means the autonomous intelligibility of an individual person or thing or landscape—the hermeneutics of nature and natural objects—and Hopkins' poems famously aspire to be inscapes.

The-thing or the-word-for-the-thing? "a horn" or "horn"? "The various lights under which a horn may be looked at . . ." Despite the apparent disjunction, there is no need to choose one or the other. Hopkins, deliberately or not, accepts the subjective and therefore distinctive nature of human knowledge. He does not set out to solve a philosophical problem. He sets out to catch a cornucopia of subliminal apparitions and to name them with sounds that fit. Because this journal entry is a meditation on a word in its relation to an organic form, it has very limited logical content. If rational flow and logical content were engaged to form a conscious structure of words, a different "horn"—actually a poem—would probably come into being. Yet the journal entry hints at wholeness. When, and to what extent, does even this list become an object in its own right? Is a poem the sum of its words, or a whole that is greater than the sum of its words?

Variation in the form of semantic series occurs strikingly in the Litany of the Blessed Virgin, one of the most Hopkinsian parts of the extended Catholic liturgy. Here are epithets declaimed antiphonally to a repetitive refrain, whose rhetorical resemblance is apparent enough to the litany Hopkins rings out under "horn." Among the titular-epithets are several which work on the mind at more than one level:

> Mirror of justice,
> Seat of wisdom,
> Cause of our joy,
> Spiritual vessel,
> Vessel of honor,
> Singular vessel of devotion,
> Mystical rose,
> Tower of David,
> Tower of ivory,
> House of gold,
> Ark of the covenant,
> Gate of heaven,
> Morning star.

Compare, for effect:

> a projection,
> a climax,
> a badge of strength,
> power or vigour,
> a tapering body,
> a spiral,
> a wavy object,
> a bow,
> a vessel to hold withal or to drink from,
> a smooth hard material not brittle, stony, metallic or
>   wooden,
> something sprouting up,
> something to thrust or push with,
> a sign of honour or pride,
> an instrument of music.

The technique is primitive and noncommittal. It verges on scientific neutral but is full of hint and implication. It "says" nothing, but how effectively does it say without saying!

Language and music may be usefully distinguished in these

terms: language is sound with specific meaning, and music is sound without specific meaning. With language, if communication of a complete idea is the norm—in the standard relationship of subject and predicate—then isolated words, disconnected words, are not really language as such; they are heard as latent subjects but not as real grammatical subjects. Accordingly, a dictionary has meanings, but not meaning. Given Hopkins' penchant for making lists, both in his prose and in his poetry, what is really a subtler form of language begins to take shape. Meaning, such as it is, is aggregative from the words chosen and their tesselated arrangement. I think that this is a borderline area between language and music. Such use of words has the strength of conceptualization and reference that language involves, but it adds associative tones and unique forms of crescendo, decrescendo, climax, dynamic variation, tempo and especially ritardando and rubato that music deploys. This artistic device is most obvious in lists, i.e., semantic series (which can be distinguished into spatial and temporal forms), but once the confident poet trusts himself, he can work poetic wonders, as Hopkins goes straightaway to, by dislocated syntax, and he can achieve the effect of polyphony by dissociating a single or predominant meaning of a word from its salient sound. One sound has several latent meanings. To write poetry like this is necessarily to slow poetry down, to make repeated readings necessary for the harmonies and timbres to be recognized. For the reader, this is not necessarily an unpleasant experience: one looks up a basic word in the dictionary and sees there in one place what is gathered and arranged under the rubric of a single sound conventionalized into spelling. The presentation of a dictionary entry is simultaneously spatial, logical and historical—paradoxes and even contradictions that the reader sees there may be enlightening and even amusing, but the effect is not jarring.

In the summer of 1864, ten months after the entry on "horn," when Hopkins the philologist was temporarily supplanted by Hopkins the phenomenologist and epistemologist, he wrote a ten-line poem beginning "It was a hard thing to undo this knot," which provides the subtitle for the present volume.

The poem in substance begins only with the second line, "The rainbow shines, but only in the thought / Of him that looks." Vivid phrases and eloquent simplicity more than compensate for the lack of conclusion. Hopkins loosens the knot but does not wholly undo it. This poem of reflective observation stops far short of definition or statement. If he were too scientific, the aesthetic achievement would suffer.

The fifty-five essayists who have made this book were invited to describe their links to Hopkins, to share with readers not just academic and scholarly responses to Hopkins, but how his person and his words have made a difference in their lives. Each contributor to this book has a self-defined perspective on our common subject. So here we are, fifty-five of us standing round a waterfall. If we as essayists have been true to ourselves in what we wrote, as Hopkins was true to himself in what he wrote, then none of us will have made "rainbows by invention." So what if there is "one bow each, yet not the same to all"? There is uncommon diversity in the body of Hopkins' readers, which is reflected in this volume, but I doubt that the effect on the reader of this collection will be cacophony. Not quite euphony, and certainly not monophony. Nor white noise canceling out each other. Here, the report of one enriches the report of another, and even the table of contents becomes a semantic series of its own. Every rainbow displays a range of colors for every observer, no matter where that observer stands. Transparent, translucent and luminous are the colors of a rainbow—as are the personal reflections here recorded.

Joaquin Kuhn
Toronto

MATCHING CREATIVITIES

"... things counter, original ..."

"Incertus" as GMH as Seamus Heaney

John Dryden talks about having been "transfused" by his reading of certain poets, and his choice of word will certainly appeal to readers of Hopkins. One of the pieces I'm sending was the result of my own transfusion when I was an undergraduate at Queen's University, Belfast, in the late fifties and early sixties. It appeared in a student magazine called *Q* and was one of my first poems to be published. I called myself "Incertus" in those days, but the pseudonym could equally well have been GMH. And even if the Hopkins style has been absorbed, the trace of that early reading will never disappear. "Seeing the Sick" is a recent poem now published in my new *Electric Light*, but it will surely find itself at home in *Hopkins Variations*.

OCTOBER THOUGHT

Starling thatch watches, and sudden swallow
Straight breaks to its mud-nest, home-rest rafter,
Up through dry, dust-drunk cobwebs like laughter
Flitting the roof of black-oak, bog-sod and rods of willow;
And twittering flirtings in the eaves as sparrows quarrel.
Haystalks, straw-broken and strewn,
Hide, hear mice mealing the grain, gnawing strong
The iron-bound, swollen and ripe-round corn-barrel.

Minute movement millionfold whispers twilight
Under heaven-hue, plum-blue and gorse-pricked with gold,
And under the knuckle-gnarl of branches, poking the night,
Comes the trickling tinkle of bells well in the fold.

Aged 19

SEEING THE SICK

Anointed and all, my father did remind me
Of Hopkins's Felix Randal.
                And then he grew
(As he would have said himself) "wee in his clothes"—
Spectral, a relict—
              And seemed to have grown so
Because of something spectral he'd thrown off,
The unbelonging, moorland part of him
That was Northumbrian, the bounden he
Who had walked the streets of Hexham at eighteen
With his stick and task of bringing home the dead
Body of his uncle by cattle-ferry.

Ghost-drover from the start. Brandisher of keel.

None of your fettled and bright battering sandal.

Cowdung coloured tweed and ox-blood leather.

•

The assessor's eye, the tally-keeper's head
For what beasts were on what land in what year . . .
But then that went as well. And all precaution.
His smile a summer half-door opening out
And opening in. A reprieving light.
For which the tendered morphine had our thanks.

"BY THE GATE OF THE SACRED"

As a visual artist I have found in the poetry of Gerard Manley Hopkins a wellspring of energy. I am convinced that his spirit can be equally enlivening to all manner of artistic creativity. I remember back to 1989 when there was a great diversity in the celebration of the centenary of his death. One such event was held at St. Malachy Church in North Philadelphia. The arms of celebration opened wide with a reading of Hopkins poems by actor Michael Toner, the music of Henry Purcell, a Hopkins favorite, performed by a brass ensemble from historic Christ Church and a lecture "Remembering Gerard Manley Hopkins" by Rev. Joseph Feeney, S.J. I was commissioned to produce a woodcut representation of this great poet to be used on the invitation and program covers, and prints from the limited edition were given to key participants in the event. (It is the present book's frontispiece.) The poet and pastor, Rev. John McNamee, hosted this gathering in an inner-city parish in Philadelphia. This in itself was a reminder that Hopkins had served as a priest in the large industrial cities of Glasgow, Liverpool and Manchester (Bedford Leigh). The commission granted me all the necessary freedom of size and condition of the image. It came like a joy which time had made ripe.

My first encounter with Hopkins' poetry and ideas took place in my student days in the mid-fifties. I recall how my efforts at creativity were enlivened by the radiance of his words. His poetic structures and concept of "inscape" challenged my own processing of life's experiences. In short, I was well taken by the phenomenon of the man, his ideas and his poetic works. I would find myself inspired by his spirit as I sat before landscapes I wished to paint or as I applied dappled brush strokes to abstract designs. However, prior to 1989 I cannot recall a desire to portray him. My work over the years experimented with different approaches and materials for making art—realistic, abstract, expressionistic and so on. But by 1989 my working approach, providentially, was well prepared for this challenge. I had already employed photographic sources for my paintings and representations of long deceased family members and even modern saints, e.g., St. John Neumann, John Henry Newman, St. Thérèse of Lisieux, and for revisiting all but forgotten locations and residences of my childhood. I consider photography a great art form but, for me, it is also a source. The photograph is not for copying but is another voice in a visual dialogue. Bringing its information to my mind activates memories, tools and materials and if I am lucky, this information mingles with that from other photographs thereby enriching the dialogue. Through these different photographic moments, each with its captured light, there emerges a new compressed moment. Like a sleuth I was armed with a magnifying glass to detect the clues of the larger event that pivots in the frozen instant. Is this a subjective adventure? Yes, it is.

After considering all the photographs of Hopkins that were available to me, the one that anchored the visual enquiry was the likeness in the Catholic Club of Oxford taken in 1878. For me, all the photographic moments, older or younger, seemed to relate themselves to that image. There in this gathering of more or less individuated men, Gerard stands far to the side looking out. In a way, the others are looking for a constellation to be a part of, while he is like a star that sends light back to the viewer. I reflected that it must have been a difficult moment for Hopkins because he is revealing the right side of his head. In the majority of the available photographs, he is shown from the left. This picture is rare among the mature representations of Hopkins. It may be a kind of hidden side, even a possibly begrudging revelation of self. Perhaps his location in the group arrangement was the luck of the draw; in fact no one seems particularly comfortable. But there Hopkins is, head cocked back to the door frame and eyebrow raised. I lingered long over this phenomenon of sight as if I were poised at the threshold of one of his "inscapes," but in reverse. With the magnifying glass I could catch a degree of activity in his eyes, in contrast to their quietude in other adult images. These eyes exuded a power he may not always have wanted to reveal, a force brewed from turmoil, self-doubt and self-discovery. It was a power that did not fear the darkest chambers of the human mind, somehow visually confirming his powerful and brave spirit. From such a vantage point, God's grandeur and rightness of beauty could be all around the poet. His mind was absorbing both the lightness and darkness of life's experience.

For me the task was only at its beginning. Yes, the little-seen side of Hopkins was in the range of the magnifying glass. Here was something more than the stoic, non-assertive Victorian gentleman. Now I had to be able to gather up this glimpse of the poet and convey the findings to the viewer. I relied on gesture as the apt agent for the task. Gesture is most strong when its depiction has a mental sense of its past, present and potential future state. I hoped that this would come through in the complex unity of the separate factors: the head, three quarter positioned, tilted back, rising tortoise-like from the collar and cassock while the back of his head rested on the stone arch of the doorway. Yet presiding over all are the eyes holding us in an attitude of discernment. The right eye with its raised brow became the nucleus for the unity of all the actions. Then came the "fun"—the brush drawing, the cutting with knife, chisel and gouge, all playing their part in the communication. It is worth noting that to have a woodcut image print the right way the image has to be cut in reverse. Therefore the awareness of the forms of the gesture was well informed from the right and left. By preparing the cuts from drawings made on acetate, I greatly reduced surprises when the block was printed. For the woodcut I used a smooth block of basswood, known in Europe as linden. Often these trees are planted to commemorate honored poets, teachers and philosophers because the tree grows strong and true toward the light. It was the wood I most wanted to use to remember Hopkins. Proofs were pulled and corrections followed. The finished prints were pulled on fine Japanese rice paper with artist's oil ink. The paper, like the poet, appeared fragile yet was strong—strong enough for all the years to come. If held to the light, it is translucent as the light fills its fibers. The print measures 11" x 18" but appeared on the program cover as 5.5" x 8.5".

The title fell into place when I studied what was happening in the shaping of the representation. The dark unknown was being cut into by the white of the paper. The background was moving up and out, stone texture gave way to air. So there it all could be, the poet, his gesture, the discerning raised eye, with his "inscape," and surely we could be "By the Gate of the Sacred."

HOPKINS AND I

I first encountered the poetry of Gerard Manley Hopkins in a high-school anthology at Creighton Preparatory School in Omaha. I was sixteen, the instructor was probably twenty-six, and neither one of us had the foggiest idea of what "The Windhover" was all about, we just knew it was full of hard words and peculiar stress marks. I was not immediately a fan.

I did, however, fall madly in love with the poetry of Dylan Thomas. I purchased his *Collected Poems* with money I earned as a greenskeeper for the Omaha Parks & Recreation Department, and was sorely put out when I heard that Robert Lowell had said Dylan Thomas was the author of five good poems and no one knew which ones they were. I did, and there were far more than five.

About one-eighth of my bloodline is Welsh, so I fabricated a jocular friendship for the word-drunk Welshman, and since I was then feeling quite a lot like "a windy boy and a bit and the black spit of the chapel fold," Dylan Thomas was my flamboyant hero. I even executed a fairly good pen-and-ink portrait of him that hung over my bed. I have no idea where it came from, but Constantine Fitzgibbon's biography of Dylan Thomas found its way into my family's library, which was then primarily Reader's Digest Condensed Books, and I found myself, in the funk of being eighteen, wholly absorbed in the young Dylan's wild and reckless life, wanting to flare and blaze as he did, deciding that his wife's name, Caitlin, was probably the most beautiful on earth, and discovering that one of Dylan Thomas' foremost influences was Reverend Gerard Manley Hopkins, S.J.

My fascination with Thomas forced me to give Hopkins another try in college, and I felt an affinity I hadn't in high school. Difficulty was no longer so off-putting for one thing, his Ignatian theology was no longer something I was ignorant of, the chromatic concreteness of his imagery was just what I was trying to add to my prose, and I was newly enlisted in the cult of those who find delight in etymologies and woefully little-used words. Wanwood, sillion, cumber, throstle. I had trouble fitting them into conversations, and yet my life was richer for hearing them.

We considered five of Hopkins' poems in the freshman English survey at Creighton University, and only one, "The Windhover," in my senior-year course in Modern British and American Poetry. But Hopkins was present enough in my consciousness that when I felt affronted by one of my peers in my junior year I recall writing, "Wert thou my enemy, O thou my friend, how wouldst thou worse, I wonder, than thou dost defeat, thwart me?" The friend never answered, but stayed far away for a while.

At lunch with a Jesuit friend a few years ago, I was approached by Paul Locatelli, S.J., the president of Santa Clara University, who said, "I have an offer you can't refuse." We had dinner and he described a professorship in creative writing that would be funded with an endowed chair. An attractive offer, but I was gainfully employed elsewhere and wasn't sure I ought to change jobs, so I secretly prayed to Father Hopkins about whether I ought to take it or not. The next night I got a call from Father Locatelli asking for my decision about the job, and adding, "We'll call it the Gerard Manley Hopkins chair. Does that mean anything to you?" It did. And I imagined Gerard in heaven, smiling.

Other poets have been important to me—W. B. Yeats, Wallace Stevens, Sylvia Plath, Elizabeth Bishop, John Berryman—but Hopkins has remained my favorite because he, like T.S. Eliot, is not so easily solved. Any interpretation insists on further interpretation. An infinite number of layers seems available for peeling.

What Hopkins did extraordinarily well is imitate in poetry the operations of the mind and spirit at a heightened moment of graced perception. We have all had the experience of a song or a photograph igniting an explosion of tangential feelings and memories that we struggle to contain. Whether through psychological acuity or sheer force and clarity of intellect, Hopkins could find the unifying factor among wildly differing things, and rejoice in their being fathered-forth by God.

Concentrating solely on the poetry, however, is in some way to miss the point, for Gerard Manley Hopkins, the man, seems to me as inspiring as his work. Who among our finest poets has lived as sane and honorable a life? Contrary, kind, opinionated, humorous, prone to depression, ill-at-ease in public, fond of puns, jealous, Hopkins was nevertheless an English gentleman and the opposite of dissolute: an abstemious, disciplined, hardworking teacher, a wise and meditative homilist, an affectionate son and brother and friend, a good priest. Even his most quarrelsome biographers portray a life of fidelity, integrity, and service, with a Christ-like devotion to his calling. He was a gift to our time, if not to his own. Praise him.

Afterthoughts: GMH

Although I'm honored by your invitation, and deeply sympathetic to your cause (in this philistine age), I feel that I've said, in words, all I have to say about music. And about words-&-music. When Harold Bloom recently announced that the best way to know a poem is to memorize it, I must add: or set it to music. There's little a composer can say about his music that the music itself can't say better.

Yes, there are certain poets (among the odd two hundred I've used) that I'll never return to. But GMH is one I revert to over and over again. Beyond those settings you listed in your letter, there is the unpublished "Felix Randal" (1946). And two others from 1994 in a cycle called "Songs of Sadness" for voice, guitar, clarinet and cello: "Strike, Churl" and "Binsey Poplars."

In many of my books I've written of Hopkins, and of my first brush with his verse. *Knowing When to Stop* lists, in the index, several references (which are erroneously under the name "Don Hopkins"). And yes again, I have written a bit about the meaning of "Spring and Fall." I was only 22 when that was composed (on a Monteverdian ground-bass), and couldn't do as well today—mainly because I did it yesterday.

Forgive the brevity of this note. Know that Hopkins continues to speak to me, almost erotically, as doubtless he speaks to you. But I can't translate that speech except through music.

HOPKINS AND I

> It is the blight man was born for,
> It is Margaret you mourn for

were the first lines of Hopkins which really made an impression on me. A boarding student at secondary school, in love with literature, I was touched by the poem and by the sudden, startling, insight it offered into the human condition. So much so that "Spring and Fall" has kept its place, down all the years, among my favourite poems—even as Shelley, Yeats, Dylan Thomas and others including Lorca fell by my wayside.

Initially, mine was an enthusiasm with nowhere to go: Hopkins poems were not on the curriculum for the Leaving Certificate examination in Ireland then (as they have been since), and no follow-up was possible until I reached University.

There, in Maynooth, I was lucky to have Fr. Peter Connolly as a lecturer. He proved an ideal guide in focussing my enthusiasm for literature. Among his own special interests at that stage Peter included Hopkins, and I suspect he had been working toward a book on "the inscape man" (as he called Hopkins in a letter, many years later), who now began to emerge as a landmark in the literary landscape unrolling before me.

The seed had been watered—but it was still in shallow ground. Perhaps I was not mature enough. Though the young can take to some early Hopkins poems, his finest work is for one's mature years, as surely as that of some lesser writers is not. So, much as I admired the poet, he had to yield to other undergraduate enthusiasms and did not make a profound impact during those days—and none at all on my occasional, stumbling efforts to write. A neurotic phase, I think: one when I had a real urge to write, coupled with a paralysing awareness that I had nothing whatever to say. I even remember one particular moment, and the time, the exact place, when it struck me with devastating clarity that I knew nothing about anything. (Some things do not change.) Somehow, that is not a Hopkins time.

So, real involvement with Hopkins' poetry had to wait a few years longer.

In fact, it was an interest in the work of John Berryman which led me back in Hopkins' direction, in the late 60s. Berryman was deeply influenced by the Jesuit poet: the convolutions of style of the American owe a great deal to that of Hopkins, something acknowledged by Berryman himself. He even refers to GMH in a poem from his last collection, *Love and Fame*, published in 1970, two years before his suicide:

> Father Hopkins said the only true literary critic is Christ.
> Let me lie down exhausted, content with that.

"Father Hopkins": I had never thought of the poet in that way. It made him more real as I began to familiarise myself with his poetry, urged on by those who admired him. There were lines like these,

> . . . For Christ plays in ten thousand places,
> Lovely in limbs, and lovely in eyes not his
>   To the Father through the features of men's faces

and these,

> All things counter, original, spare, strange;
>   Whatever is fickle, frecklèd (who knows how?)
>   With swift, slow; sweet, sour; adazzle, dim;
> He fathers-forth whose beauty is past change:
>   Praise him.

Among other excellences these embodied a calm sense of the coherence of things, something I badly needed at the time. There was also a detachment, an authority, and an ease with language which one could find equalled, perhaps, only in George Herbert.

I was studying and teaching some Hopkins when my first

book of poems, *Midland*, took shape in 1972, and the poet Thomas Kinsella shrewdly detected some traces of Berryman "and at bottom, Hopkins" (as he wrote) in it. Now I began to realise the importance which Hopkins had begun to assume for me. From being an acquaintance, he had turned into a friend.

More years flit past, too many alas, but the friendship continued. Cut to 1987, when I was invited to give a poetry reading in Monasterevin. The Committee assured me that it was the first poetry reading ever in that small Kildare town (pop. 2,500) and were surprised at the size of the audience it attracted. In the inevitable pub afterwards, I suggested to Richard O'Rourke and company that they should commemorate the Hopkins link with Monasterevin. After all, he considered the place and its people, including his friends, Miss Cassidy and her sister, Mrs. Wheble, "one of the props and struts of my existence." This was news to the Committee. I can still hear Richard ask, "The connection of who?"—but bravely they decided to have a go, urged on by Fr. Denis O'Sullivan, the genial Parish Priest and great supporter of the arts. So The Hopkins International Summer School came into being and has become an annual event. It celebrates the poet and his interests—art, music, philosophy—as well as his own writing. To our surprise, the School has spread and prospered—and even more, has survived. In the year 2000, the thirteenth Summer School, Monasterevin hosted visitors from twenty-two countries, and the School was described in *The Sunday Tribune* as "one of Europe's most exciting cultural forums."

The town itself can also boast of a permanent fringe fest: a magnificent Hopkins monument in limestone by the great sculptor James McKenna, a Hopkins Lane, a beautiful Hopkins garden leading down to "the burling Barrow brown," and even a pub named The Manley Hopkins.

This kind of enthusiasm does not come from a void: it is fuelled by the energising presence of Hopkins' poetry, an inspiration to us all in our different ways.

There are poets in various languages whose work means a lot to me—Rilke, Machado, Tsvetayeva, Verlaine, Ritsos, some Irish poets—but right now, Hopkins is probably my favourite poet in English (though Patrick Kavanagh comes close). Why so?

I see poetry as an attempt to say something, to master some aspect of human experience and open a door into it, using all the resources of language. Hopkins' convoluted style has excited a lot of attention—but it is the content of his poetry that I value and am nourished by: the depth, the coherence of it; the assumptions behind it. It takes on a universal resonance because it is grounded in an intense feeling for the reality of things. Easy to see why GMH valued the philosophy of Duns Scotus, with its emphasis on the *haecceitas* of reality, its physical intensity. I believe there can be no real poetry without such an awareness, this kind:

> I noticed the smell of the big cedar, not just in passing it but always at a patch of sunlight on the walk a little way off. I found the bark smelt in the sun and not in the shade and I fancied too this held even of the smell it shed in the air.

Such a hold on the real, transubstantiated by Hopkins into poetry, allows the sensuous response to move easily from the physical to the metaphysical:

> Summer ends now; now, barbarous in beauty, the stooks rise
> Around; up above, what wind-walks! what lovely behaviour
> Of silk-sack clouds! has wilder, wilful-wavier
> Meal-drift moulded ever and melted across skies?

One could illustrate the point by opening almost any Hopkins poem at random, not excluding "The Windhover." A thing has to be apprehended as totally itself before it can begin to take on any wider relevance; Hopkins' quasi-mystical sense of God's creation is rooted in a delighted awareness of the glowing reality of the ordinary: of grass, cloud, birds, animals, trees, weeds, the everyday people one meets.

"If the doors of perception were cleansed," said William Blake, "everything would appear as it is, infinite." Few poets could match Hopkins in the cleanness of his perception or in his rejection of anything that might cloud it. He has the necessary humility of the artist, that refusal, as creator, to get in the way of things. Rilke in his ninth Duino elegy writes,

> . . . Perhaps we are here in order to say: house,
> bridge, fountain, gate, pitcher, fruit-tree, window,—
> at most: column, tower? ... But to say them, you must
> understand,
> oh to say them more intensely than the Things
> themselves ever dreamed of existing.

No great ambition, it might seem; and yet more than most people can handle:

> Not of all my eyes see, wandering on the world,
> Is anything a milk to the mind so, so sighs deep
> Poetry to it, as a tree whose boughs break in the sky.

At the end of his life, Cézanne was seen hugging a tree, weeping. Morandi spent his life painting the same few household objects, shaking in the face of their existence so that he cannot even render their precise outline. The world of Beckett and of Giacometti seemed to get smaller and smaller. None of us, not even the great ones, can cope with much: but what little we can, we must do with total intensity, knowing that "Million-fuelèd, nature's bonfire burns on" and that life is full of such glorious waste, most of the time.

Rilke's was a lesson which Hopkins never needed. (Unfortunately, I did—but that's another story.)

As for Hopkins' style: it interests me only as the means he needed to contain the fierceness and complexity of his vision. Virtuosity for its own sake, in any of the arts, holds little appeal for me. In a letter written to Bridges in May 1878, Hopkins says, in exasperated response to the former's criticism of his opaqueness, "Obscurity I do and will try to avoid so far as is consistent with excellences higher than clearness at a first reading." It was a problem he had faced in another letter to Bridges, in the previous November, when he insisted, memorably,

> Plainly if it is possible to express a subtle and recondite thought on a subtle and recondite subject in a subtle and recondite way and with great felicity and perfection, in the end, something must be sacrificed, with so trying a task, in the process, and this may be the being at once, nay perhaps the being without explanation at all, intelligible.

Bravo! How important is this statement, for any understanding of the necessary obscurities of art.

That accepted, and indeed as a corollary, it is what Hopkins has to say which matters and which I find so moving: his struggles in the country of King Lear or of Philoctetes—where Beckett also lived, and Thoreau—"to drive life into a corner, and reduce it to its lowest terms, and . . . publish its meanness to the world; or if it were sublime, to know it by experience, and be able to give a true account of it . . . ." Thoreau's words have a special aptness when applied to Hopkins and the almost desperate integrity of his life and writing. Lately I have come to the opinion that faith is not merely some kind of intellectual assent but a mysterious impulse which finds its truest expression in the tone of one's life.

The world has its fair share of talent. Most Creative Writing teachers, for example, would lay claim to having one or more gifted practitioners in the class—but the literature which matters, which we need, has come from writers who could push through technique into that other space where the truth lurks and where the soul can take a deep breath. I read Hopkins now, not for the brilliance of his writing but to understand life a little better and to accept it a little more: for lines like these,

> . . . Flesh fade, and mortal trash
> Fall to the residuary worm; world's wildfire, leave but ash:
> In a flash, at a trumpet crash,
> I am all at once what Christ is, since he was what I am, and
> This Jack, joke, poor potsherd, patch, matchwood, immortal
> diamond,
> Is immortal diamond.

When I had the honour of being invited by the Jesuits to read a poem at Hopkins' modest grave in Glasnevin, Dublin, on the centenary of his death, June 8, 1989, I finished as follows:

> . . . your steadying gaze has turned inspiration has
> uncovered the audience which you had hidden in
> the future where your mind lived
> people like us who admire your indifference
> your quiet which pierces the empire of noise
> to mould things into themselves
>
> your spirit darts through our human June.

I have no doubt that it will continue to dart through mine.

PHYSICAL MATTERS

" . . . bones and veins in me . . ."

LESLEY HIGGINS

FOLLOWING HOPKINS

I have always wondered what his hands were like: were the fingers long and tapered, graceful in Englishmanish repose, or were they short yet extraordinarily capable, like the rest of him? Could one somehow tell, in a flash, that they were the hands of a priest, a poet, an artist, a prankster? How did they behave, when they held the host aloft at Mass, when they scribbled corrections upon the umpteenth undergraduate exam, when they wrote "our night whelms, whelms, and will end us"? Having spent so many hours deciphering (or not) the written works of Hopkins' hands, I would like to know if the exceptional character of the man, "the forgèd feature" of his intellect and soul, was somehow legible in the palms and fingers. He could feel the impress of God's "finger," or vividly imagine the sacrificial hands and wrists, the "lovescape," of a crucified Christ or a stigmatized Francis; he reckoned too harshly when his God's "poising palms were weighing the worth" of his own abject self. I imagine his own "arch-especial" fingers working away, literally translating heart, mind, and ink into the words and images ("I kiss my hand / To the stars, lovely-asunder") which constitute, for us, his gifts.

Eventfully, happily, Hopkins has been leading me astray since the early 1980s. The adventures began in graduate school. There I was, a first-year doctoral candidate keenly prepared to write the (next) definitive dissertation on George Eliot and Thomas Hardy, when I began the readings for my "Hopkins, Yeats, and Eliot" poetry course. Good-bye ponderous prose fiction; hello a poetic discourse so demanding that I had to know more about how it worked its linguistic thaumaturgy, how it worshipped, how it reawakened the possibilities of English. I simply had to focus on Hopkins' texts, resonant because of a Catholic upbringing and academic training in Victorian literature, but remarkable for their own intellectual and emotional richness. And so I planned a new project, a comparative study of intertextualities among the writings of Pater and Hopkins (the latter had been Pater's student while at Oxford; the connections were startling) and Pater and Eliot (whose critical writings rejected Pater's "aesthetic" appreciations with homophobic hauteur, but whose poetry told another story). But those plans went astray when I discovered the wealth of Hopkins' undergraduate writings, including essays for Pater, housed in Campion Hall, Oxford. Adieu, the "perpetual weaving and unweaving of personality" in *The Waste Land*; I was determined to untangle the threads of Hopkins' Oxford life and prepare the manuscripts for publication. (And, because my supervisor wisely insisted, I also wrote the dissertation on Pater and Hopkins.) Thus began the months of transcribing the twelve "Oxford" notebooks, preparing the annotations, trying to reconstruct, at an *nth* remove, the many discursive threads of his essays and notes. (Writing about the poetry was something that would come much later.) Locating sources and documents by then-contemporaries took me, gladly, to some of the dankest basements in Oxford (the location of choice, it seems, for a college archive or special collection) and allowed me to meet the remarkable, unsung librarians and their assistants who make our scholarship possible.

Following Hopkins has always led me to the diverse company of exceptional people. The pleasure of having my dissertation supervised by Dr. Norman MacKenzie always outweighed the trepidation of having my efforts read by *Dr. Norman MacKenzie*. Whatever I now do best as a teacher, supervisor, or academic adventurer comes from a well-honed understanding of "what Norman would do." His recommendation made it possible for me to visit Campion Hall and inspect the Hopkins collection in its archives. My work there was particularly enabled by the energetic and welcoming Master, Fr. Peter Hackettt, who not only found a place for me in the cool, book-hushed elegance of the Hall's library, but allowed me unparalleled access to the Hopkins collection. It was at his behest that I returned to Campion Hall to re-catalogue the notebooks and manuscripts, photocopy them for future academic use, and organize their preservation through the auspices of the Bodleian Library's manuscript conservation department. In the process of reconstructing the life of Hopkins' manuscripts in the Hall, I learned about the special friendship with Fr. Francis Bacon which helped to sustain Hopkins in the Society; how Fr. Martin D'Arcy, the first master of Campion Hall, brought Hopkins' poetry to the forefront of Oxford's intellectual society in the 1930s (imagine a dinner featuring D'Arcy reading Hopkins, and T.S. Eliot reading Eliot; Auden and Spender were among the fascinated auditors); how Fr. Anthony Bischoff and Norman MacKenzie had laboured to find and protect the papers. (The day that I discovered, in Fr. Bacon's scrapbook, the holograph of Hopkins' final vows and translation of the Chrysostom sermon remains a special highlight of those endeavours.) It was in the midst of the recataloguing project's organized havoc that Robert B. Martin first visited Campion Hall, hoping to consult various papers and "the diaries" (still, in the mid 1980s, more vaguely infamous than widely read; that was only possible with the publication of *Early Poetic Manuscripts and Note-books*). I had already spent several grim days deciphering the personal journals—no, not grim, but oppressed with sadness as Hopkins' pencilled notations became more and more self-reflexive, more self-loathing (to my mind, Canon Liddon has much to answer for). Robert Martin began his work with characteristic and genial zest, but, due to an eyesight problem, found the over-scored handwriting too difficult to read. So we improvised. I read the diaries to him as he took notes, pausing to ask questions or to compare interpretations. In this way "my Hopkins" was tested against the portrait of Hopkins he was beginning to fashion.

Oddly enough, it was Hopkins who introduced me to academic feminism (something that professors at Queen's neglected to do). I was trying to find a way to write about the intensely homosocial, masculinist culture of mid-Victorian Oxford, the privileging of male beauty in Oxonian aesthetics, and wanted to distinguish between uneasy inferences about "homosexuality" in the critical commentaries and the homoerotic yearnings I discerned in Hopkins' writings and Pater's.

Fortunately, my questions coincided with the publication of Eve Kosofsky Sedgwick's first book, *Between Men*. Suddenly, I had the resources of a new vocabulary and intellectual matrix, and a truly groundbreaking theoretical approach to gender, textuality, and sexual difference that I could apply in my research. The 1984 Hopkins conference in Dublin, my first, introduced me to two women who confirmed for me the possibilities of other voices in Hopkins studies: Rachel Salmon, who, having delivered a superb paper, was steadfast yet poised when rudely dismissed by a member of the audience; and the wonderful Alison Sulloway. Like everyone, I had learned a great deal from Sulloway's study of *Victorian* Hopkins, but there she was, in the washroom at Lower Leeson Street that had been commandeered for the "ladies," welcoming a mere graduate student into the scholarly fold and giving me the lowdown on how to work at a conference.

Nothing is so beautiful as the soundscape of a Hopkins poem, or so demanding. And yet, not surprisingly, my most visceral response to his texts is awakened by the visual life of the manuscript, poetry or prose. Does it feature the well-rounded, affirmative features of the confident student's handwriting, the tensile strength of the post-"Wreck" script, or the chaotic, anguished appearance of the Dublin notebook's contents? Which phrases gave him the most pause; which did Bridges try to amend, to make more decorous; which did Hopkins stubbornly, rightfully, re-revise? I try to share this experience with my students, in several different ways: in literature classes, we compare the facsimile manuscripts and the published texts and discuss the implications of the variants for comprehension and commentary; in the bibliography course that I direct for our M.A. students, I introduce them to the complex world of textual studies by having them edit an unidentified Hopkins poem. "Spring" is a favourite choice for this exercise. In addition to tackling some thorny transcription issues (is that "weeds" in "wheels"?), the would-be editors learn first-hand the implications of distinguishing between "the poem" and its paratextual elements, of dispersing meaning between the text and any notes they need to create. And in the process, I ensure that they have all read at least one Hopkins poem before they consider themselves a "master" of the discipline.

As we pursue our scholarly and teaching interests in Hopkins' writings, I think we all invent a working myth of Hopkins, grounded, as he has instructed, in a mystique of place. For some, he is always already the tormented Dubliner; for others, the exuberant wordmaker of Wales. My Hopkins is Oxford-bound, twice-over. In the 1860s, he was the "star of Balliol," a consummate insider, discovering the myriad possibilities of his "park" and "pleasance" and its people, yet painfully learning the price of independent thinking and believing. The outsidership which conversion brought was intensified in 1878-1879, when he returned, as a priest, to work at St. Aloysius' church (then, surely one of the dreariest churches in Christendom). Some probably hoped he would be Newmanesque, charismatic, and win Oxonian souls for Rome; he knew better, and experienced worse: the outsider's life. Yet, as I retraced his steps (as we all do, if fortunate) from Balliol to the Bodleian, across Port Meadow and rambling towards Binsey, I realized that he always held within his imaginative grasp the half-musky smell of a Plato volume; the burnished light of late afternoon, after a rain, as it illuminates the sandstone spires and makes livid the gargoyles; the restless whispering of poplars; the tolling of Great Tom in Christ Church's tower; the musical sounds of *gloria* as choristers' voices rebound within the walls of Magdalen or New College chapel; the malicious and protesting laughter, coming from Balliol's inner quad, as the mattress of a smells-and-bells papist was hauled down the stairs by unsympathetic peers and dumped on the lawn for public display. When, in Dublin, he held in his hands the journals, notebooks, and letters of other years, there was little comforting to be had; he felt a "sadness" akin to "madness." Yet the Word and such words as he could muster sustained him.

An academic could not ask for better scholarly editions than Norman MacKenzie and Catherine Phillips have provided for us; I have spent so much time reading alongside House and Abbott and Devlin that I wish I could thank them, personally, for their efforts. But to get inside a Hopkins poem, to define its linguistic and imagistic challenges and begin to understand the way in which it makes meaning, I go back to the manuscripts, the work of those hands, and start all over again.

A HOPKINS APPRENTICESHIP

The memory plays tricks and I have no notes to ensure that
I am being accurate but my introduction to Hopkins was, as I
recollect, unusual in that I began not with a published text but
with reproductions of the manuscripts. It all occurred when I was
sixteen and in need of a summer job at a time when such things
were not plentiful. My father, Norman MacKenzie, set me to
work distinguishing Hopkins' interlineations from Bridges' hand
in MS B. I can also remember spending many hours that summer
scanning the Oxford Dialect Dictionary column by column for
Hopkins' contributions of which, in proportion to the entries I
scanned, there were not many but enough to please Dad. Later,
perhaps even that summer, came the task of tracing on
transparent sheets samples of Hopkins' handwriting, letter by
letter, from the diaries and correspondence. I subsequently
suggested dates for nearly all Hopkins' poems, taking a day to
absorb each manuscript, using what was already established and
the transparencies to narrow the likely range of dates, then
comparing my target poem with dated pages close to it in time
until I felt the hands comparable. The irrational element of this
last part of the process, one that we use every day in recognition
of friends but which forces one to trust to unanalysed
impressions, was a considerable strain. It was like taking part in a
bizarre quiz and I longed for Hopkins to appear with
confirmation or rebuttal. So, my exposure to Hopkins was from
the beginning to the poetic manuscripts within the context of
diaries and letters and, despite concentrating on stray words and
phrases for their letter-shapes, I enjoyed the witty correspondence
and the beautiful verse. Dad was a generous boss and, had I not
had a desire to give value for money, I could have learnt a great
deal more than I did but I seldom took time to explore. What I
did absorb was the pleasure he got from reading widely for

annotation; editing was fun. I did other summer jobs too over the years, checking library orders for the English Faculty at Queen's University, preparing an index to Doug Spettigue's *F[rederick] P[hilip] G[rove]: The European Years.* Then, in the summer after I graduated, Dad took me to Oxford as his research assistant and there I had the thrill of working on the originals of the pages I knew, noting things that are not particularly obvious in reproductions, such as the fold down the middle of the second page of "The Woodlark."

During these years there was no obvious connection between the research I was assisting in and my work for my degree. It was actually when I was doing an M.A. at Toronto that I first formally studied a poem by Hopkins in detail. The poem was "'As kingfishers catch fire'" and I loved it, producing a seminar paper for David Shaw. And only when, as a doctoral student at Cambridge, I prepared my little York Notes study guide did I come to try to make sense of all the mature poems and then I worked as any student does, from the published guides, including my father's. The project was sent my way by Dad in an attempt to provide me with some additional income at a point when my Canada Council Scholarship was badly dented by the exchange rate. It also provided a welcome break from a bad patch in my dissertation on Robert Bridges' intellectual and poetic development. The dissertation too involved the use of poetic manuscripts and a large volume of correspondence and it brought me the enjoyable friendship of Donald and Maryanna Stanford. I later expanded the thesis into a biography of Bridges.

It was a publication deriving from one of my three previous Ph.D. topics that provided the next stage in my education as an editor, and Dad and David Clark provided the opportunity. The task was the presentation of all the manuscripts of W.B. Yeats's *The Hour Glass* for the Yeats Manuscript series and this I did on my own, struggling to decipher Yeats's hand and learning how to cope with larger and much more chaotically incomplete manuscript groups. Warwick Gould and Stephen Parrish later salvaged the series as it was passed from publisher to publisher and gave me support. Had Liam Miller's *Noble Drama of W. B.*

Yeats not been published, I would probably have developed as an Anglo-Irish specialist. As it was, Miller removed any need for a Ph.D. on the subject and, cajoled by my supervisor Philip Gaskell, and the news of the availability of Bridges' papers, which my father told me, I obtained instead a useful self-education in the areas in which Bridges was interested.

As my doctoral thesis was nearing completion I think Dad began to share my worry about how I was going to get a job. He phoned me in Cambridge and we proceeded to argue, he urging me to take on the proposed Oxford Authors Hopkins, which he said he would not have time to do. He would let me use his OET text, he said. If my name was going on the book, I said, it would have to be my work. Reluctantly, I took it on, thinking that there would be little to do to the fourth edition, given the constraints of providing a text bare of the deferred decisions that abound in the manuscripts. However, I soon found that if I tried to work to the principles of disentangling Bridges' taste and following Hopkins' last thoughts, there was in fact plenty to do and I spent some very enjoyable months arriving at a text of the poems and the first chronological ordering of all the poems integrated with the fragments and translations. Aware that I must have absorbed much more from my work as Dad's assistant than I could recall, I tried to acknowledge those places where I knew that he would be making changes even when I had no idea of the details of the new text. The Oxford English Texts series are very different from the Oxford Authors and I frankly admire Dad's *Hopkins* as an exceptionally creative as well as immensely informative work to which, like all Hopkins scholars, I turn. Our textual disagreements, and some of what I have learnt from his OET, find muted expression in my World's Classics edition, hobbled as it is by the restrictions of that series.

I have also along the way edited at the request of OUP a selection of Hopkins' letters and, thanks to Howard Erskine-Hill, completed the Critical Heritage volume devoted to the reception of John Donne from 1873-1923. I am now, when other commitments allow, absorbed by a contextual study of Hopkins and art and music.

I owe my father a great deal in making my academic career possible and I am also deeply indebted to Norman White, who has generously sent many invitations my way. The world of academia is often thought of as vicious but I had an incredibly privileged introduction to it and have met with amazing kindness. I hold increasingly precious the opportunities I have been given, the friendship and the stimulus of exchanging views.

HOPKINS AND ME

How I came to Hopkins or what Hopkins means to me are not topics which spark off in me a need to write and I am not sure that my responses would interest a reader. I first met Hopkins' work when I heard a lecture on him given by Noel Lees (the Francis Noel Lees of the Hopkins pamphlet, number 21 in the Columbia Essays on Modern Writers series). This was part of the series of lectures for undergraduates on nineteenth-century writers at the University of Manchester and what I remember most is Lees's remarkable ability to imitate Frank Sinatra by keeping smoking throughout the lecture without interrupting the flow of his argument. What the argument was, I cannot remember.

While I was a junior lecturer at the University of Newcastle upon Tyne I found myself given the task of lecturing on the Victorians in a course which James Maxwell (long time editor of *Notes and Queries*) had left when he went to Oxford. I began to work on several of the Victorian poets, including Hopkins. Like Topsy, my interest in Hopkins just growed, and I cannot be precise about when or how or why I decided to write my book about Hopkins which came out from Arnold's the publishers in 1971.

I have a clearer picture of how I came to collect the material for *All My Eyes See*, the exhibition and book which explores Hopkins' visual world. I knew Chris Carrell, who was at that time director of the Ceolfrith Arts Centre in Sunderland, and he asked me if there were any writers around whom it would be interesting to construct an exhibition. Writers are notoriously difficult to make visual displays of; illustrators of Tennyson crossed my mind, and Browning's painters, but the subject which looked an interesting possibility was Hopkins. I did not know when I started exactly how interesting it would be.

Hopkins' love of the visual arts was obvious from his journals and his accounts of visits to exhibitions, with comment on the pictures there. I was familiar with the drawings which are illustrated in the editions of his diaries and journals. But the richness of the material proved astonishing. We made a number of contacts. I can't remember how we got into contact with Jerome Bump, who was then working in Oxford, but he was a welcome contributor and a vital connection with the Humanities Research Center in Texas, who owned a number of photographs and drawings which would be central to the exhibition. I remember visiting Jerome in Oxford where he seemed to be enduring everything that the English climate and the English apology for a heating system could contrive to make life miserable. Snow outside, draughts all through the house and a totally inadequate gas fire were making his visit to England less than comfortable, but he and his family were warm and welcoming. He helped to make the exhibition possible, and he contributed an article to the eventual book. Norman White too offered all kinds of help in suggestions, lists, contacts and material. Galleries were unaccountably willing to lend their works, so we managed to borrow things like Frederick Leighton's *Clytemnestra*. Lord Bridges made for us a large reproduction of the portrait of Hopkins which he owns. The project went well.

Most importantly we made contact with Leo Handley-Derry, grandson of Gerard's brother Arthur, and he allowed us to use the sketchbooks which Hopkins had drawn in, along with one or two separate drawings which we were able to suggest derived from those sketchbooks. He also showed us Arthur's sketchbooks and paintings and we were able to identify the sketchbook which Arthur had used alongside his brother when they went sketching on the Isle of Wight. Leo Handley-Derry and his family were the epitome of an old-fashioned courtesy and were enormously helpful and supportive. Campion Hall too made available the manuscripts and drawings in their collection, which we were able to photograph and reproduce, so that we were able to collect a large proportion of Hopkins' drawings, to photograph them, and to get a real sense of Hopkins' visual world.

Perhaps the most curious of the discoveries and one which has perhaps not yet yielded up all its treasures is the collection at Stonyhurst. There Father Frederick Turner was in charge of the library and he too was remarkably hospitable and helpful. He showed us the copies of the *Stonyhurst Magazine* and other books and documents that are kept there. These had of course been pored over before by several Hopkins scholars. But what had not been asked for was the visual record; and when we asked if there were any pictures associated with Hopkins, Father Turner led us to a cupboard, opened the doors and revealed a large collection of scrapbooks and photograph albums which cannot have been looked at for years. They dated from the nineteenth century and indicated the interest that the Jesuits and their pupils had in photography, and were in some ways a legacy of a bygone social practice. Many collections had been left to the college by alumni, sadly with little annotation. Some of the photographs were of Stonyhurst before and after the big restoration and rebuilding. We could date the rebuilding and could relate this to the dates of Hopkins' periods at Stonyhurst. But the most fascinating and infuriating of the photographs were groups of staff and pupils and collections of *cartes de visites*. These are fascinating because they provide faces for the people who were in and around Stonyhurst at the times Hopkins was there. But they are infuriating because seldom had anyone thought it necessary to annotate the pictures with names. So we have groups of staff, which might even include Hopkins himself, but no way in which we can be sure of who is who. Some of the more obvious faces one could get familiar with, and thus recognise some fellow Jesuits, but many faces cannot be attached to names. There is still room for a systematic cataloguing of the Stonyhurst photographs, certainly to enrich the visual context of Hopkins' time at Stonyhurst, but with the fascinating possibility that another likeness of Hopkins might emerge.

What Hopkins means to me in the end is the friends and colleagues I have met through a shared interest in his work. I hope he wouldn't be unhappy with that.

T O M I K O   H I R A T A ,   S . P . C .

The Incessant Calls from Hopkins:
From a Tributary,
a Winding Stream to the Main Current

It is more than twenty-five years since Hopkins' name reached my ears. The poet appeared to me at a thunder-purpled seabeach-like parlour of the Jesuit House in Tokyo. He seemed indeed a great stormfowl with its palmy snow-pinions—greatness only scholars could touch. Only they could recognize the scattering of the colossal smile off Hopkins. Many factors have been argued in my mind and heart, and hindered me from flying up with full-fledged confidence.

On that occasion, his poems were not recited; the speakers only referred to famous lines such as "degged with dew, dappled with dew" and these phrases have remained ringing inside me. Ignorant as I was, a large vocabulary both strange and lovely, both annoyed me and attracted me by the unheard melody. Unable to design an exact image or get the meaning from the verses, my supposition made me hurry to a conclusion: not to encounter Hopkins for a while. However, someone had thrown a stone of Hopkins into the well of my heart.

A long time had passed before I went back to the poet. He seemed to have sent me his waves, calling and warning: would I be really wise enough or would I run away from him? The reflection made me answer, No, I am not wise enough. Then my reading of Hopkins' poems aloud gave me my primary proof of my insight: I will approach Hopkins through recitation.

Then the relationship with Hopkins began—the first little stream I began to follow. The secondhand books were still not easy to get in Tokyo, yet I could purchase them with a store master's kindness. Once I had decided to access his poetry, other chances ushered me to him. The second one was the 1982 publication of *Hopkins' Poetry*, a Japanese translation written in a colloquial style which complemented the literary style of the 1968 version. Soon after, I learned that Margaret Drabble declared Hopkins a major poet in *The Oxford Companion to English Literature*, which I found in our college library. It was at that time my first poem about him arose from my heart, and I dedicated it to him on June 8, 1985, celebrating the glorious dawn with him. My friends said it had a shadow of the Hopkinsian beat.

Hopkins' rhythm was also an essential energy in his poetry. When it reached me the understanding of things and his self as well became clear. The rhythm reveals the thing itself, himself, and my self in consequence. I surmised that his rhythm exceeded in charm that of Wordsworth's own, even though this Lake Poet had the idea of common-language rhythm in poetry. In the following final lines, it seemed that Hopkins transcended and I was the witness. I saw Hopkins becoming a determined self: his perception, his reasoning, and his objective realization of self within the poem brought this about.

> It is the blight man was born for,
> It is Margaret you mourn for. . . .
>
> Long live the weeds and the wilderness yet. . . .
>
> I am so very, O so very glad
> . . . .
> . . . I balance and buoy
> With a sweet joy of a sweet joy,
> Sweet, of a sweet, of a sweet joy
> Of a sweet—a sweet—sweet—joy.

I take up one stanza—31—from "The Wreck of the Deutschland,"

> . . . lovely-felicitous Providence,
> Finger of a tender of, O of a feathery delicacy, the breast of the
> Maiden could obey so, be a bell to, ring of it. . . .

The outriding foot and sprung rhythm tied me to him even if I had not yet become as involved as many scholars had. On reading his poems, I was often left with a feeling enlivened and uplifted, and on a much higher and more worthwhile level.

I happened to give a talk of my harvest from my Hopkins research. Its theme was "Poetic Energy of Hopkins." What I did was read his poems aloud, as Hopkins insisted to Bridges: all his verse was oratorical. This was the least I could do, and the most, to give pleasure to the listeners. Apprentice as I was, Prof. Yasuda spoke well of me on this. It was because of this trial reading that my research proceeded on the precious experiences: Milton's counterpointed rhythm, the music of Bach canons, Henry Purcell's brilliant interpretation of "Ode on St. Cecilia's Day (Hail! Bright Cecilia!) (1692)," the music of M. Tippett and B. Britten, and Eliot's poetry.

Equipped with these, I found myself more keenly aware of Hopkins' consciousness. He ordinarily expresses honest pathos and ethos through poetry. The expressions are indeed himself, and they portray what he is in God's eye. Then I still said to myself that his consciousness must have been most rightly "ghost guessed" as C. Day Lewis evaluates in his *A Hope for Poetry*. And it seems that he effectively expresses himself of "what heart heard of" in a total consideration—unlike Eliot's *The Waste Land*, where the poet simply recreates a "mood of mixed memory and desire," as the critic mentioned.

Even then, my early concerns frequently returned and detained me from involving myself fully in Hopkins research. The first concern was how ordinary people could come to know him deeply and the other was how young Japanese students could see and understand the poetic integrity of Hopkins.

My investigation of the solutions to these concerns started. When I was in communication with the people I met in England, I was told of their interest and appreciation of Hopkins' poetry, because they had good teachers. I also noticed most of the lecturers with high distinction such as R. Pinsky, and Anthony Thwaite, and Donald Hall read Hopkins' poetry and acknowledged their high appreciation of him. My first concern was blotted out through this information. The students of my Shirayuri College released the second concern during classroom discussion. Some of Hopkins' poems began to be included in a certain anthology of poetry for the university students in Japan. Such texts surprised and pleased my ear, containing poems such as "'Thou art indeed just'" and "The Wreck of the Deutschland" from stanza 17 to 28, whose editor was Jon Silkin. Editors of poetry books believed that young Japanese students were capable of deep understanding. And indeed, our students did well in oratorical reading, and as a reward, they came to understand the artistic form and rhythm, and figures of poetry. Moreover, they took pride in Hopkins' attitude and endeavour in harmonizing his self with his environment as an indispensable necessity. Young as they are, the students have their own problems, and stresses. They would hope to be encouraged, as Hopkins hoped to be, discovering the creative power within themselves. They perceived nature and felt this line very much, "Nothing is so beautiful as Spring—." Then, motivated by intuition, they inquired as Hopkins did, "What is all this juice and all this joy?" The affirmation follows: "A strain of the earth's sweet being in the beginning / In Eden garden.—Have, get . . . / . . . worthy the winning." This process let the students reach the final step of full understanding and knowing, quite naturally. With full consciousness, I noticed what process was going on in their souls, starting with basic sense perception, then to intellectual understanding and finally to the experience of growth: reason, affirmation, judgment, and choice-making.

In 1994 I happened to attend the 150th birthday service of Hopkins at St. Bartholomew's in Haslemere. It was all by the kindness of Mr. Richard O'Rourke's family. There Rev. Michael E. Allsopp, as an honoured preacher, gave an inspiring sermon. I had indeed precious consciousness of Hopkins and was greatly encouraged. It was that afternoon the words of his sermon transformed into words of energy and integrity through the Spirit, and I experienced a wave of appreciation. He assured me in our short talk to each other that Hopkins could work still for the good of men in this world through his poetry. This experience I am sure came by the help of Hopkins. So, what working for the good of man was reaffirmed providentially by Rev. Allsopp on the day of celebrating Hopkins' birthday. His words sounded solemn and my journey to knowing Hopkins was confirmed.

Hopkins' musical rhythm in poems signified for me the meaning of each poem, and because of that I was able to approach nearer to its vast richness. Newman identifies the music with thought (*The Grammar of Assent*). By the following line from "The Windhover" Hopkins signifies and affirms Christ, himself and the bird with the final glorious glow of energy as seen in the embers:

> . . . and blue-bleak embers, ah my dear,
> Fall, gall themselves, and gash gold-vermilion.

It can only be obtained in the reflection and choice of falling and galling by the ember itself, or by himself. This happening is altogether both natural consequence and willful outcome in human action. In this way, first comes the image, then expression wells up in rhythmic verse, then finally confirmation of decision. Thus we feel there is a continuing experience of ascending towards an atmosphere of loftiness.

Lewis remarked that Hopkins' imagination in his verse is decked with dramatic presentation. In the case of "The Wreck of the Deutschland" the poem appeals to students who wish to understand Hopkins' situation and his sensibility. Then students, naturally, in seeing his commitment came to honour the poet's interpretation. Moreover, they gained an insight that the more they read in an oratorical way with rhythm, the more they understood. As a result, this rudimentary procedure led to the students' better understanding of Hopkins' involvement in the hardships of the sisters and passengers, inasmuch as they applied this technique. The indirect influence of the poet awakened them into involvement. They had chances of hearing the lectures with the powerful and delicate oratorical reading by the Jesuit Fathers, Peter Milward and Joseph Feeney. The researches of Dr. Norman MacKenzie and Catherine Phillips were enormously precious, and they let us imagine and suppose our interpretation is possible. At this point, the tributary began to grow wider.

Hopkins has been declared "a true revolutionary poet." Indeed, one may be amazed and point out Hopkins' abundant use of multiple images with overflowing vocabulary rich and appropriate. Lewis explains the visage of his poems: "Hopkins used an intense concentration of images in such a way to give the reader a series of sensual shocks. . . . There is a perpetual interplay between the surface images and underlying dramatic situation or series of situations." This also affirms the poems of Hopkins should be oratorical.

With the view of Lewis on Hopkins' poetry and of what happened to my students in understanding, I realized his philosophical reflection and spontaneous knowing of all the beings and Being, Himself. He had simply appropriated what he had known to be good in his life. Bernard Lonergan called that kind of knowing the Five Steps of Transcendental Precepts, a principle which had its beginnings in the philosophy of Thomas Aquinas and Aristotle. Lonergan explains that in all our knowing, man proceeds in sequential order before truly knowing something. The steps consist of the experiences from the basic sense perception to higher acquisition after judging something right or just. In Hopkins' case, he proceeds to the final higher reality so as to appropriate what he judged just. This quality is the source of pure attraction within the persons with whom one communicates. Lonergan's steps go up from the bottom in a spiral form to find the appropriateness of thought and conduct. These are the five steps:

1. Being attentive to the data of experiences: Sense perception
2. Being intelligent to experienced data: Work of insight
3. Being rational to experienced intelligence: Rational affirmation
4. Being responsible to the reasoning: Responsible reaction
5. Being in love with the best: Total commitment.

Let us trace these steps in the poem, "'Thou art indeed just.'" We become aware of Hopkins' sensitivity to life experiences, of his intellectual understanding, his reasoning, and reflection, and finally the longing of his heart.

First, the poet seeing his state calls to God, "Why do sinners' ways prosper? And why must / Disappointment all I endeavour end?" These dramatic questionings are very factual *data* that he has perceived in life. (1)

Then, he no more *questions*, but he appeals to Him, showing his judgment. Hopkins wishes that He could be more just to him. *His argument* is that even creatures live a good life; "birds build— but not I build; no, but strain"; unfair reality is the issue. (2)

Hopkins indeed enumerates a series of what he is and how his life is, compared with all the creatures expressed in the octave and the first tercet. *He understands* and *expresses himself*: He is "Time's eunuch." (3)

Then he *judges*: if He is sincere, He could do anything to Hopkins, as the poet is submissive to accept himself with no fruit of his hard work. (4)

Finally the poet does what he can, *chooses*, asking for Him to be his giver of life, to "send my roots rain." (5)

Thus reassured, Hopkins followed the innate process of knowing his self and things; and wrote the poem. It was quite spontaneous, innately done. Hopkins' poetry has proved that it should be very capable of understanding to everybody. It was not just a product of religious reasoning, but was purposely written with images to enrich. Hopkins' poetry treasures not only his art of poetry and priestly devotion, but also his philosophical mind and his longing to be in love with the Being of life. He then transcends his reality into another, and appropriates what he judges just for self—"worthy the winning," of being in Love. This is what Lewis praised of him, pure poet.

And finally, through Lonergan, I am facing the main current of Hopkins' treasure: the magnificent structure, within his poems, of Hopkins' spiritual growth, which had been in his intention and seen in the poem "Summa."

WHY HOPKINS MATTERS TO ME

Until the late spring of 1946, I had never heard of Hopkins. Then during a course for servicemen about to attend universities, a Welshman read to us "Hurrahing in Harvest," "The Windhover," "Felix Randal," and "God's Grandeur." To this day Instructor-Lieutenant Bevan's renditions of these poems remain the most inspiring I have heard. They left me unshakeably convinced that Hopkins is above all an aural poet. One of my few triumphs as a teacher came during a semester course on him in which I had every student prepare and justify an oral reading of one poem. An honours student's version of "Spelt from Sibyl's Leaves" proved word by word more ominously meaningful than anything I, or probably an actor, could have produced. In this age of literary theory, to believe that some poems are best apprehended aurally is a heresy, but one for which we can cite Hopkins himself. "Spelt from Sibyl's Leaves," he tells Bridges, is "made for performance . . . not reading with the eye but loud, leisurely, poetical (not rhetorical) recitation, with long rests, long dwells on the rhyme and other marked syllables, and . . . almost sung . . . in *tempo rubato*."

Almost everything else that Hopkins means to me was implicit in Bevan's reading: feeling for nature and its denizens in "Hurrahing" and "The Windhover"; sympathy with a man's suffering coupled with admiration of his former prowess in "Felix Randal"; awareness of nature as infused with divinity and so "never spent" in "God's Grandeur." Opportunities provided by this association are mainly responsible for what insights have come since.

At some time before "the environment" supplanted "Nature" or, for many young people, "God," it transpired that Hopkins' feeling for the natural world implied something other than the anthropomorphism of the hymn "All things bright and beautiful" or even the odd passage in Wordsworth. For me, it is supremely evident in "Binsey Poplars," "Henry Purcell" and, in a quite different way, in the "The Wreck of the Deutschland." Hopkins does not simply face the ocean's terrifying and irrational power, but seems to identify with the "burl of the fountains of air" and "sea-romp over the wreck" in stanzas 16 and 17 like a hostage identifying with a captor. By contrast Wordsworth, even in the sublime description of the Alpine descent in the *Prelude*, almost always writes as an observer. The same identification is even more true of "The Windhover" and of the "storm-fowl" in "Henry Purcell."

Since then other poems have, as it were, come on stage, among them "Binsey Poplars." What if any part this poem played in the decision to replant a certain river-bank in North Oxford is for others to say. What fascinates me is the fusion of elements which together constitute the quintessence of what might be called "pre-Dublin Hopkins" and which, in isolation, can arouse some response in a variety of readers. An average high-school student, in my experience, hears the echoing vowels and consonants of "Quelled or quenched in leaves the leaping sun"; a sensitive one hears the nostalgic cadence of "Sweet especial rural scene." An undergraduate who has heard of Duns Scotus perceives the implication of "especial." But I have known a geologist, previously unaware of Hopkins, seize on ". . . like this sleek and seeing ball, / But a prick will make no eye at all" when I read him the poem upon hearing him denounce the Reagan government's "open sesame" for industrialists and developers.

The opening of "Binsey Poplars" would not be the best example, however, of the poet's habit of beginning as though pointing out something noticed: "Look at the stars! look, look up at the skies!"; or responding to something told him: "Felix Randal the farrier, O is he dead then?"; or addressing someone encountered: "Margaret, are you grieving / Over Goldengrove unleaving?" His best openings compel our attention to whatever he is about to say.

Some of his most compelling and touching reflections concern the feelings of children, the boy wrought by love to lip-biting tension as he watches his younger brother perform in a play; the little girl wrought to tears by autumn leaves dropping. In common, I imagine, with most readers, I prefer the latter poem because its originating incident is less commonplace than that of "Brothers" while its conclusion is more direct and of more universal import: "It is the blight man was born for, / It is Margaret you mourn for." That the displaced egoism underlying so many human emotions is a consequence of the Fall not only calls attention to the intended ambiguity of the title "Spring and Fall," but is really quite difficult to restate in secular terms.

The Hopkins I do not enjoy is the priest to whose instruction the bugler-boy yielded "as a pushed peach," or the repressed homosexual who admired the rippling muscles of Harry Ploughman. For "The Bugler's First Communion" the high-school group I was teaching at the time shared my unspoken distaste, but about "Harry Ploughman" I feel ambivalent, for no poem in English offers a more exact and sensitive portrait not only of its subject's appearance, but of his rhythmic movements. In an age when the word "manly" has fallen into disrepute, it is good to find in a "churl" a grace all his own, yet a strength that is God-given.

In late middle age, when invited to address the Hopkins Association some time after being privileged to hear Norman MacKenzie on the Dark Sonnets, I chose to compare "'I wake and feel the fell of dark, not day'" with two other poems on insomnia. Since then, reflection on this and other Dublin sonnets has led me towards their appreciation less in religious than in existential terms. In these poems, it seems to me, Hopkins records in a very few perfectly chosen yet apparently spontaneous words the essential quality of inner experiences we might equally well call "psychological" or "spiritual." Everyone sensitized to aging and mortality by the stresses of middle life has stood on "cliffs of fall," has known prayerful entreaties that seem "dead letters," and has experienced the self as "gall" or "heartburn." Almost every immigrant has served time as "a lonely began"; everyone in a responsible position has known when "To seem the stranger lies my lot." In late middle age what creative worker has not known that "winter world" wherein, however expert in a craft, he or she lacks "the one rapture of an inspiration"? Perhaps because of having travelled in Southeast Asia, I feel that insofar as these sonnets are religious, they are so in the way that, as C.S. Lewis says, an orthodox Christian may have "more in common with a *real* Jew or Muslim" (or, I would add, Buddhist) than with a modernist or fringe Christian. It is a case of deep calling to deep.

And so over fifty years I have come to find in some two or three dozen poems by Hopkins a power not merely to arrest the ear and provoke the mind's immediate and developing response, but to call attention to human spoliation of a world "seared with trade; bleared, smeared with toil" long before Rachel Carson, and to echo my innermost experience of all the heart's deepest feelings save romance or wedded love.

KUNIO SHIMANE

HOPKINS MADE ME

—What shall I do for the poet that made me;
His songs and sounds that sought and found me? —

In my salad days as a postgraduate student and also as a university lecturer, I tried to establish a methodology for studying English poetry by analysing Hopkins' works. With a modest M.A. (there were no young Ph.D.s in English literature in the 1960s in Japan—it was regarded as more or less an honorary title), I went down to a provincial Catholic women's university to take up a lectureship recommended by my mentor, Father Peter Milward.

Had I not been a student at Sophia University, I would not have read Hopkins, as I believe that it was probably the only place in Japan where he was taught then. Also if I had not met Peter Milward in my undergraduate days, I would not have aspired to read much poetry, much less Hopkins. The English literature taught in this country consisted mainly of the novel with a possible exception of Shakespeare and very few other poets; it was taught and studied through translation. As a student at a Jesuit university, I decided to focus my attention on Christian literature. For my B.A. thesis I chose J.H. Newman, being completely ignorant of the fact that there was a bond between him and Hopkins.

Embarking on my postgraduate studies, I was determined to tackle Hopkins under the same mentor in whom I found striking similarities to the difficult poet. The circumstances and conditions favoured me: the university, the mentor, my knowledge, though yet elementary and in many ways inadequate, of Christianity and English phonetics.

Hopkins puzzled and overwhelmed me; he made me feel utterly powerless. If I had been confident of my English ability, I would certainly have given up further efforts to continue reading him. For if my English had been as good as the average educated native speaker's, I would have blamed the poet for being too difficult and unnatural, just as the editor of *The Month* did, and even Robert Bridges. I did not blame him but myself. At the same time I became vaguely aware that even for the most educated of native English speakers, Hopkins was almost impossible to understand.

With much care, I went on reading Hopkins steadily until one rapture of inspiration struck me: *Is it impossible that sound has meaning*? Look, no, *listen*, to such lines as:

> *M*ay is *M*ary's *m*onth, and I
> *M*use at that and wonder why.

There must be a clear reason for this exaggerated bi-labial alliteration; the poet tries to convey, if not an extra-meaning, at least some feeling through it. Otherwise it is ridiculous. At least it is obvious that together with the title, "The May Magnificat," the emphasis of the bi-labial *m* supported by another bi-labial *w*, is so great that Hopkins would not forgive the reader who fails to pay attention to it. What do the bi-labials, *m* and *w* signify? In my ear the poet's words began ringing: *take breath and read it with the ears, as I always wish to be read, and my verse will be all right.* I followed this and another piece of welcome advice—*if it is obscure do not bother yourself with the meaning*—and practised reading poetry (not only his) aloud. This sharpened my ear and I came to trust it. Then the following lines came to take on an extra dimension in my mind:

> I caught this morning morning's minion, king-
>   dom of daylight's dauphin, dapple-dawn-drawn Falcon in his riding . . .

These are typical Hopkins lines where individual sounds and techniques work together to create an extra meaning which fuses with the literal meaning. The poet was interested not only in the literal meaning but also the description of the magnificent flight of the Falcon. This is a fusion which only a genius can create.

If each sound had a meaning, so would each technique; and his techniques are far too many to be confined in the traditional category. I could no longer rely on my ear alone; I felt a keen desire to acquire a firm and objective basis for phonetic analysis. Also a very strong wish to study the Hopkins MSS which could be treated as the indispensable source for re-producing his voice as well as for tracing his poetic creation.

Hence my study of experimental phonetics in the postgraduate course and again, a few years later, extensively at the same institution on a grant during a sabbatical after I became a university lecturer. A few of my King's English (the RP) speaking friends of both sexes living in Tokyo helped me by becoming the subjects of my experiments to analyse their pronunciation using elaborate equipment. Father Milward was one of them, and it was rather curious that I tended to identify his pronunciation with Hopkins'. My "literary study" of Hopkins went on simultaneously.

The time came when I felt that I had done all (or almost all) I could in Japan for my Hopkins study; the basics for my methodology having been laid, I felt an intense necessity to study in England. Fortunately just then I was given a British Council Scholarship to study there. Professor Francis Berry, then professor of English Literature at London University, kindly consented to supervise my study. He is one of those rare people who know poetry as a poet and also as a scholar. Based in London, I was completely free to study at Oxford and anywhere I found necessary and to do phonetic fieldwork at a few places in Britain.

At the Bodleian Library, Oxford, I enjoyed every minute of deciphering, tracing and copying every possible word (including canceled ones), punctuation and metrical marks in all the MSS of Hopkins' finished works, though it was laborious and especially exacting to my eyesight. Because of this experience (and examining and copying many of Tennyson's MSS), I could truly appreciate and value Professor Norman MacKenzie's work.

After returning to Japan, my study of Hopkins continued in spite of heavy teaching duties. I decided to write a book in English by which I hoped to share my ideas with a greater number of people. The basic framework had already been laid in my book in Japanese (still unpublished) on Hopkins, written before I went to Britain. I now tried to make the most of my study there. The efforts resulted in my *Fusing Point of Sound and Sense* (1983).

After its publication, the general scene in the academic world, especially the universities here, began undergoing changes; along with them my life has changed and I am now at my fourth *remove*—at the fourth university in my career. During these years my interest in poetry has widened to a few more poets besides Hopkins. But he is the *home* where my carrier-witted mind always bounds. It is his exaggerated lines that had first troubled me and later made me wonder about the possibility of a methodology combining phonetics and MS research. Hopkins helped me. He made me. I shall continue to enjoy exploring his poetry whose immortal beauty is sound with sense.

STUMBLING ON HOPKINS

It must be impossible not to have seen him there with all the others. An undergraduate at a good university, invited to join a senseless few in burrowing athletically through the not-yet-dubious canon at the rate of about 1000 pages a week, agog over words and the feeling of thinking, moderately cocky about one's powers in a kind of formalistic analysis then the fading rage, and yet at odds with some intellectual fashions of the day, partial to difficulty in poetry and to poetry in literature . . . and merely a century apart. How I missed him I can't now say.

But it is true, though improbable, that I first stumbled on Hopkins in German and in Germany, during a post-graduate year, when a *Kommilitonin* at the Ludwig-Maximilians University brought me the *Untergang der Deutschland* and asked if it had a beginning, a middle, and an end. The poem made a small impression. A family oddity of language had sapped, beyond the ordinary anemia of translations, this able labor overseen by a very eminent Ordinarius: Hopkins falls more naturally, so to speak, into German than into English. Not that such a thought could have occurred to me at the time. In retrospect, though, it is hard to escape the impression that by mining English for its proper inscapes, Hopkins found his way down to its Germanic bedrock, which he "translated" up into a modern alloy. Translating him into modern German normalizes the tense foreignness of his idiom, enfeebling it.

So much so that I don't believe I had stumbled on Hopkins himself, really, at that time. Gerhard was much less startling than Gerard would be and even—strange to say—than Gérard, in Pierre Leyris' exceptional French renderings. These I stumbled on in the stacks of a great library while looking for something else. It was very likely the hand-lettering in white ink on a brown canvas spine — *Hopkins* — *Reliquiæ* — *Vers* — *Proses* — that caught my eye.

The thing seemed improbable. How could this most peculiarly English poetry possibly be put into a language and a poetic tradition so thoroughly at odds with the original? Some such question must have crossed my mind as I made for this temptation, scanned the table of contents for *Le Naufrage du Deutschland*, and came up short. But "The Windhover" was there, predictably unringing as "Le Faucon," and, curiosity gaining over ungenerous pity, I made the acquaintance of these prodigious translations. To be sure, they did not sound like Hopkins; but neither did they sound like any other French poet I knew and yet they often crackled with a like linguistic charge and sometimes rolled with an arch-especial cadence. But that was not all.

(I had in the meantime certainly stumbled on Hopkins in his English translation.)

Leyris mentioned in his Preface the best commentary on Hopkins then available in French, an essay that had appeared in 1953, in the journal *Critique*, by a D. de Grunne. Oncle Dodo? Some years later, when this brilliant, learned, and eccentric relative of my wife's visited us in New York and approved, mildly, of my cooking, I was able to present him with a sloppy xerox of "Technique du poète Gérard Manley Hopkins," which he could not recall having written.

But I was groping towards a doctoral dissertation topic on late nineteenth-century poetic language, having, for my French example, battened on Mallarmé and—no less than my predecessors and betters—been elegantly retroflected by him into the mise-en-abysmal theorizing of *Tel Quel* and its identical opposites. It was, I think, while wondering if the *chora sémiotique* would ever be less mystical to me than divine afflatus (with which I suspected it had an underground link) that I *realized* that I had stumbled on Hopkins, whose work possessed the strong strangeness-yet-rightness that poetry in one's native language never quite has and at the same time the echoing fulness and immediacy that *only* poetry in one's native language quite has.

Translated from an earlier or deeper level of language, and with the strangeness of the rendering alive in the lines, this poetry came by elective affinity and as a natural obstacle.

Why Hopkins Matters to Me

I still remember vividly the moment that I first heard the name of Gerard Manley Hopkins. At secondary school, my English teacher, a Roman Catholic monk, told the class one day that Hopkins had been a great poet, and then read "God's Grandeur" to us. What struck me most of all, while listening to the teacher's beautiful, sonorous voice, was the strength of the rhythm, and the forceful interplay of vowels and consonants. Difficult it was, though. What did it all mean? What for instance were the "last lights off the black West"? Meanwhile outside, the gathering gloom of a late October afternoon descended upon the square, surrounded by quaint step-gabled houses, in the centre of Den Haag. A daring poetic image was brought into sharper focus by what happened in a quiet part of a Dutch city.

My teacher started to unravel the lexical, grammatical and conceptual density of the poem, but never forgot to dwell on the music of the words, such as the deep low sound of "ooze," and the sudden, strong crash of "crushed." I now realize how lucky I was that my first encounter with Hopkins was not spoiled by being inundated with the usual, long explanations of the poetry's depth of argument. The poem's intense verbal magic was not forgotten, even appeared to interest my teacher more than the meaning. When he became a monk, he had taken the name of Willibrordo, after the great English missionary in the Netherlands. Perhaps because he lived in a monastery, he also read "Heaven-Haven." I will always remember the fine alliterative string in "sharp and sided hail" —all the more so as a few days before, during a violent storm in Den Haag, I had felt once again how sharp and painful hail can be.

Willibrordo was indeed the ideal person to introduce Hopkins since he taught both English and music; he was also a good violin-player, sculptor, and painter. He is 85 years old now, *and* still plays the violin, paints, and reads English poetry. I think that as a teacher, he was perhaps more inspired by form and sound than contents. Later I read that for Hopkins, "Some matter and meaning is essential to it [poetry] but only as an element necessary to support and employ the shape which is contemplated for its own sake. . . . Poetry is in fact speech only employed to carry the inscape of speech for the inscape's sake." Profound words which, I think, are sometimes overlooked in the study of his work.

The poetry's formal perfection supports its pressure of feeling. I think of lines such as "O the mind, mind has mountains; cliffs of fall / Frightful, sheer, no-man-fathomed." The lines are almost physical in their impact, and often send a cold shudder down my spine. Almost unawares I also frequently recite to myself from "The Wreck of the Deutschland" the line: "And frightful a nightfall folded rueful a day." Over the years, its music has become dearer to me than the meaning. Had not Hopkins written, "My verse is less to be read than heard . . . ; it is oratorical, that is the rhythm is so"?

Hopkins' prose too has a strong immediacy, although less than the poetry. My teacher recommended the Penguin edition when he noticed how interested I had become. I still have that old edition with its reproduction of a detail from Ivon Hitchens' vigorous "Warnford Water" on the cover. My notes, in pencil, appear on almost every page. Yes, here are the opening lines from "On the Origin of Beauty: A Platonic Dialogue." They had, and still have, a great directness for me; the Professor "came one day in the evening to New College gardens and found John Hanbury a scholar of the college walking there." Since then, I have often been to New College, and have also walked in its beautiful gardens. How excited I was to discover that one of the College's most famous wardens, William Archibald Spooner, had been a friend of the poet. Once, while sipping my tea under Spooner's portrait in New College's impressive Hall, it almost seemed to me as if I saw them both engaged in a learned philosophical discussion, sitting at one of the long tables.

When I became interested in Hopkins at secondary school, I was also deeply engrossed in the Sherlock Holmes stories by Sir Arthur Conan Doyle. In them, one of the police-inspectors from Scotland Yard is Stanley Hopkins. His name may very well be modelled on Manley Hopkins, although there is as yet no evidence that Doyle and Hopkins met at Stonyhurst. Hopkins was a scholastic at the seminary, St. Mary's Hall, and Doyle a student at the College. I think it likely that the paths of two men of such great intellectual and imaginative talent crossed. Inspector Stanley Hopkins was an "exceedingly alert man," and he asks Holmes's help in tracking down the three Randalls. A reference to Felix Randal?

Impossible to prove, but as a member of "The Sherlock Holmes Society of London," I have not yet given up all hope of one day finding firm evidence linking Doyle and Hopkins. Moreover, it is certainly true that Hopkins too was interested in sudden deaths: in his journal for 30 December 1872, he gives a lucid analysis of the mysterious death of a fellow Oxford scholar near Paris—an analysis in the style of Sherlock Holmes that is certainly "exceedingly alert." Years ago when staying at Stonyhurst, I used to watch the fog and snow swirling round this enormous, rambling structure. I was reminded of Holmes's fog-shrouded Baskerville Hall and its Yew Alley, which in Doyle's description corresponds almost exactly with the one at Stonyhurst. I also thought of the "whírlwind-swivellèd snów" in "The Wreck of the Deutschland." Hopkins' long poem and *The Hound of the Baskervilles* are strongly connected in my mind since they have never given up all their conceptual mysteries to me.

Roman Catholics in the Netherlands have always shown deep social concern. In the nineteenth century, the workers suffered grievously in the country's factories and mines. The effects of the Industrial Revolution did not pass the Netherlands by. In our history lessons, we were told that miserable social conditions had been caused by the Protestant Reformation. It would, it was asserted, have been different if the country had remained loyal to the true faith. I was not surprised to learn that Hopkins had seen such a link for Britain too. He wrote of the

Reformation, "As it at present stands in England it is itself in great measure founded on wrecking." The working classes "got none of the spoils, they came in for nothing but harm from it then and thereafter." In Hopkins' letters and in poems such as "Felix Randal" and "Tom's Garland," I could feel warm empathy towards the working classes. When I was looking for a subject for my Ph.D., a lecturer at Amsterdam University, Rinus Stam, suggested social ideas in Hopkins, which in time appeared as a book, *The Random Grim Forge: A Study of Social Ideas in the Work of Gerard Manley Hopkins* (1992). Rinus Stam had always been an admirer of Hopkins' poetry, which surprised me at first since he is a Freemason. Now I am no longer surprised, but feel happy that Hopkins can appeal to people of different philosophies of life.

If I have to sum up why Hopkins matters to me, it is above all because of his great social concern revealed in great poetry. Here is a man who felt the moral and emotional complexity of everyday life, "the random grim forge" of "Felix Randal." His prose certainly contains the strict and theoretical insights of nineteenth-century Roman Catholic social thought in the Ultramontane tradition. About a dozen of his most beautiful poems, however, show in their vital and strong style how uncertain he was about the implications of the social question. It matters to me that in this poetry, honest tension and honest unrest get beneath his rational guard.

PHYSICAL RESPONSES

" . . . my heart in hiding / Stirred . . ."

S E A N   D A V I D S O N

FOR THE SAKE OF SELVING

> Sake is a word I find convenient to use . . . . I mean by it the
> being a thing has outside itself, as a voice by its echo, a face by
> its reflection, a body by its shadow, a man by his name, fame or
> memory, and also that in the thing by virtue of which especially
> it has this being abroad.
> — G.M. Hopkins, May 26, 1879

Unlike most writers in this volume, I have not been a
student of Hopkins for very long. I first encountered him about
six years ago in a freshman poetry class. At the time, I didn't take
too much notice. I was a philosophy student, after all, and had
more serious things to think about than poetry. It wasn't until my
second year that I began to read Hopkins seriously. It was "'As
kingfishers catch fire, dragonflies draw flame'" that first caught
my attention. I don't know what it was exactly. I remember
sitting alone in a room somewhere, longing for a bit of relief from
the academic grind. Turning to page ninety of my used copy of
the *Poems*, I sunk into my chair and began reading, quickly at first
and somewhat haphazardly—anything to cultivate a bit of
distraction. But as I finally settled into the rhythm of the first few
lines and allowed the poem to have its way with me, my tongue
starting to move in my mouth, I found myself returning to the
beginning to read it aloud and with deliberation. The second
time through I experienced something quite strange. It began at
the point when my now unrestrained tongue managed to register
the concatenation of monosyllabic feet in lines three and four:

> . . . like each tucked string tells, each hung bell's
> Bow swung finds tongue to fling out broad its name . . .

This "something" intensified through the alliterative "Deals"
and "dwells" and "Selves—goes its self" of lines six and seven and
culminated in the parting cry "*What I do is me: for that I came.*" I

paused and listened as the last few words resounded off the walls and echoed in my head and I realized for perhaps the first time in my life that it's possible to be in two places at once. Hastening to the sestet, I was disappointed to find that the "something" that had pursued me through the first part of the poem began to retreat, perhaps because of Hopkins' expressed need to "say more." But as quickly as it had withdrawn, it returned with "Christ" in line twelve and as I scanned his "Lovely . . . limbs, and . . . eyes" and turned to the "Father through the features of men's faces," my ground gave way and a peculiar mixture of satisfaction and longing took hold of me.

There are many ways to describe an aesthetic experience. Emily Dickinson likens it to the top of one's head coming off. David Foster Wallace refers to it simply as "the click." I'm not sure that I have adequate words for what I experienced back then. I can say, however, that this experience and others like it are the reason why I chose to study English literature and Hopkins in particular. I wanted to explore what could move me in and out of myself in such ways. Over the last few years, I have returned to "'As kingfishers catch fire'" many times and tried to observe what's going on at the knotty intersection of word and self. The closest I have come to an objective view of the whole thing is yet another sequence of images and sounds that appear and reappear in my mind's eye. Of course these secondary images and sounds do not turn up with every reading. They come during those in-breaking moments when I manage to give myself over to the poem and allow it to penetrate. I see everything craze inside me and there's usually a crack from somewhere difficult to find, and my ceiling and walls fall to the floor of me in tiny shards. Then everything elasticizes and dilates and I find myself no longer inside but outside, moving upwards and outwards along the slippery edge of a new periphery. I have reflected on these images and sounds often and tried to relate them back to Hopkins' poem, but the more I reflect and relate, the more I sense the encroachment of another set of images and sounds that threatens to put me at one more remove from my original experience. Perhaps there is no direct language for this kind of experience. Perhaps my search for objectivity is without end. But one thing seems quite clear: at a certain point in the poem, my readerly self manages to forsake its desperate need to remain a monolithic entity. There is no longer an essential "I" that I can point to with confidence and say, "That's me." Something else has taken place that leaves me hanging in the midst. And as I hang there and feel the vestiges of my substantive self fall away, everything begins to shift and I feel myself fling to an otherly There and Thou. What shall I call this? Thomas Browne refers to it variously as "annihilation, exstasis, exolution, liquefaction, transformation, the kisse of the Spouse, gustation of God, and ingression into the divine shadow." There are many vocabularies. Whatever it is, it's what Hopkins' poetry does to me.

I say more. While it is true that my experience of "'As kingfishers catch fire'" has something to do with the rhythm of the poem and the strange alliterative twists, there's more to it than sheer aesthetic effect. It also has something to do with existential concern. Or perhaps it has to do with concern *and* effect. Throughout the poem Hopkins talks about dealing out being and speaking and spelling himself and the ludic activity of Christ in the world's doing-be, which are fairly mind-bending ideas in themselves, but then he couches the whole thing in a form that activates untapped synapses tucked away deep in my psyche or spirit or mind or whatever that inner region is that quickens these fingers moving across the keypad. What's going on here? Did Hopkins find a way of doing what most poets only dream of? Did he manage to integrate the form and content of his poem in such a way as to enact the very thing he envisions? Or perhaps this is the deception on which the entire poem turns. Maybe Hopkins wants us to believe that such an integration exists even though we know (or think we know) that the reality itself must be perpetually deferred. Whatever the case, it's clear that Hopkins does not write at a distance from his subject or value the sound of his language for its own sake. In fact, he seems to resist these impulses at every turn. Hopkins lashes himself to his words, sometimes violently, and then sets them adrift in the liminal space between self and other. And the most extraordinary thing of all is that he holds out the same possibility for his reader. This is why Hopkins is important to me and it is the reason I turn to him again and again.

B R U N O   G A U R I E R

How Did I Come to Gerard Manley Hopkins?

There is nothing through one's life to happen only "by chance." Would I have been speaking in such a way during childhood or during my youngest time? Probably not. Such a statement takes place in a long process, coming from our deepest experiences, sufferings, creative thoughts. Through my own poetic paths and trials, or being close to poetry in the very whole of my life, I mean close to its "stress and instress," I now feel able to "assess" how my ways might have crossed Hopkins' ways all along and so deep inside poetry.

I do clearly remember the very circumstances of my first meeting with Hopkins. Now, after years, it does not any more come into question for me to wonder, whether I came to Hopkins, or Hopkins came to me. Like people in love with poetry, Hopkins definitely "came" to me. And he came with his "Wreck," inspired by both a real wreckage of a real ship with real crew members and passengers inside of her bows, some of whom met death and among whom were five sisters exiled from Germany, and his own judgment upon what was happening, then just as nowadays, in some sort of an industrial society killing human beings instead of providing them with any progress. Also probably, my dream of being a seaman, as I was a kid, which continues up to now, came across such a poem.

One of my best friends is a Franco-American citizen living in France for many years since his early childhood, most skilled and creative in music, especially medieval and ancient, with whom—as well as with Claire, his wife—I experienced my most moving musical ventures as a tenor singer. Berry and I alike are in love with poetry, are used to writing articles and books, of speaking together of the important and deepest things of Life and even Death. Hopkins came to me thanks to you, Berry, in January 1995, and you will surely allow me to quote these quick words:

"Bruno, take this small book, read it and let's speak together about it afterwards." Now I am conscious and delighted to tell about what I should call an "event," a most spiritual event, alike a true tale: *Once upon a time I was given a small old Penguin book: "read that," was I advised by my best friend, "something will happen."* As a matter of fact, something happened. A few days after, I was sitting in a bus, crossing Paris. I opened the book, whatever the page. Long, long poem: "The Wreck of the Deutschland." I was quickly so struck that I felt obliged to get off the bus, walk, find a bench, cry in solitude and discreetly, soon recover and decide: this has to be read among my people, this is one of the most marvelous poems ever met, I will translate it into French. So I did, and so was it published one and a half years after. Such a translation task was a year and a half long jubilation. Month after month, the book accompanied me wherever over the world, and I step by step entered the words into my own language, to be set up in a French rewritten version of one of the most difficult British poems to be translated. Definitely, translating poetry is a true and full poetic task, by which from an original poem you draw, discover, invent, achieve another poem.

I don't serve in a university. I don't work as a researcher, nor as an English language teacher. My current involvements and personal commitments are taking place in the social field, at a European level, with all developments throughout the European Union and Eastern countries as well. Every day I work in several languages, especially in English, sometimes more than in my own mother tongue. Every day I experience the ideological, political, philosophical difficulties and misunderstandings among people, just because of words and all sensitivities in their very background. Words are arms, words can kill, words make love, words are one of each person's windows to the world from the sunrise to the sunset of life. Words are the way, the mainstream to sound, leading to poetry. Translating sensitivities into sensitivities, cultures into cultures, sufferings into sufferings, tears into tears, love into love, mother tongues into non-mother tongues, really constitutes one of the best experiences one can meet in his / her life.

The publication of my "The Wreck of the Deutschland" translation came as the occasion of my meeting a most wonderful Irish poet, Desmond Egan, organiser of a yearly summer school in Monasterevin, County Kildare, about and furthermore around Hopkins. The Jesuit poet used to come to that small village not far southwest of Dublin, when he moved to Ireland as a teacher in the National University. There, in Monasterevin, did we meet and every day of the week share our breakfasts, Father Joe Feeney and myself. I love Joe's culture, humour and smile and being together. Gerard Manley Hopkins is the one who gathers people around poetry, author of one of the richest bodies of poetry ever written during this modern time in Europe. "*To seem the stranger lies my lot, my life / Among strangers . . .*" did Hopkins write before falling in love with the small place of Monasterevin and its inhabitants? Egan's *Elegies* produced a second shock on me: I translated and published the *Elegies*. For three years already I have been attending Monastervin, at the end of July. Summer school about Hopkins, with friends, all poets from all over the world, so many languages spoken, all meeting around THE poet Hopkins: from Japan to South Africa, from the U.S. to Russia, from Norway to Italy, from Helsinki to Madrid, Budapest, Dresden, Rome, etc. And me, why not in such a context? I am now quite honoured to be acknowledged by Desmond among his friends as a possible person to be charged with a certain responsibility to bring French poetry lovers to a better knowledge and feeling of Hopkins' poetry.

Therefore have I to resume: back to Hopkins. One after the other, I'm aiming to publish Hopkins' poems in French. This do I consider as one of my new poetic tasks, this is "*my lot, my life / Among strangers . . .*"

Hopkins sometimes felt so lonely when experiencing his third removal, the one to Ireland, the last one. "*This to hoard unheard, / Heard unheeded, leaves me a lonely began.*"

May I here quote closely a recently discovered poet entering my poetic world, the African (Congo), Tchikaya U Tam'si. He used to be a high-level representative in UNESCO Paris, as well as a most committed companion of Patrice Lumumba. As a child, he met an accident during a game with his school mates. He broke his right foot. He remained disabled after such a bad . . . chance? Rejected by his relatives, rejected from the children's games, experiencing rejection from all close and further surroundings, nature, seashore, sand and desert, imaginative thought had become his new companions, familiars, very siblings and family. He was obliged and pushed within the deepest of his Self to find the way to cope with life, loneliness, every day wilderness, violence of life: "*What choice is to be met when getting lonely? Either might you meet craziness, including behaviour never understandable to others, or better, do become a poet*!"

HOPKINS AND ME: HOW AND WHY

I went to one of those English second-level schools, mainly in the North and Midlands, which had to prove their superiority over better known but namby-pamby public schools further South by beating everyone within sight at team-sports and by gaining more entrance scholarships to Oxford and Cambridge. A short cut to the latter was by focussing on classical studies, where the number of students competing for each university award was disproportionately small compared with any other subject. In the form above me, all the classics prizes were regularly won by a spotty youth, now Sir Peter X, reputedly the original of Sir Humphry in "Yes, Minister," the convincing BBC television satire on who runs British politics. Sir Humphry, an obsequious and self-serving top Civil Servant in Whitehall, specialises in employing arguments and language so obscure and dense that his political masters stand no chance of ever introducing any improvement, or indeed any alteration, into the existing governmental system.

The usefulness or otherwise of classics in everyday life was never discussed at school, but all other subjects received short shrift. Even though D.H. Lawrence had once been a pupil there, English was a very poor relation, being taught, along with Religious Instruction, in a low key by the form-masters, no matter what their university degree-subjects had been. As the only specialist English pupil in the school I had to take the subject with historians, for whom it was their subsidiary. Then out of the light blue of Cambridge an energetic young English-master was appointed, full of I.A. Richards, F.R. Leavis, and Practical Criticism. For Fred we suddenly found ourselves with totally different perspectives: strange prose-passages and unfamiliar short poems were put in front of us for very close scrutiny and detailed comment, all without any helpful information about the author's identity or the piece's contexts. We learned a lot about the nature, composition, and structure of a poem, and by hard puzzling out acquired practical skills I still find useful. We also knew in the deepest way possible the nature and worth of literature—it was the only set of values the school taught which I found, at the age of fourteen, and still now find, solid.

I vividly remember my frustration at failing several attempts to describe under the heading "Tone" and otherwise account for the peculiar intense pangs of wild beauty conveyed by a poem called "Spring and Fall: to a Young Child," an anonymous exercise placed in front of us, just as Richards had used it on a university class thirty years before. Some poems I eventually seemed to know all about and have under my control (though I was always puzzled and uneasy when I found the task of composing original pieces incredibly difficult by comparison). If ever there were a work of art which could not be paraphrased or explained away or accounted for, it seemed to be this poem, written by, so Fred told us, a priest called Hopkins, whom I'd never heard of. And I remain in a state of amazement, deeply moved by the poem, and unable to say why, though, as an amateur painter, I sometimes imagine I can see its peculiar colours.

Reacting against the ethos of the school I eventually went to an evening college of London University founded in Victoria's reign for working adults with full-time day jobs. Compared with most undergraduates at other colleges we all knew precisely why we were studying, and when we chose to join a particular seminar it was for a good reason. I selected a ten-seminar course on Hopkins because of the extraordinarily intense integrity and human helpfulness of its teacher, who remains a good friend, thirty-five years later.

Each of those seminars was a true and wonderful Voyage of Discovery, to use a Leavisite phrase, with no previous knowledge of where it would finish, or what we would have discovered. One period we were due to examine "Spelt from Sibyl's Leaves," and after the hour was up we had not exhausted the complexities of the first line. The teacher set us the task of discovering in the interval before the next seminar why Hopkins used "hearse" rather than the more obvious "tomb" at the end of line 2: "womb-of-all, home-of-all, hearse-of-all night." During the next seven days, when I was not checking page-proofs or selling advertising-space for the journal on which I worked, or demonstrating for nuclear disarmament, I looked up things in the university library, and wrote forty pages on "hearse." At the end of two further seminars on "Spelt from Sibyl's Leaves" we had still not exhausted the poem, and in fact had opened up further and limitless complexities. How could a mere fourteen lines contain such a vast and frightening universe, a survey-history of world art and philosophy which acted as context for the outpourings of a terrified and deeply depressed lone individual at the end of his tether? And be a wonderful work of art itself, which one could never get to the bottom of, which continuously intrigued and puzzled me deeply?

My experiences with this poem altered my life. Before I had completed my first degree, but armed with two publications on "Spelt from Sibyl's Leaves," I told the head of the department that I must do a full research thesis on this sonnet. He walked with me to Warren Street tube station, talking about Hopkins. He stopped above some workmen digging up the pavement. "White, do you seriously think these men would say you were justified in spending two whole years writing about fourteen lines of poetry?" The men concerned didn't seem prepared to offer an opinion, but I wasn't allowed to cover such a limited area. When I had completed an M.Phil. thesis on the Dublin poems, my supervisor sent it off to a publisher, with an accompanying note saying that I intended to spend the rest of my life on Hopkins. At that time I hadn't thought in those terms, but thirty years later I still haven't written all I want to about him and his poetry, and find new things. (By the way, did you know that Peter Carey based the Reverend Oscar Hopkins in *Oscar and Lucinda* [1997], a film by Gillian Armstrong, partly on our Gerard Hopkins? Oscar's father is the Rev. Theophilus Hopkins; Gerard's father, Manley, used "Theophilus" as a *nom-de-plume*.)

"THESE THINGS WERE THERE"

Someone once pointed out to me that, while Catholics believe everything, Presbyterians believe nothing. My thoroughly Presbyterian upbringing in New Zealand provided me with equal measures of Bible-based training and scepticism, and laid the foundations for my love of poetry (we used the King James Bible, to my mind the most elegant and poetic version in English) and for my propensity to look for the narrow fissures of doubt and contradiction in the spaces between the brilliant peaks of any work I read.

In the sixties my family moved to Cleveland, where I attended Case Western Reserve University. I don't remember when I first encountered Hopkins' poetry; clearly, I knew some of it quite well by my junior year for it was at that time, one autumn night, that it called to me.

I was reading "The Windhover." This was *the* Hopkins poem for me, although I had little idea of its implications. But the words! The words! I read it for sound, and for music. I didn't care what a minion was, or a sillion. I wasn't even sure what a windhover was, come to that. But there I was, glorying in the language when epiphany struck. Not a Saulian scouring of the soul, nor a Joycean slap of truth: but the sort of enlightenment that a dour Presbyterian might expect. Something meagre and banal; appropriate, perhaps, to the works of a man who declared that a man with a dungfork in his hand, a woman with a sloppail, give God glory— of a man who could write magnificent words about one of the least members of the hawk family, the kestrel, fit for a knave.

My epiphany was this: "The Windhover" was a sonnet. Well, I told you. But what a sonnet! An octave in which the four feminine lines picked up and repeated the rhyme of the other four lines; in which the sestet played with two more rhymes; in which alliteration and assonance and internal rhyme and chime and caesurae and run-on lines and outrides all deflected attention from the form and pointed it at the ideas. Yet the form was magnificent! Even before it meant anything, "The Windhover" was a masterpiece of sound and shape and silence.

I had several friends, Catholics, who were "doing" Hopkins for their honours dissertations. I spent much of the rest of that night looking for them to tell them of my discovery. None of them was at all amazed by it but to me it was vital. Here was complexity of form subordinated to something else, as the windhover and his movements were. Not a grand poem; not a grand bird: but both exhibiting immense control and exuberant loss of control simultaneously.

More important, perhaps, was the idea of immolation as imitation of divinity. Again, my Catholic friends professed no surprise at this theological revelation; but sacrifice did not seem to be a dominant idea in Presbyterian theology. To someone whose religious education had focused on an empty cross betokening Christ's rising in glory, rather than on a cross carrying a broken sacrifice, it was an essential insight. Even the text beneath the burning bush that was the only other churchly adornment of my childhood pointed in the opposite direction: "and it was not consumed." Added to the emphasis on Communion as no more than a metaphorical link with God, I had little to help me understand the apparently seamless unity of selfhood and Godhead which appeared in so many of Hopkins' nature poems.

I was not allowed to choose Hopkins for my honours dissertation—my friends had "done" him the year before. I turned to Blake, no mean consolation prize, and stayed with him through the Master's thesis that I completed at Otago University in New Zealand. Many years later, when I applied to the University of Western Australia to work on a doctorate, I was permitted to return to Hopkins, although Daniel Brown was already "doing" him. I was fortunate to be guided by Hilary Fraser, who once had also been refused permission to work on Hopkins as he had been "done." I was thus blessed both in my associations and in my ability to work on that aspect of Hopkins that I and, I suspect, every other reader, most love: his poetry.

I was still Presbyterian enough to look for flaws in the works, and in the ideas they conveyed. Others have commented on their disquiet with phrases or concepts in various poems, and my own experience with a life-or-death situation at sea has damaged my appreciation of the tall nun in "The Wreck of the Deutschland"— if I'd been there, listening to her, I would have brained her with a belaying pin. But this wasn't the sort of thing I meant. I felt that Hopkins was still approached by many readers (including those who thought that Hopkins had been "done" and there was nothing more to do with him) as a quintessentially Roman Catholic poet. The many new literary theories and methodologies which abounded by the time I came to study Hopkins allowed new approaches to his thought and work. Indeed, recent work by scholars such as Rachel Salmon and Dan Brown demonstrates that there are worlds of insight to be gleaned from approaches that do not prioritise Catholicism. My own work on Hopkins' Tractarian background was in part an attempt in the same direction.

The dark fissures in the poetry, which expanded to become gaping crevasses in the Terrible Sonnets, suggested that there was something to be found. But, again, I was exploring what others had already mapped. My insight was something that I had discovered earlier in the form of "The Windhover" but had not properly applied. The windhover, however humble in hawk hierarchy, is still a miracle of complexity and grace and achievement and control whose most brilliant moment comes when it buckles. Hopkins' sonnet, a similar miracle, undergoes the same transformation. And neither is destroyed, but made greater again. The dark fissures of contradiction disappear, as an apparently dead coal breaks open and reveals an inner glory. In the darkest night, at the lowermost pit, the thing that we grasp as we struggle is God.

It is not a conclusion I am happy with. Perhaps we only ever read literature to confirm and contextualise what we already believe. For me, an empty cross connotes absence. How can I deal with poetry that sees, even in apparent absence, the perpetual presence of God?

I guess I'll just have to keep on reading.

E Y N E L W A R D I

Birds, Nests and Aerial Spaces, or: Why Hopkins Matters to Me

There are many reasons why Hopkins matters to me. One of them is his sensitivity to space, especially to aerial space, and another is his fondness for birds, both of which I deeply share. This must have something to do with the privilege I had, in my younger days, of spending a year and a half in the high mountain area of St. Catherine's, Sinai, in constant view of the immense spaciousness between cliffs and boulders of red granite, softened into benevolence by thousands of years of erosion that have taken nothing away from their reassuring solidity; and with my having been free as a safe bird to spend my days among them and in the pure air that surrounded them, and daily to note the peculiarities of the behaviour of black wheatears (*Oenanthe leucopyga*: a species of small black song-bird, with a white rump in the grown males). My job was to identify the language of courtship and nesting habits of these birds, their boasting gestures to demarcate their territories, and their occasional "mobbing" to scare away cats and snakes and of avoiding the preying glance of a passing windhover, or a pair of even more majestic eagles, whose "brute beauty and valour and act" made me focus my binoculars with an awe that by far exceeded my pseudo-scientific curiosity and the desire to "catch" its objects. I was going to become an ornithologist after that glorious time, until I realized that the scientific research I was taking part in was no more than an excuse for being there and focusing my attention, and that the significance, for me, of what I was inhabiting and—well, yes—*inscaping* and *instressing* in my keenly attentive looking, listening and feeling, was of the kind I might find echoed in poetry rather than zoology. And so I went and registered for English Literature, and it was eventually in Hopkins' poetry that I found what was and still is most intimately significant for me specifically in the imaginative experience of air and birds.

Something of what that personal significance is, will, I hope, emerge from my reference, in the following pages, to the relevant images in Hopkins' poetry. Indeed, I have gone into such detail about my stay in St. Catherine's because what matters to me, and I think for Hopkins also, is first and foremost the literal images of air and birds in their irreducible reality—or the reality of their phenomenal experience. In this (phenomenological) respect I wish to say only that these images most palpably evoke a sense of embodiment in space—of being in the air of the world—which varies to include actual and wishful experiences of well-being and ill-being in accommodating or unaccommodating, open or closed spaces (not respectively). The spatial imaginary in Hopkins' work (as in any poet's, perhaps) reflects on the poet's experience of inhabiting the world in a most basic and primal sense, and it is easy to discern, from his poetry as a whole, that Hopkins was not, generally speaking, someone who lived comfortably inside his skin. This may account, in part, for his great sensitivity to space in general, as well as for the more uneasy, obsessive, stressed or constricted aspect of his spatial imagination. However, it is his capacity to go far beyond this aspect and to imagine such inviting, accommodating spaces which makes me so enjoy and admire his work.

In "The Windhover," the air is *not* an accommodating place, with the exception of one very short but golden moment. In the larger part of the poem, being is obtained not through the intimacy of a containing space, but rather by an audacious gesture of conquest. Here, the "big wind" sustains the bird in the air by way of friction, by way of resistance, like ice that sustained the almost horizontally bent skater. "My heart" too stirs "for the achieve of, the mastery of the thing," but even more so for the vertiginous thrill at the prospect of suicidal loss of control: taking its momentum from the run around the ring coached by the wind ("he rung upon the rein of a wimpling wing"), the "dapple[d]" horse-falcon ecstatically breaks loose of the coach's control and the ring's boundary—to lose himself to the centrifugal force that exceeds both the wind's and the bird's. It "rebuff[s] the big wind" by kinaesthetically taking "*off, off forth on swing,*" away into the free space of the air, where it will become prey to gravity and disintegrate into burnt out pride and floating plume. The magnificence of it, for me, is in that moment of vertigo, where virtuosity ventures to appropriate a force that is not one's own by relaxing into it—in what is at once an overreacher's leap and a letting go that are irresistible despite, or because of, the intuition of the consequences. And I don't call it pride (though Hopkins does), or the death drive (though I used the word suicide), because what is at stake here is something else. This poem enacts a desire to be imaginatively freed of a self-imposed notion of existence by resistance and stress—a notion that is configured by the controlled friction whereby the bird sustains itself in the air. This notion is prevalent in Hopkins' poetry: as I have suggested elsewhere, his poetic imaginary as well his verbal practice often project a constricting sense that one's existence depends on one's constant, strenuous assertion of it *against* something (or its absence)—a mode of "doing," or, indeed, overdoing, that is self-defeating in that it in effect prevents its subject from simply "being" in the world. Though Hopkins affirmed this mode of stressed "doing" in his conception of human "selving" through "instress," his longing to break away from the confined and confining mental disposition that generates it is what yields what I take to be the greatest moments of imaginative flight in his poetry. The windhover's final gesture before breaking is one such moment of imaginative flight—not only away *from* the vicious circle, troped by the horse's ring, of constraining fear and control, but also *to* a felicitous space of momentary but nonetheless absolute freedom. This is the freedom, taken as a conscious choice with its full consequences and temporal limit, of appropriating the open sky.

"The Caged Skylark" evokes the sense of being uncomfortably embodied in the human "bone-house, mean house," and it does so most effectively through the comparison between the respective living conditions of the caged bird and its free counterpart. The caged skylark and "man," whom it represents, forgetting their shared condition of imprisonment—

> Both sing sometimes the sweetest, sweetest spells,
>   Yet both droop deadly sometimes in their cells
> Or wring their barriers in bursts of fear or rage.

Now, it is

> Not that the [free] sweet-fowl, song-fowl, needs no rest—
>   Why, hear him, hear him babble and drop down to his nest,
>   But his *own* nest, *wild nest*, no prison.   [my emphases]

But the comparison works both ways, and especially the other way: the "wild nest" imagined from the caged bird's cell is so wild that it actually opens the cage, with its powerfully suggestive condensation of safety and freedom— of the immensity of the open air of flight and the safe intimacy of a home, of a lightness of being and a suitable ground for its embodiment. This happy combination is often represented, in Hopkins' poems, by *both* the air *and* the bird images in their reversible metonymical relations. In this poem, it is beautifully troped by the image of aerial lightness of providential grace in the phrase "meadow down is not distressed / For a rainbow footing it." And we find it in the archetypal "Wild air, world-mothering air, / Nestling me everywhere" in "The Blessed Virgin compared to the Air we Breathe," to whom the poet prays that she may "fold [him] home" as in the following "fast fold thy child," but also, I think, into the folds of her iconographically "azured" robe that is also the sky.

Such aerial nestling-folds are also found at the end of the sonnet "God's Grandeur," in the air pockets under the brooding "bright wings" of the Pentecostal dove. In their grace-full lightness in the sestet, these wings embody both the freedom of flight—indeed, from gravity itself—and the home which the "generations" who "have trod, have trod, have trod" in the octave were lacking, despite their nomadic mobility and the solid ground under their "shod" feet. The lightness is further enhanced by the clearing air of the morning that over "the brown brink eastwards, springs," whose ascending movement liberates "the dearest freshness" that was trampled down by the migrating generations, from "deep down things." And finally, a similar aerial image of relief in happy spaciousness is to be found in "'My own heart let me more have pity on,'" which is a kind of interlude to the self-torture in the "Terrible Sonnets." Here, the poet's heart, tired of obsessively grating on itself ("Patience"), consents to "let be," and consequently gets to imagine its own expansion in a

> . . .joy [that] size[s]
> At God knows when to God knows what; whose smile
> 'S not wrung, see you; unforeseen times, rather—as skies
> Betweenpie mountains—lights a lovely mile.

This image of God's smile in the lighted mile between mountains is one of my very favorite because it is, to use Gaston Bachelard's words in *The Poetics of Space*, at once so immense and so intimate; because it is so free of the controlling expectations of the mind yet so accountable for the heart when it is open, that, as Bachelard again puts it, the world itself becomes "the nest of mankind," a "nest of immensity" wherein we experience an "expansion of being."

In contemplating the image of the nest as the perfect image of the oneiric house, Bachelard cites Jules Michelet's book on birds, where he notes that birds shape their nests with their own bodies. The female "presses and tightens its materials" with her breast "until they have become absolutely pliant . . . and adapted" to the needs of inhabiting. "The nest," Bachelard explains, is thus "a house built by and for the body, taking form from the inside, like a shell, in intimacy that works physically," and so, he quotes Michelet again, "The house is the bird's very person." The nest is, then, the perfect habitat, a primal image of the function of inhabiting whereby we begin to be in a *suitable* space (like a fitted garment), "where being starts with well-being." It is, in short, an image of living comfortably inside one's skin, whose function, as I have tried to show, is sometimes fulfilled in Hopkins' poems, by the nestling air. Thus, Hopkins' sense of well-being in the hospitable house and its surroundings in "In the Valley of the Elwy" (Wales), is accounted for by the animating, animated "cordial air" and the "comforting smell" there. The "comforting smell breathed at every entering" ushers us into the house as if it were the subject of the breathing (only in the following line, after the enjambment, will it become the syntactic object that it is: "Fetched fresh . . . off some sweet wood"). And as we go in we discover that the "house where all were good / To me" derived its goodness from the animated air inside it, which built it from within, like a nest: "That cordial air made those kind people a hood / All over, as a bevy of eggs the mothering wing / Will." And as we are ushered out by yet another aerial simile—that of "mild nights" that also make a hood over "the new morsels of Spring" —we find ourselves facing the scenery where the comforting smell came from expanding panoramically: "Lovely the woods, waters, meadows, combes, vales, / All the air things wear that build this world of Wales." The "air" that "all things wear," signifying both *appearance* and actual *air*, now comes to be like the maternal "robe" that "mantles the . . .globe" in "The Blessed Virgin compared to the Air we Breathe": it at once houses the world of Wales and renders it visible—or sharpens the defining contours of its otherwise generalized "things" —as does the Virgin's material "wild air" on such "glass-blue days . . . / When every colour glows," and "Each shape and shadow shows."

The movement of the air between the inside and the outside of the "things" which it both houses and shapes, enhanced by the descriptive movement and by syntactic ambiguity, assists in the expansion of the poem's imaginary from the space of the house of well-being into the "nest of the world." The nestling quality of the world of Wales is further ameliorated by the syntactic ambiguities that blur the distinctions between inside and outside—which guards against exposure to friction of the sensitive skin. But the turning inside out of the aerial house in the poem does more than that: it annihilates the limiting binarism of inside and outside—that "dialectic of division" which, as Bachelard puts it, "blinds us as soon as we bring it into play in metaphorical domains." That dialectic blinds us by the judging perspective (or "tick") that it embodies, which is hostile to the imagination of grace—be it poetic or metaphysical grace.

In "Peace," the dialectic of division between inside and outside is nicely resolved. I read this poem as being about making space for God—a space that transcends the division between inside and outside by the ingenious device of duplicating God's bird-image. In the first stanza, the speaker, who is a kind of bird himself, complains to Peace, the "wild wooddove," for being too restless—or wild, or free—to give him the real peace of constant faith that he needs. The peace he wants is "pure peace," by contrast to the "poor," inconstant, "piecemeal" peace that visits him only every once in a while. Such peace will give him ground for perching and nesting: "When will you ever, Peace . . . shy wings shut, / Your round me roaming end, *and under be my boughs*?" [my emphasis]. The speaker nags and frets until he realizes that the peace he needs can indeed be cultivated, or domesticated, on condition that he should be willing to let go of Peace and his own desire to control it. This realization comes to him in the form of a substitute bird bearing the exotic name of "Patience exquisite," which God provides him with for the asking. Once settled in, the new bird "plumes to Peace thereafter," so that when he occasionally does come and "here does house," having much work to do and little time to coo, he has the nest all prepared for him "to brood and sit." Patience relieves the speaker of his anxious need to pin Peace down (as in to wring God's smile in "'My heart let me more have pity on'"), while building a nest for his visitations—and for the speaker! She creates a space of freedom from the urgency of need, which leaves room for the possibility of its fulfillment—and perhaps even for the actual fulfillment itself? The wooddove comes when the patient speaker has prepared the nest—but the nest is all the speaker ever wanted to begin with! And if Patience really replaces Peace in terms of giving peace, who needs Peace anyway? Perhaps clearing a *space* for God is enough?

Or is this all one can do, anyway? This is what the sister tells me here, in the monastery of the Sisters of Bethlehem in Beit Jemal, Israel, where I have come from nearby Jerusalem to write this paper. It is very quiet here, and it feels like the right place to think about Hopkins. Following the lead of St. Bruno, the nuns here devote their lives to contemplation in extreme solitude. She is the only nun I can really talk to, because she is in charge of the contact with visitors. And she obviously knows a lot about patience. Naturally, she does not share my idea of possibly finding contentment in a birdless nest (in clearing an inner space for God, or Godot, and patiently brooding on its emptiness forever after. Do I?). Nor does Hopkins, for that matter, for whom the inner space is no private domain, just as the outer can be his personal nest. For this reason, he imagines the two birds that are one—and not one: the space in the heart opened by grace *is and is not* the realization of the divinity that endows it. By his poem, where would Patience exquisite be without her love and double, and *where* would *he* (Peace) be? But, surely, "where" is not the question where the intimate elasticity of nests is concerned. This is made clear in the poem by the images of a duplicated peace-dove that annihilates the either/or dialectics (this way both inside and outside can each have a dove), and of a nest that becomes the ultimate site of freedom for all the birds in the poem, including the speaker, as well as the reader who comes to visit.

The reader who came to visit Hopkins in Beit Jemal found herself in a space quite different from where she first got involved with birds and the air. There, in St. Catherine, I went bird watching in the area around a monastery I hardly ever cared to visit; now, I am sitting in a monastic cell with a remarkably low ceiling, watching Hopkins' imaginary birds grow into their infinite aerial nests—and back to the size of a nun's, or a monk's, hood. What am I doing in this space, which is so austere and confined? Naturally, I think of the caged skylark in his cell . . . . It is amazing how spacious such a small room as this can become when you read poetry that, like the collocation "wild nest," expands your imagination as well as your heart.

J O S E P H J . F E E N E Y , S . J .

SWIMMING AND DIVING WITH HOPKINS

I am a latecomer to Hopkins. I swam early, I dove late.

The swimming: I came to know and enjoy Hopkins in my high-school days at Saint Joseph's Prep in Philadelphia. I again read him during my Jesuit studies, and—with perhaps an unrealized bow to him—I asked for, and was granted, tertianship with the British Jesuits at Hopkins' own St. Beuno's College in Wales (1966-67). Yet even there, and during doctoral studies at the University of Pennsylvania (1967-71), Hopkins was never my focus. I was not even a Victorianist: at Penn I worked in Modern British and 19th/20th-century American literature. Nothing on Hopkins, nothing.

Such were my years of swimming.

I dove into Hopkins, much by chance, in 1977. I had gone to England that summer for the first time since tertianship and, on a bulletin board at the Jesuits' Campion Hall in Oxford, I saw the announcement of a conference at St. Beuno's on the centennial of Hopkins' ordination. Unable to attend—I'd be back in the States by then—I wondered about some American celebration. Opting for an essay in the Jesuit journal *America*, I read all of Hopkins' work from the perspective of priesthood, wrote a text of fourteen pages, had the essay accepted, and to my surprise found it the cover article for the December 7, 1977, issue: "'Nature's Round Makes Jubilee': Hopkins' Priestly Centenary."

Having finally dived in, I explored the depths: coral reefs, fish "that swim," bits of seaweed, a few sharks ("Henry Purcell" perhaps, and "Tom's Garland"), and many pearls. But first I explored Hopkins on the priesthood, and wondered where his views came from. From his Eucharistic piety as an Anglican? From his readings in Scotus? From his theology courses at St. Beuno's? New questions arose from my research: What happened in his final theology examination at St. Beuno's? Why was he so often transferred from place to place? For answers, I expanded my research from London to Dublin to Rome, found new material and unexplored resources, published more and more on Hopkins' Jesuit background, edited two early obituaries, and suddenly found myself a Hopkins scholar. I was diving on my own, and still breathing.

Through the years I've been diving mainly in three parts of the sea: Hopkins' Jesuit context (his third-year theology examination, frequent reassignments, reputation among the Jesuits, friendships with Robert Curtis, S.J., and other Jesuits); catalogues of the Hopkins collections at the University of Texas at Austin and at Gonzaga University, Spokane; and editions of seven Hopkins manuscripts I happily discovered—a comic poem, a poetic fragment, four letters, and a short story—editions published in *TLS: The Times Literary Supplement* and *The Hopkins Quarterly.* Over the years I recall four special pleasures: the 1984 Dublin Conference (organized by Norman White) that gathered a rare group of international scholars for learning, conversation, and the passing libation; the 1989 centennial year when I lectured and published all over the place, enjoyed Carl Sutton's exhibition at the University of Texas, and (with Jude Nixon) hosted an International Conference at Saint Joseph's University; the special spring day in 1989 when my university presented an honorary doctorate to Norman H. MacKenzie, dean of Hopkins scholars; and the 1998 day in London when I discovered an unknown Hopkins poem, the 48-line comic caprice "'Consule Jones.'" From these and other times—the annual International Summer School in Monasterevin, the now-annual Hopkins Conference at Regis University in Denver, the hours of co-editing *The Hopkins Quarterly* with Joaquin Kuhn—I cherish the dear friends I have made in my years of diving.

But why does Hopkins interest me? To begin, we share common traits. We love words and language—roots, wordhistories, sound and soundplay, fresh combinations—and we invent new words with panache. We both love beauty. We care about our prose. We care about God. We're both Jesuit priests.

We share a probing curiosity, a love of the unusual perspective, and (if truth be told) we both have a strong sense of self.

But I am just a diver, he a genius of the waters—a genius in his topsyturvyflow and vitality of image ("cobbled foam-fleece," "Wiry and white-fiery and whirlwind-swivellèd snow"), his weird angles of vision ("The down-dugged ground-hugged grey," "half hurls earth for him off under his feet"), his granitic strength of line ("All felled, felled, are all felled," "Our heart's charity's hearth's fire, our thought's chivalry's throng's Lord"), his fresh vitality of language ("dappled-with-damson west," "braggart bugles," "gash gold-vermilion," "His rollrock highroad roaring down"), his sometime sheer simplicity of phrase ("O is he dead then?" "Long live the weeds and the wilderness yet"). He is a genius of the waters, I add, in his celebrations of divinity ("God! giver of breath and bread; / World's strand, sway of the sea," "ah! bright wings," "[my God!] my God"), in his ability to strike deep emotion ("I kiss my hand / To the stars," "does set danc- / Ing blood," "I am gall, I am heartburn"), and the stark terror of

> O the mind, mind has mountains; cliffs of fall
> Frightful, sheer, no-man-fathomed. Hold them cheap
> May who ne'er hung there.

Swimming and diving in Hopkins' poetry and prose, I recall his own love of swimming or (to use his word) "bathing." In 1863, on the Isle of Wight, "the sea [was] brilliantly coloured and always calm, bathing delightful." In 1871, in Lancashire, "we bathe every day if we like now at a beautiful spot in the Hodder." In 1872, on the Isle of Man, Hopkins and some fellow Jesuits went "bathing at a cove," and in 1873 "went down to the sea and bathed in a little shingly bay." In 1874, near Runnymede, he "bathed at their osier-grown and willowy bathingplace." A poem of 1879-80 remembers "a diver's dip." In 1886, on holiday in Scotland with Robert Curtis, he regretted that "we got no seabathing," and again in 1888, in North Wales, lamented that "we have got no bathing (it is close at hand but close also to the highroad)." A poem of 1888 still idealizes a swim in Lancashire or Devon: "Bathing: it is summer's sovereign good" when a man "will the fleet / Flinty kindcold element let break across his limbs." Alone in a woodland pool, the bather "frolicklavish . . . looks about him, laughs, swims."

To swim and dive with Hopkins: I dare beg for wateryears more in these mysterious deeps.

An Ascot for Astronauts:
Riding the Eternal Carousel
with Gerard Manley Hopkins

I am an urban amazon, a woman who rides side-saddle to work and play. I set aside my Diesel jeans and Abercrombie t-shirts for the elegance of a favourite red and black riding coat, jodhpurs, and Spanish boots, handmade in Mallorca. I'd like to think that I am in Galway, pitching my hat on a post, as Mary Danaher did for Sean Thornton. Few cities conjure as much romanticism as Galway does for me: at once I hear the thunder of hoofs and feel the smoothness of wood in Skeff's, arguably the most beautiful bar I've ever seen. If I'm not in Ireland—riding a regal stallion through Connemara or Dingle Bay—then I am on an exiled Arabian in Boracay Island in my native Philippines, or on the road to Santiago, riding with friends through medieval Leon, Celtic Galicia, and the beautiful villages in the north of Spain. The movie in my mind does that to me: inspired work comes through creative play, and there is nothing like the imagination to bring divine enchantment to daily life. I aspire to the privileged sorority of the *Amazones de France*, the chic *équestriennes* who ride side-saddle to Paris, in a costume that has changed little since the time of Napoleon III: wide black skirts, high-collared blouses, tailored jackets, neat chignons tucked under a veiled hat. This is one of my many dreams, hitched to a gold star on my list of new and exciting things to aspire to and try at least once in life.

But in the meantime, I make do with my local Ascot: Warrington's Victorian carousel in Princes Street Gardens, Edinburgh, Scotland.

I am a regular at the carousel. It is my fleet of noble horses below Edinburgh Castle. I am their princess, and they stand loyal and waiting. I choose my horse carefully. Misty of Chincoteague, Manila Galleon, Medea, Rhapsody in Bleu, Evinrude, Holly Golightly, Goyescas, Troyanos, Sabrina Fair, O'FFlahertie, Oscuro Wildegoose, Duns Scotus, Christopher Robin, Ben Bulben: they are named after childhood anecdotes and adult aspirations. The horse that carries me is a bearer of dreams, a guardian of soulful hinterlands. They are baptised in an ocean of joy. The barkers greet me with the conspiratorial wink, smile, a giggle in the rain: I am a diehard jockey, and nothing gets in my way of riding towards heaven. Nothing, be it tsunami, snow, sleet, or the wet confetti of an Auld Reekie wind. I am Julie Jordan, lifted off a lacquered horse by handsome carousel barker Billy Bigelow. I look at the world and ask why not: if I loved you I would do this and this and this . . . and because of these dreams I never walk alone.

For as long as I could walk and dangle my legs I have been in love with carousels. They are my passion, my toyland, my live music box, my Renoir menagerie, my Saint-Saens carnival, my heaven-haven, my whirling world of lions, tigers, bears, kingfishers, and dragonflies.

In a figurative sense, I have always been riding horses. My family and I emigrated from the Philippines to the United States when I was two. I rode in the silver Pegasus of an airline fleet. I arrived in Wilmington in a coltish car, beige and brave as it sped through a concrete tierra. A minotaur of ten horsepower brought us to New Jersey. He paused for an oily nightcap by the Delaware River, before leaving us in the labyrinth that was our new home.

My first carousel in the New World was a carnival regular at Trenton's Cadwalader Park. Dad worked the night shift, which allowed him to indulge me in my mid-morning Black Beauty ride. I was a restless, garrulous child, with a passion for animals and books. To this day, I am known by friends and colleagues as the doctoral student with a teddy bear in one hand, and a Yeats volume in the other!

It was only natural that I would ride carousels: it was an iconic signposting of actual and imaginative journeys. It was the naming of places, an intimate cartography in which my soul remapped the world. It was a road map of the human heart, in which boundaries and differences are intentionally blurred. There had to be a way of expressing the displacement that so often marked my nomadic life. A citizen of the world rides perpetually with Magellan: she circumnavigates the world with him, finishes where he left off. As a Filipina, I am haunted by the circles of Magellan. Given the chance to re-write history, I would like to resuscitate him in Cebu and join him in his outward journey towards infinity. My Magellanic heart has given me a weakness for circles: I am biased towards spheres, spider webs, celtic knots, ceilidhs and Bach inventions. If my mind were a subway map it would be the Arachnid loom of the Paris *métro*, rather than the masculine linear logic of London's—mind the gap, please! — Tube. I am Sisyphus in the city: sorting through a problem, I engage myself in a moving meditation of a horse ride through musical time and memory.

Riding a carousel, I ride through life. I look at it from all angles. Time is leveled. Sound reigns and rains. An impressionist takes my life and blurs it in a wash of paint and Giverny water. Memories are shaken, not stirred, in a Martini hourglass. I am an Astronaut, at a Royal Ascot race on the moon. I am not alone. I am riding in between two persons: myself as a child, holding for dear life to the reins, and myself as a wise old woman, calm and tranquil on her wooden hobby-horse. Given this autobiographical triptych, I meditate upon the accidentals of Fate, and the beauty of relationships that occur not out of choice, but chance. Riding the carousel, I wonder what hand rested there before me, what foot secured itself in the stirrup, what body gave warmth to the seat. How often do we meet people, without really meeting them? How often have we passed by someone years ago—in a queue, through a carousel door, through a crowded place—only to meet them again, in a more pivotal and fateful future? Wislawa Szymborska captures the beauty of an uncertain Other:

> I want to ask them
> if they don't remember—
> a moment face to face

in some revolving door?
perhaps a "sorry" muttered in a crowd?
a curt "wrong number" caught in the receiver? —
but I know the answer.
No, they don't remember.

Even before I met him, I rode the carousel with him. He was always there, beside me, behind me. A taciturn man, he was the first to board and the last to leave. He chose his horse carefully: I could see him peering closely at the chipped paint and elaborate designs. He looked so closely and intently at things that I thought to ask him, "Excuse me, sir, but have you lost your eyeglasses?" I can understand, as I myself suffer from severe myopia and astigmatism.

Even before I met him, my father's footsteps covered his. As a student in Oxford, Dad frequented his church, the Roman Catholic parish of St. Aloysius.

Most of the time he was alone. He said little to others, but a lot to himself. He kept his lips tightly pursed, lest the verbal volcano within him erupt into a liquid Oxford English Dictionary.

One day I was surprised, because he brought a few friends along. They seemed to have followed him, for he hardly noticed them when they shouted something in the wind. There was a man who called himself William Butler. He spoke of a woman named Maud and muttered time and again, "Horseman, pass by." Beside him was a well-dressed man with a rather long name: Oscar Fingal O'Flahertie Wills Something Something. He carried a suitcase, claiming to have been born in it. I learned from William Butler that what Oscar really wanted was to return to his summer home in Moyntura, on the west coast of Ireland. He never stopped talking, and the others ignored him when he declared, "I wish to be a Cardinal of the Catholic Church." And then there were the two men who never left the quiet man's side. One was called Bridges. He was a doctor. He argued continuously about a ship known as the "Deutschland." The other was a young man, called Digby, I think. Like Oscar, he was handsome and a sort of dandy, but he surprised us all by his unusual outfit: he was dressed in the brown habit of a Franciscan friar. When the ride ended he ran towards a lake, and the quiet man tried to run after him.

Sometimes I could hear the quiet man. A faint whisper that soared above the music: "When will you ever, Peace, wild wooddove, shy wings shut, / Your round me roaming end, and under be my boughs? / When, when, Peace, will you, Peace?"

Like me, he was tempted to shut his eyes. But both of us knew better. We rode through eternity, and it was only fitting that we should ride with our hands open, palms cupped and deep, to catch the freefall of beauty and bounty.

I remember the day when I met him formally. We were introduced by a Winnie the Pooh look-alike, Father Joseph J. Feeney of Saint Joseph's University, Philadelphia: "Leonora, this is Father Gerard Manley Hopkins, an esteemed member of our Jesuit community."

Father Hopkins asked the class to read aloud a poem that he had written: "Spring and Fall: to a Young Child."

He seemed to wince at our singsong attempts. Finally, he stood up himself and read it the proper way: "Márgarét, áre you gríeving / Over Goldengrove unleaving?"

And then it hit me. This special way of speaking, which he called "sprung rhythm" (something that Fr. Feeney and the people of Ireland do quite naturally) was best done on the carousel. Riding with the wind towards Eternity, you are uninhibited by convention. A primeval rhythm overwhelms you, and you cannot help but mimic the irregularity of wings bracing against wind.

After all, what better place to feel the goldengrove unleaving, than on a moving globe, the world in miniature that spins on a frenzied axis.

I tried it. Riding Warrington's carousel, I recited Father Hopkins' words. It felt so natural, so at ease with the pull and push of air:

> Winning ways, airs innocent, maidenmanners, sweet looks,
>   loose locks, long locks, lovelocks, gaygear, going gallant,
>   girlgrace—
> Resign them, sign them, seal them, send them, motion them
>   with breath,
> And with sighs soaring, soaring sighs, deliver
> Them . . .

As a Warrington jockey, I am at ease with anachronisms. Guided by my cardiac map, I delight in the re-creation of the world. I revel in Paris, Texas, Paris, Timbuctu. I serve Colcannon with Pad Thai, Yorkshire Pudding with Tempura and Peking Roast Duck. A straw cowboy hat is an elegant accessory to a white silk shirt and long black skirt. Purists shudder at my fusion witchery, my bold alchemy of lofty art and ordinary experience. In their eyes I am irreverent, iconoclastic, bold. Like a charlatan, I am studded with vices, but am anything but boring.

It is just another day in the life of a Hopkinsian protege.

We are good friends now. He urges me to be independent. It helps, he advises, to write for an absent audience, one that you can never see nor hear. Artistic integrity is important. His quaint juxtapositions have become my literary Angelus:

> . . . sheer plod makes plough down sillion
> Shine, and blue-bleak embers, ah my dear,
>   Fall, gall themselves, and gash gold-vermilion.

We ride the carousel together. It is a sacred ritual, as important as Mass and morning writing. It is an exercise in observation and imagination. It is an amateur club for ornithologists.

I tell Father Hopkins my dream: given the money, I would construct a carousel especially for him. It would be the most wonderful and original carousel. The flying horses of my dreams would indeed be a flock of feathered steeds like pegasus: kingfishers, dragonflies, windhovers, kestrels, skylarks, doves, hawks, falcons, robins. Trees, as in his mythical "Binsey Poplars," would be curved and rounded, to make a seat for couples. "Deutschland" would be diminished, to hold a cluster of children. Each figure would be painted differently, according to the *inscapes* of the given day, the *instress* of the artist, as he felt at that particular moment. The background would be a wallpaper montage of Duns Scotus' Oxford: spires and trees, grounded by the Cherwell and the Isis. And the music: all of Purcell, Monteverdi's "Beatus Vir," Pachelbel's "Canon," Puccini's "Humming Chorus," the overture to Gilbert and Sullivan's

Patience, the overture to Rameau's *Platée*, Bach's *Inventions* and *Goldberg Variations*, "Waltz for Jazz Orchestra" by Shostakovich, orchestrations of Hopkins' piano compositions, Delibes' "Flower Duet" from *Lakmé*, Mozart's "Rondo alla Turca."

There is a poignancy to his joy, an urgency to my dreams. Both of us are overcome by an avarice to grab the *inscape* that God pours, monsoon-like, upon an unsuspecting world.

He whips open an umbrella, and we are shielded from the benevolent rainfall. We sit down under a parasol of leaves, and he outlines the shapes of his shadows. Sketched in Dublin charcoal, they conjure images of a midnight Goya. I am not frightened by what he tells me. In fact, I have experienced it to some extent in my own life. I tell him of the iceberg, ferocious and thick, as it enclosed within its walls the pen and ink of my imagination. He half-smiles, conspiratorial in his empathy. He knows all too well the necessity of play, the warmth of a nurturing home. He tells me about his Divine Father, who so loves artists that he does all He can to save lost works. Hide a work, suppress it, stuff it in a drawer, burn it, ban it, handcuff it, imprison it, feed it to the birds and fish, make it into confetti, throw it into the sea, and God ultimately fetches it and throws it back at you. Or, if you're too stubborn, at the world, and some unfortunate harbinger.

I catch him winking to the sky. And then he whispers, so softly—"Bridges."

That iceberg is not frozen. It's God testing you. It's God awaiting the right moment to make you his Lazarus. Artists, he sighs, are children at heart. And when children get scared, they run, they hide, they give themselves the dunce cap and sulk in the corner, they stop talking altogether.

> And what to do, given that dilemma?
> Again, that half smile of irony and bittersweet memory.
> Do something you're not accustomed to doing—
> And that is?
> Stop riding the carousel, for a change.
> What?

In other words, just sit on the other side of the fence, for a while. And just take time to watch others enjoy themselves. Be a part of the world. Look at it, listen to it. Feel it, touch it. Don't immerse yourself in yourself. Wake and feel the dark of day and night. And that is when the iceberg shall melt.

And that is what we do. Every now and then, I sit with Hopkins. I welcome silence into my life. The peace and patient calm of an artist who watched life pass him by.

He has taught me the importance of being a spectator, and not just a rider. From where I sit I hear music. I hear the familiar gallop, the precious grinding of an antique machine. I am tempted to jump from my seat and hop on my favourite horse, but he stops me.

Leonora, if you don't mind, let us have some hot chocolate. It need not be Lent. I would like to show you the fog and foam that form on its surface.

INTELLECTUAL RESPONSES

". . . delight that fathers thought . . ."

U W E   B Ö K E R

G.M. Hopkins, the Transparency of Language and Modernist Word-Skepticism

Sifting through the volumes on the shelves of my Dresden bookstore recently, I found, by mere chance, a collection of Sarah Kirsch's poems from the nineties, *Bodenlos*. Kirsch has been honored with the Hölderlin (1984) and the Büchner (1996) literary prizes , to name only the most prestigious ones, and has been called one of the most important living female poets of the German language. She introduced this slender book with a quotation from Gerard Manley Hopkins: "June 19. Two beautiful anvil clouds low on the earthline in opposite quarters, so that I stood between them." It was this epigraph that sent me straight back to W.H. Gardner's edition of the *Poems and Prose of Gerard Manley Hopkins*, republished several times since 1953; but Gardner's, alas, is a very select selection, reducing the 130 pages of the House-Storey edition to thirty pages, leaving out the passage just quoted. Nevertheless, the Gardner edition has been and still is my main source of knowledge on the Victorian poet. I had originally become acquainted with the author of "The Wreck of the Deutschland" through German translations, published around 1960, and—not being a Hopkins scholar—I subsequently deepened my knowledge by using the popular Penguin Hopkins. I am sorry to say that I never really taught Hopkins in class, though I have, again and again, used some of his poems to introduce my students to the *Beowulf* poet's prosody; I have also, in seminars on contemporary poetry, demonstrated what can be done in terms of musicality, rhythm and tone by quoting—or rather, reading aloud—my favorite piece, "Binsey Poplars." But as I can see now, I reproduced nothing but what was common knowledge at that time.

To return to the initial stage of acquaintance, my first
knowledge of Hopkins goes back to Hans Magnus
Enzensberger's anthology *Museum der modernen Poesie* (1960).
Enzensberger, a poet himself, was obviously unable to include
Hopkins amongst the moderns, though he mentions him side by
side with Gérard de Nerval, E.A. Poe, Emily Dickinson, the
Comte de Lautréamont, Jules Laforgue, Alexander Blok and
William Butler Yeats as one of the "lonely, deep-thinking natures"
prefiguring modernism. Enzensberger's anthology and a number
of other selections published during the late fifties and the early
sixties were ultimately responsible for shaping my image of
Hopkins as well as my ideas of poetic modernism.

During the last five years I have, however, acquired a more
intimate knowledge of the poet by attending Desmond Egan's
Hopkins Summer School in Monasterevin, Ireland, although I
have been less interested in the theological aspects of his poems
than in his concept of language immediately before the advent of
modernism. In order to place him from the literary historian's
point of view, but also from the translator's, I'd like to quote
some of his journal entries that at first glance seem to be out of
the way. On May 2, 1866, Hopkins remembers:

> Same day, I believe, Case at one of the cricket grounds saw
> three Ch. Ch. men laughing loudly at a rat with back
> broken, a most ghastly sight, flying at the dog. He kicked
> away the dog, put his heel on the rat's head and killed it, and
> drove away the crowd of cads.

When I read this I wondered why Hopkins had put this short
episode down at all. Cruel as it was, the hunting of rats was
nothing unusual on Christ Church meadows, as an article in the
Cornhill Magazine of 1865 tells us. The author reports that there
used to be "persons of highly unprepossessing appearance, with
small cages and sharp-looking terriers: these cages contain rats,
and on a moderate payment, a rat-hunt at once takes place." The
rats, I promise the reader, will reappear at the end of my essay.
They play a significant role in an imaginary letter written by the
German poet Hugo von Hofmannsthal. His "A Letter" (1901) is

one of the most important documents of Vienna modernism, expressing growing doubts about the possibilities of creating a philosophical or poetic language adequate to describe or embody reality.

Let me come back to Hopkins' journals. When I recently read them once more in the Gardner selection, I began to see why Sarah Kirsch had selected the remark about the two anvil-shaped clouds, although she could have chosen others. It was not the first nor the last time that Hopkins had looked at the sky and the ever-changing shapes of clouds. Take the following entry for April 27, 1868:

> Generally fine between hard showers; some hail, which made the evening very cold, a flash of lightning, a clap of thunder, and a bright rainbow; some grey cloud between showers ribbed and draped and some wild bright big brown flix at the border of a great rack with blue rising behind—though it was too big in character to be called flix.

Hopkins had started describing "scapes" and "inscapes" like this around 1868, e.g., during his journey to Switzerland and Germany: "Before sunrise looking out of window saw a noble scape of stars" on July 9; or describing Swiss trees as "well inscaped—in quains" on July 7. Hopkins is not the tourist admiring the picturesque mountains, waterfalls or glaciers. It is not the landscape as such he is interested in, but the "scape" of natural objects that appear to him to be "original and interesting"—above all the clouds' constantly changing shapes that, for Hopkins, generate ideas of singularity, individuality, oneness. Sometimes Hopkins makes mention (at least in my Gardner selection) of other natural "objects," of a cuckoo on June 16, 1873, for example, singing somewhere amongst distant trees. Human company obviously tends to distract him: "Even with one companion ecstasy is almost banished: you want to be alone and to feel that, and leisure—all pressure taken off" in the Alps on July 25, 1868. He is, as Norman White remarks in his biography of Hopkins, experimenting to re-experience linguistically his confrontation with nature. He obviously sensed danger in the shapes, textures, and movement of human beauty, but his responses to sky could be indulged. Hopkins had found a conventionally acceptable way of expressing, and perhaps masking, some of his most powerful sensuous responses.

Responding to the ever-changing shape of the clouds is nothing less than a "spiritual exercise" in the sense of St. Ignatius Loyola. Hopkins is obviously becoming acutely aware of the singularity of natural phenomena—of their randomness—as he is confronted with "the prismatic colours in the clouds," "great bulks of brassy cloud hanging round, which changed their colour to bright reds over the sundown and to fruittree-blossom colour opposite," or "endless ranges of part-vertical dancing cloud, the highest and furthest flaked or foiled like fungus and coloured pink." As the quotations demonstrate, Hopkins seems to be convinced that he is ultimately able to translate his impressions of absolute oneness as well as of the underlying pattern into human language. Both seem to be in danger of being destroyed by human intervention—by the "pressures" he experiences, e.g., the moment he learns of the felling of an ashtree: "I heard the sound and looking out and seeing it maimed there came at that moment a great pang and I wished to die and not to see the inscapes of the world destroyed any more." It is the contingency of nature, its randomness, its subservience to chance that ultimately, however, discloses to him a non-chaotic or meta-chaotic order. Oneness and pattern are two sides of a coin:

> All the world is full of inscape and chance left free to act [!] falls into an order as well as purpose: looking out of my window I caught it in the random clods and broken heaps of snow made by the cast of a broom.

It is true that the seeming randomness of natural phenomena at times becomes painful and threatening, as with a thunderstorm killing people:

> Flashes lacing two clouds above or the cloud and the earth started upon the eyes live veins of rincing or riddling liquid white, inched and jagged as if it were the shivering of a bright

riband string which had once been kept bound round a blade
and danced back into its pleatings.

But as this quotation shows, Hopkins is trying to "imitate"
nature or non-human reality; he is looking for a "natural
language of things" by making use of, as in his poetry, alliteration,
assonance, onomatopoeia and the like. Hopkins gives the
impression that he will be able to find his personal, sometimes
even semi-private terminology—the means and medium to
translate his communications with nature into a language
adequate to embody both the oneness and the pattern. Thus, his
poetry is informed with the idea of "making words not just
represent but become the thing itself," finding its equivalent

> in the contorted syntax and extreme "chiming" . . . whereby
> everything "rings, tells of" its involvement with the thing it
> denotes, and simultaneously is perceived as interdependent,
> because its harmony is not a product of itself alone, but of its
> interaction with all other objects, or words in a poem, and the
> reality they express together.

A Hopkins translator should be aware of these ideas. One
has to be aware of the fact that poststructuralist critics have tried
to decenter not only prevalent humanist notions of self and
individuality, but also the idea of the "transparency of language"
that is at the basis of Hopkins' poetics; thus, emphasizing the
"opacity" of language. Language is held to be "a system which
pre-exists the individual" and in which the individual produces
meaning, and it is said "to speak us." According to Linda
Hutcheon, "an organization of the world which seems natural is
not necessarily so." If the world we experience is more or less the
world differentiated by language, "then the claim that realism
reflects the world means that realism reflects the world
constructed in language." And she adds to this, " . . . if literature
is a signifying practice, all it can reflect is the order inscribed in
particular discourses, not the nature of the world."

Leaving aside post-structuralist deconstruction, it is
nevertheless necessary to draw attention to the widespread

"word-skepticism" of modernist writers. In Hugo von Hofmannsthal's fictional "A Letter" (1901), the crisis of identity leads to a crisis of expression. As we know, Francis Bacon, Lord Chandos' addressee, considered nature to be a system of signs that had to be and could be deciphered by means of empirical science. Chandos, on the other hand, who formerly had seen "the whole of life as a great unity," admits:

> I have completely lost the capacity to discourse or speak about anything at all in a consistent way. . . . [A]bstract words . . . were crumbling in my mouth like moldering mushrooms. . . . Everything broke apart into pieces, and these pieces again into pieces, and there was nothing left that could be spanned by means of abstraction.

He goes on to describe his new life that finds its fulfillment in sudden revelatory but everyday moments that resemble James Joyce's epiphanies. One of these moments occurs when he is watching the death throes of rats poisoned by himself, and he goes on to describe the horrible scene at some length and in some detail, emphasizing the sympathetic or emphatic spilling over of his own suffering being into the dying creatures. It is an altogether different attitude informing his description: the horror, the word-skepticism and the non-verbal epiphany seem to be one, encapsulated in objects of ugliness. Hopkins obviously took a different attitude, as the journal entry quoted at the beginning of my essay shows. He is, and rightly so, enraged from a moral point of view, but he is still able to speak about it (about the world, that is) from a relatively detached observer's point of view.

To come back to the first part of my essay: Hopkins was obviously looking, because of his doubts in the efficacy of the contemporary Victorian poetic idioms, for a new and more adequate, but nevertheless "transparent" language. He wanted to convey to his readers the oneness of nature as well as its underlying patterns. The natural phenomenon was more or less a metonymy, pointing at the overall structures in terms of time and space, whereas the far-going word-skepticism of certain modernists resulted in the loss of the metonymic quality of words and sense-impressions, in the emphasis of the moment, the significance of which is left open to interpretation, as well as the use of the private cipher, as we find it in the poetry of Paul Celan. However, contemporary poets are using again all sorts of new and old techniques; they have, diverging from extreme modernist or post-modernist attitudes, regained some of their predecessors' confidence in the dignity and worth of poetic language. And a poet like Sarah Kirsch is even able to grasp and render Hopkins' attitudes towards nature, as the very last poem in her 1996 collection demonstrates. The first lines read like this:

> *Franziskus*
> As nature communicates with us
> the way she does he talks to her
> creatures in his own language
> it breaks out of his body volcano-like
> a long oration urgent fiery a pure
> gesture accompanying in the mangy
> public park of Feldafing a fountain
> whose mouth has been silenced five
> miserable beheaded trees in the snow
> he attributed to them courage and beauty . . .

Is this not Hopkins praising nature as he did when he saw "the beautiful anvil clouds low on the earthline in opposite quarters"? I would say yes, in a language of his own, more than one hundred years after the felling of the Binsey poplars, still full of confidence in the dignity and force of poetic language, perhaps even moving "after-comers" to imagine "the beauty been."

ALAN HEUSER

HOPKINS IN MY LIFE AND WORK

In full-time Science at McGill, I took a Creative Writing course and wrote among my poems an ironic item on a "One-day Church," in conventional blank-verse. English Prof Algy Noad noticed it and loaned me his copy of Hopkins' Poems (second edition by Charles Williams) about 1945. Hopkins' forms and content jolted me from Deism to Theism and made me jostle with McGill's *avant-garde*—F.R. (Frank) Scott, Patrick Anderson, A.M. (Abe) Klein. Twice in 1945-47 I was an editor of the McGill literary magazine *The Forge*. Over the next two decades Hopkins was my exciting study in poetry, religion, imagery: I went from a B.Sc. (McGill 1947)—studying Hopkins under Noad and Klein—to an M.A. in English with scholarly work under G.I. Duthie and Joyce Hemlow and a master's thesis on Hopkins' poetic imagery (McGill 1949). Hopkins' Early English diction pointed by sprung rhythm and internal rhyme ("chime") made his verse very exciting to me. Hopkins had a triple impact—on my English studies (especially Anglo-Saxon), on my own poetry, on my taking orthodox Christianity seriously. I advanced to Harvard for a Ph.D. in English and a doctoral dissertation on Hopkins' "aesthetic cognition" (Harvard 1953). Here, using platonism and neoplatonism, I tried to trace Hopkins' overall aesthetic philosophy, to unify Hopkins' thought from beginning to end. But first impressions of Williams' second edition remained strong: I was following Williams' kind of Christian mysticism. Also, the *Poems* in a third edition came out in time for my master's thesis. For this, Catholic friends (Paul Orr and Charlotte Tansey, and later, Eric O'Connor, S.J.) were helpful and over the years remained loyal, so that near the end of my life and looking back I can say I have come full circle—to the Roman Catholic Church within which I have only recently been conditonally baptized or "received" (1999)—while the long interim has been spent in the Anglican Church (1951-98). In this big loop into Anglicanism I was led by my immature notions and a certain fear of outright Catholicism; I became an Anglican altar-server, and aspired to a settled married life—by the example of two married Anglicans, by the Ven. Mac Ellis and then by colleague Archie Malloch, who saw what I did not: that my attachment to Hopkins was tied up with my contradictory fear of marriage.

At Harvard my teachers included George Sherburn, Hyder Rollins, Douglas Bush, W.J. Bate; my fellow-student friends were Anglo-Catholics: Bob Regan, Orville Conner, Dick Van Fossen, contacts made first through T.S. Eliot's Harvard lecture "Poetry and Drama" (1950). Anthony Bischoff, S.J., kindly sent copies of Hopkins' unpublished letters and journals to Boston College for my use. But I remained Anglo-Catholic in sympathy. My Episcopalian home was the Church of the Advent, Boston; in Montreal, the Anglican Church of St. John the Evangelist. Avoiding the RC Church as too strict, I took Anglican instruction at "the Cathedral," Montreal, Summer 1951; was confirmed there, took my first communion at "the Advent" in Boston. I made retreats at an Episcopalian monastery, like Hopkins but with a non-priestly outcome. Then I taught two years at Princeton. Renting a piano at the Princeton Library, I played over and over Henry Purcell's keyboard works (Hopkins' favourite composer) for the precision and authentic cadences of English baroque music. I wanted to write a book from the inside—on the creative process within Hopkins' poetry and prose, art and music, prayer and thought. But I felt isolated and so, given the opportunity, returned to Montreal and McGill, where I remained in the English Department until retirement.

Before returning to Montreal I travelled to the UK with a Princeton grant to look at Hopkins manuscripts and visit his old territory, Summer 1953; I met Hopkins scholar Humphry House and Hopkins' nephew Gerard W.S. Hopkins, as well as Jesuit Fathers Philip Caraman, Thomas Corbishley, Christopher Devlin. But I was still in an Anglo-Catholic crowd. Then, with a McGill grant, I returned to Cambridge, Mass., to draft my Hopkins book, Summer 1955. I made my daily communion at an Episcopalian monastery before my work day in a hotel room, tuning to a Christian muse. All the while I was encouraged by my friend and colleague Archie Malloch.

I was continuing to be active in writing poetry, completing a long poem "Selving Time" which John Sutherland—well known in Canadian letters—published in his *Northern Review* (1954), where my Anglican confirmation became "baptism's print"; he took that literally, as well he should. When I came back to McGill to teach, Sutherland asked me to be sponsor at his RC baptism; realistically I could not; I had (unwittingly) misled him by my poetic licence. However, I kept on writing the occasional poem marked by "religious enthusiasm" and imitative internal rhyme ("chime") after Hopkins. The "triple impact" of Hopkins on my studies, my poetry, my "Catholicism" continued.

At McGill I taught a nineteenth-century English course, ending with Hopkins as the pinnacle of nineteenth-century poetry; then a seminar on Hopkins, Yeats, and Eliot. In the interim years between teaching I tried for the Anglican priesthood—Hopkins had his way at last—I became a seminarian twice, but that did not work out: I was no Hopkins of self-denial! Resigned to my fate as a university teacher not a priest, I taught twentieth-century literature for the rest of my time at McGill. From 1945-60 Hopkins was my steam-engine. In October 1957 I sent my book-in-manuscript to Gerard W.S. Hopkins at OUP London; it was published in October 1958, but without some crucial acknowledgements!—and too condensed for the public.

After the Hopkins book was out of my system, I married, and my exhilarating marriage led to children: I was a very happy family man. Life in my forties with teaching, a wife to love and cherish, and two youngsters was very demanding; so my studies on Hopkins lost their zest. However, I was still inspired to write the occasional poem, once or twice a year, no more; some of my poems were published in journals from *The Sewanee Review* (1955) to *Encounter* (1972). But the triple impact of Hopkins thinned out: my original poetry became less and less, and the Hopkins influence less Hopkinsian. My last Hopkinsian poems were three sequences or canticles: "Atlantic Farewell" (1960) published in *Canadian Forum* (1961), followed by "Atlantic Letter" (1966) and "Atlantic Soundings" (1969)—long variations on themes.

Two revolutions in Hopkins publishing took place a decade apart: in the UK, the Oxford University Press was publishing an expanded prose Hopkins (five vols. 1955-56, 1959) and a fourth edition of Hopkins' *Poems*, edited by W.H. Gardner and N.H. MacKenzie (1967, revised 1970). I had seen much of this prose for my book, but not all, and I left it to others to comb through the expanded fourth edition of *Poems* for further insights. My work had been done. I left it at that. My later scholarly research was on D.H. Lawrence (a blind alley for me) and on Louis MacNeice (I edited three books of his neglected writings through the Clarendon Press).

New teachers were arriving at McGill in the 1960s, among them medievalist Prof. David Williams, who was to be very helpful in my final growth into Roman Catholicism. This became apparent in my later communications with this good friend after I had retired and he had published his scholarly award-winning work *Deformed Discourse* (1996).

But for Hopkins it was Prof. MacKenzie's work which struck me and others. When MacKenzie's *Reader's Guide to Hopkins* came out (1981), Hopkins scholars joined in a Hopkins Conference at Wilfrid Laurier/Waterloo Universities; I met counterparts, happy to pay respects to Norman H. MacKenzie for his many scholarly contributions. I was invited to join *The Hopkins Quarterly* Advisory Board on which I've enjoyed serving. Prof. MacKenzie's three meticulously edited volumes of Hopkins' poems (1989-91), especially *The Poetical Works of Gerard Manley Hopkins* (OET 1990), must be acknowledged as the major Canadian contribution—not my earlier stubborn book written in a too-condensed prose. One can spend weeks, nay months, contemplating Prof. MacKenzie's Commentary to Hopkins' *Poetical Works* with great profit.

After retiring I moved to Vancouver and came at last to the Roman Catholic faith through communications with my friend

David Williams, whose work seriously questioned the negative philosophy of neoplatonism on which some of my Ph.D. thesis on Hopkins had been based. I undertook instruction from Father John Horgan at Saints Peter and Paul RC Church (1998-99: five months of reading and discussion), and made my Profession of Faith at Easter 1999. Hopkins was central to my life and work, but not as central as my family and faith.

Thus 1945-60 was a fully Hopkinsian phase: 1962-80 a domestic phase, during which I spent a year or two struggling with Greek; 1981 was an opportunity leading to the *HQ* board. As reader for *HQ* and for Prof. MacKenzie at Queen's I have gotten some idea of recent Hopkins research. In all it has been a fascinating and rewarding experience working on Hopkins.

I began with emblems in relation to Hopkins in my M.A. thesis; went on to over-elaborate platonism and neoplatonism in the doctoral dissertation; and in my book tried to unify diverse influences of creativity—"inscape," "instress," "pitch"—doing too much in too small a space. Later, I gave a paper on poems by Hopkins, D.H. Lawrence, and Ted Hughes—a paper published in the *HQ*; but that was all.

This has been a personal review of the influence of Hopkins on my life and work; I trust it has not been too subjective. Ultimately it was he who brought me to respect and then reverence the RC faith and gave me much poetic inspiration—though my spiritual development was different from his, taking place a century later and in a very different culture. The big question is: why did it take me so long to convert? The answer: blindness and sloth—failure to do my homework in the RC tradition—failure to proceed from the aesthetic level to the ethical level and further on to the leap of faith. I will always have great affection and admiration for Hopkins—who converted in his early twenties and went on to write some of the finest religious poetry in English. I am grateful to my friends who have been patient with my blind spots.

But I can't end here. My Hopkins steam-engine turns to a wish-list: (1) for an inclusive (including newly discovered letters), chronological "Collected Letters" with unified index; (2) for a book on Newman and Hopkins; (3) for links in Jesuit zeal—especially English geniuses St. Edmund Campion, S.J., martyr to the old religion, and Gerard Manley Hopkins, S.J.; (4) for the role of drama in Jesuit education and Hopkins' dramatic efforts within that context.

A POET WHO CAME TO BROOD AND SIT

My first encounter with Gerard Manley Hopkins was at a relatively early age. By the mid-seventies, he already figured as a major precursor of twentieth-century poetry in my A-level English literature course. I think I can sum up my initial feelings—as well as those of my school companions—towards him in two words: baffled and impressed. On the one hand, here was a man (clearly something of a misfit) who seemed to have appeared unheralded from out of nowhere and whose poetry was so surprisingly different from anything we had been studying until that moment. On the other, although a good deal of it may have proved to be rather arduous for us at the time (attention was mainly focussed on "The Wreck of the Deutschland," I must add), we could not fail to sense the urgency and immediacy of a profoundly lyrical and powerfully dramatic voice. It being a Catholic school, much emphasis was inevitably placed on the doctrinal aspects of his verse. But that was certainly not what drew me to him then. Nor is it so now.

What I have personally always found exciting about Hopkins is his experimentation with metre and his use of language, though it was not really until years later, when I had to teach Hopkins myself, that I learnt to appreciate his prosodic virtuosity and semantic density more fully. One is constantly learning as one teaches and, as a result, Hopkins has reinforced my own sense of the importance of the study of prosody in poetry in general. Indeed, I think it is to be regretted that this fundamental aspect of verse is still generally neglected (taken for granted dare I suggest?) in both schools and universities around the world. I believe a knowledge of the metrical and stylistic aspects of versification is of fundamental importance if one is to get at the heart of what Hopkins is doing, for the very fact that these are so heavily foregrounded and play such a key role in contributing to the drama and tension in his poetry. Reading Hopkins certainly made me aware of the various ways in which the apparently over-familiar forms of traditional prosody could be so skilfully stretched as to become almost completely unrecognisable, as in the long rambling lines of "The Windhover," for example, his first sonnet in sprung rhythm, with its various "outriding syllables," or the tormented and violent rhythms of the sonnet "(Carrion Comfort)," whilst at the same time resisting total metamorphosis. Furthermore, I have always sensed tensions behind Hopkins' craft, both on a poetic level (his daring linguistic and prosodical challenges are so different from those of other poets, Victorian and modern, for the very fact that his anti-Victorianism was conducted in complete isolation) as well as on a human one (his stylistic idiosyncrasies serve to heighten the self-dramatisation of the poetic voice and ultimately of the man himself).

What actually most fascinates me about Hopkins is the conflict between the man who prayed and the poet who created, and his constant need to reconcile these two dimensions. His struggle with religion, his sense of desolation and abandonment—so powerfully and frankly expressed in the "Terrible Sonnets"—is something that speaks directly to our modern sensibility. His language is also "modern" in the sense that, unlike other Victorian poets (with the exceptions of Hardy and Browning), it can be almost tactile in its immediacy and directness and is always "charged" with energy and vitality. Like Hardy, Hopkins was reacting against the tameness of Victorian verse and proposed a return to "the naked thew and sinew of the English language," and I think it is particularly this sense of strength, and linguistic energy, coupled with the dramatic effects of his sprung rhythm, that has made him an important influence on such modern day poets as Dylan Thomas and R.S. Thomas, for example. But besides moving us, his language also forces us to ponder. It does not only "come to coo" but to "brood and sit." It stays with us and in its brooding makes us brood.

To return to my main point, Hopkins' greatness, for me at least, ultimately resides in the conflict between his candidly emotional and sensual response to life and his apparently staunch spiritual commitment. Rather than distance us from him, I feel this quality endears him to us even more. Indeed, I would go further and say that I hold with the opinion of those who insist that it is not necessary for one to share Hopkins' religious beliefs in order to appreciate the beauty and power of his work. Poems such as "Spring and Fall," "Felix Randal" or "Binsey Poplars," for example, will touch anyone's heart regardless of his creed. Set beside this is also the fact that Hopkins' tone is never a "preaching" one. Even the phrase "Praise him" is so delicately placed at the end of "Pied Beauty" as to seem an utterance of quiet reverence, rather than a loud assertion of self-confidence. Finally, what we witness in Hopkins' poetry is a whole range of extreme emotions, from the sheer joy and delight of the celebratory sonnets composed in Wales, to the torment and anguish of the "Terrible Sonnets" composed in Dublin before his death, and I can think of few poets who have laid open their souls so disarmingly. It is precisely because Hopkins is never coy about expressing the heights of human joy or afraid to probe the depths of human suffering, that we can relate to his vision and sympathise with the sensitivity of the man who lived behind the verse whatever he believed.

JOAQUIN KUHN

MASTER OF INSCAPES AS MATRIX OF INVENTION

Hopkins makes me think. His extraordinary skill in arranging words fosters my thoughtful encounter with a world rich in promise and mystery. The man, as I meet him in his writings, manifests himself to me as a best leader, *maestro, autore* "wandering on the world," relentlessly telling me where to look, how to see, as one mood after another registers on him: sensorily observant, inwardly reflective, universally inquisitive, artistically sensitive, linguistically magisterial, and affectively restless. Hopkins is never boring. Making me think, he also helps me to think, a kind of *aide-pensée*. His immersion in the world and the ways he reacted to it, for me generate personal paradigms negotiable to my own experience, casting distinctive light for me on important things such as my sensory conscious self in a world where I feel my individual contingency. I value him as a matrix of invention. For example, in his arresting formula "counter, original, spare, strange," he sets existential markers for "All things," which include himself and me. I find such comprehensive and precise tuning a conceptual mirror for self-recognition and self-knowledge. This is just one of many such matrices.

Hopkins also marks in practice and in speculation the strange nature of language as the medium of formation and exchange of my thoughts, and on a different, smaller scale, words as the incomplete pieces from which language is constituted. He elevates my subliminal perception to engage my consciousness, and he urges me to think connectively about everything. Further, studying Hopkins has led me, on the one hand, to the world of nature, literally into the fields and hills of Irish botany and physiography, and, on the other hand, to an appreciation of the systems of language, art, philosophy and science that order our understanding and interactively configure our brains.

Hopkins' medium was words, in which his genius is beyond question. His posthumously published words report and record his personal reactions to being in the world, how his thinking, reactive self functioned: first, in a middle-class London family; then, in school; next, at Oxford as an insider; after that, briefly at Oxford as a convert, a self-proclaimed outsider; then, in the Society of Jesus as a convert and unavoidably an outsider; then, an *annus mirabilis* in Wales in which years of self-denied happiness burst out of him, reclaimed him and redeemed him from self-imposed obscurity and inevitable oblivion. (That wonderful year began when he was thirty-two and ended with his ordination and assignment to external duties; if he had died then, like his master, at the age of thirty-three years, three months, how happy he would have been as a minor, unknown poet.) The mettle of the man began to be tested, repeatedly and in diverse ways, for the next twelve years. But this sourceful medium of words continued to flow, with higher personal stakes than before. Finally, this man who was never comfortable as an insider had to adjust to national, political outsidership for the last five years of his short life. For me his most painfully honest poem is "'To seem the stranger,'" where a few words are laid out that are so simple and severe they don't attract commentary: "Only what word / Wisest my heart breeds." Logos is not found; it must be made, perhaps only painfully, and of one's self. He does not accuse or blame anyone, yet he acknowledges that something is dreadfully amiss. This is a wounded bird with not much flight left in him.

*   *   *   *   *

During my first sabbatical from the University of Toronto, 1975-76, I became a serious Hopkinsian. The place was Connemara, a mountainous kingdom that rises precipitously from the sea and which the sea thrashes constantly in a vain effort to take it back. Hopkins visited there in 1884, his first summer in Ireland: "I have been through Connemara, the fine scenery of which is less known than it should be," he wrote to Bridges on July 18. But he didn't celebrate it, storing instead images of terror and abandonment for the terrible sonnets soon to come. I remember the very place on the shore where I became a serious Hopkinsian during the Christmas season of 1975. Brooding on "Pied Beauty," which I was convinced was a thoroughly ordered representation of the perceptible world and not just a random array of bright and beautiful things, I had a kind of enlightenment and saw, to my deep satisfaction, an underlying Aristotelian and Scholastic metaphysics in this small poem that gave me confidence that Hopkins' lists and catalogues were likely always to be calculated arrangements and tools for discovery. I already knew him as a master of inscapes; I began to look to him for inscapes meta-physical, for intuitive grasp of how things are ordered and named.

My sabbatical project was to turn my Ph.D. thesis, an edition of Sir Fulke Greville's *Life of Sir Philip Sidney*, into a book, but an unexpected surplus of such editorial work on Fulke Greville—two other editions were submitted to the same press in apparently the same month—left me adrift but not shipwrecked in the Renaissance. My scholarly orientation, which was till then fully Elizabethan, readjusted itself to the era of Queen Victoria. The subsequent "years with Hopkins" have been better in every respect than I would have been able to report of the "years with Greville." In fact, this turn of events was really a homecoming, for I was not new to the Jesuit frame of reference. I had been a Jesuit novice in the late 50s, continuing in the Society for eight years until I was a graduate student in English at Yale. I left the Jesuits at Christmas 1965, but rejoined the culture of Jesuit scholarship and extended family at Christmas 1975. Even now some aspects of my thinking, reasoning and rhetoric are attributed by my friends to a hypothetical Jesuit in me that I am sure the Society would not be eager to claim credit for. But I knew I was well qualified to read, teach and study Hopkins, because in relation to much of his philosophical and experiential world, I was both insider and outsider.

A new direction and an article on "Pied Beauty" came out of the sabbatical and I have found since then that I don't so much think about Hopkins' poems as I meditate or brood on them.

The seamless compression that Hopkins achieves makes the poems icons of meditation. I find them like the "well, to a poise, to a pane," endlessly self-renewing. A mainstay of my critical interest in him is that his intelligence is so keen and his philosophically guided sense of completeness, comprehensiveness, is so thorough that he somehow (intentional it can only be) always touches all the bases. I prize Hopkins too for his insights into many areas of human being in the world. He was a most keen observer in a time of keen observers. To list the objects of his attention is to evoke a Victorian Renaissance man. I like the movement of his mind: restless, agile, curious, scoping, scaping, scanting, demanding, circular at times to a fault, microcosmic, abstractive, illative, reactive, generous, self-effacing, proud.

I became a serious Hopkinsian in 1975. But I had been inducted as a Hopkinsian sixteen years earlier, as a Jesuit junior in a classroom which is lifelong unforgettable because of who taught there and what he told us. I had the good fortune to hear Hopkins practically before I had heard of him. Edward J. Romagosa, S.J., was the new literature teacher in the juniorate in 1959 when, after taking my vows, I moved from the novitiate to the juniorate. He was the best teacher I ever had—because of the chemistry between us. I might add that I was the best student I ever was, under his guidance. Early on, he read "The Wreck of the Deutschland" to us and left us in stunned silence. He read many of Hopkins' poems to us—and his readings were ideal performances. In a series of classes he read Flannery O'Connor's whole *The Violent Bear It Away* when it was newly published—he was an admiring correspondent of hers then and later. Somehow we had limitless class hours for what in retrospect was a paradise of studentry—a classroom of youths full of hungry zeal for knowledge. As students our minds were wicks for the firebringers who were the juniorate teachers. Father Romagosa had studied Hopkins with John Pick at Marquette; before that he had studied theology in Louvain. He could teach everything because he seemed to know everything, art history included—he spoke fine French (as well as Cajun French), he was a fine Latinist—and his encouraging manner of challenging inspired us to act as though we too could learn everything. We saw him as a typical, brilliant Jesuit, the blackrobe we fledglings aspired to be. That time stands out now as one in which "the last lights off the black West went." The later 1960s changed many things so much, in the Catholic Church and the Society of Jesus, that a dear person has asked if those far-off days were only a dream? But Father Romagosa's teaching endures "like the blowpipe flame": *videlicet*, a broadsheet study guide for poetry which he devised finds my students, thirty, forty years later, working their way through his questions in my adapted form, a sequence of progressive, focused cognitive points, New Criticism in its best flowering. Novices at poetry are deep into a poem before Romagosa and Kuhn are finished with them, and leave them, novices no more.

Of course there have been academic conferences, Waterloo in Ontario, Dublin, Philadelphia, Austin, Waco, Denver, where familiar names have become familiar faces, as well as the annual fellows' meeting of the Society for Values in Higher Education. In 1994, in the afterglow of Jude Nixon's Baylor conference, Joe Feeney and I took up the co-editorship of *The Hopkins Quarterly*, and from there we were "off, off forth on swing." Soon a decade of real hands-on work will have come around. I add my special praise of Joe Feeney, as my friend and co-worker, to the chorus of similar praise of him that the reader will find in this volume.

*   *   *   *   *

Hopkins does something special with words, and it is essential to my self-scrutiny here to describe my take on it. Single words, if they are detached from discourse, are effectively detached from time. Language, on the other hand, moves; it occurs in time. The name and nature of a periodic sentence invoke time and its passage. In the act of writing poetry (which may be described simplistically as a specialized form of language) Hopkins is constantly spatializing his words, teasing them, taming them, into the stillness that restless language would deny them. Occasionally, he goes to great lengths to spatialize them, as in that pregnant opening line of "Spelt from Sibyl's Leaves." As an unheard timpani marks and measures that heavy immobile line, Hopkins has to subvert syntax for his purpose, or at least render syntax sufficiently unimportant so that the static qualities of the words, rather than their dynamic qualities, predominate. This looks like dislocated syntax, but it is really more than that. It is taking an aural device of music and grafting it into an alien medium, language. He does the same thing in the final lines of "The Wreck of the Deutschland," especially in the jumble and tumble of the last line: "Our hearts' charity's hearth's fire, our thoughts' chivalry's throng's Lord." This is not the music of language; it is the music of words. So daring is this virtuoso composition that it must be admired but hardly imitated.

In parallel fashion, inscapes are spatial, although they are expressed as language in time. Hopkins makes it possible to do the unthinkable: to memorize an inscape. This is one of the remarkable powers of words. However abstract and otherwise inadequate they may be, they are exactly repeatable. The other arts (except photography, more or less) do not have this advantage. And when words are fashioned into oracular or seraphic sequences, they can be used to establish not only permanent structures, but to cross-light the lexical referents as well. Hopkins' phrases are, curiously, photographs of sound. Hopkins manages to slow down—in various ways—the temporal nature of language. His gift of phrasing is different from, say, Shakespeare's, whose phrases are dynamic in time, intentionally dramatic. (I suspect that the difference between iambic pentameter with its legato cantabile character, and sprung rhythm with its tendency to staccato, is a criterion of this difference.) Occasionally Hopkins practices dramatic phrasing, as in "'No worst,'" "(Carrion Comfort)" and in "The Wreck of the Deutschland" in crescendo and climax. But in general, I think that as he got older and his insight into, and experience of, existential discontinuity increased, his poetic language changed from intermittent temporal continuity to spatial contiguity. His masterpiece of spatialization is "Andromeda," where he used a device as simple as virtual stage directions, merging time and space, and achieving the effect of arrested motion, atemporality.

In addition, this sonnet is for Hopkins (indeed, for anyone) a rare synthesis of Hellenic-Christian iconography. Another beautiful matrix is the line in his final, farewell poem, "To R.B.": "The roll, the rise, the carol, the creation." This is contiguity implying and reaching out to continuity but respectfully not claiming it.

As early as Aristotle, the nature of genius was recognized as a talent for seeing connections that are not readily obvious to others, at least until the similarity is explicitly pointed out or the equation is stated. The originators in every area of human endeavor have seen what their fellows could not see on their own beforehand. The distinctive case of artistic genius, which has no power of demonstration or practical application which would be comparable to the demonstrations and applications of math and science, gets a bit more complicated. Not only to see—or in metaphor sometimes *to make*—the connection, but also to express it felicitously. And to do it not just once, but often, especially in arts of language.

Genius has many expressions. The scientific mind is an ordering mind. It finds provisional order in actual seeming chaos because it proceeds on the conviction that consistent, natural laws of matter have produced the after-explosion of perceptibles that are likely to overwhelm an undisciplined mind. Hopkins, in his thinking and seeing, was hungry for order in the world. He took exceptional care in his analytical descriptions of different trees and their leaves. During a summer filled with significant events—taking his degree, a trip to France, the drowning of Dolben—he recorded in his journal for August 22, 1867, his wording for the vital design of appletrees and wych-elms, elms, ashes, elm leaves, and then he imported an entry from the previous summer, July 6, 1866, which is an intense reading of elm leaves. As a young Jesuit he continued as opportunity offered. In March 1871 he wrote, "This is the time to study inscape in the spraying of trees, for the swelling buds carry them to a pitch which the eye could not else gather." He devoted a long entry to ash trees as spring takes hold. This is an application of the advice Ruskin gave in the Second Letter, "Sketching from Nature," in *The Elements of Drawing*:

> I say, first, there must be observance of the ruling organic
> law. . . . Your common sketcher or bad painter puts his leaves
> on the trees as if they were moss tied to sticks; he cannot see
> the lines of action or growth; he scatters the shapeless clouds
> over his sky, not perceiving the sweeps of associated curves
> which the real clouds are following as they fly; and he breaks
> his mountain side into rugged fragments, wholly unconscious
> of the lines of force with which the real rocks have risen, or of
> the lines of couch in which they repose. On the contrary, it is
> the main delight of the great draughtsman to trace these laws
> of government . . .

Ruskin's concentration on the ordering forces on trees,
water and clouds will sound familiar to a reader of Hopkins'
nature poems. In that time of concentrated tree and leaf analysis,
July 1866, he wrote: "Oaks: the organisation of this tree is
difficult. Speaking generally no doubt the determining planes are
concentric . . . . " He digressed to cedars and beeches, then
returned to the difficulty of oaks. Eight days later, on July 19: "I
have now found the law of the oak leaves." His scientific curiosity
was appeased by the insight of that day, which he meticulously
worked out in words.

In contrast to an observant scientist, an aesthetic anarchist,
romantic in temperament, stands before a waterfall and prizes its
wild diversity—no two spurts or jets simultaneously or
sequentially are alike. Standing round the same waterfall as the
romantic, the scientist sees the interaction, the interplay, of
bedrock, ledge, flowing water, gravity, height of fall, wind, etc.,
and knows at least the limits of what he sees before him. Hopkins
combines the scientist and the artist in an unusual way. His whole
being strains to feel his understanding of the singularity of the
phenomenon at the same time that a set of consistent laws of
physics controls it within predictable bounds. His comfort in
synthesis is that it is intelligible display. But the poet cannot stop
there. Taking it to the next step, wording the catch is the rare
achievement. Hopkins effectively announces in "The Windhover"
that first, he caught the event—the falcon in flight; second, he
caught the meaning—the inscape of sunrise and bird mastering
the element of air and the buckling of brute beauty, valor, act, air,

pride, plume and the concurrent outbreak of fire with consequent dignified humility; and third, with the "photography" that words allow, he caught the likeness of the inscape—the poem itself. No word could possibly say more than "catch" for this ambitious claim. Already in only its second word the poem is emitting a spectrum of meaning-colors, like a prism. And the hardly remarkable first word is an unpretentious "I"! When he caught inscapes in words, Hopkins mastered intelligibility, display and wording. Let him be praised for it.

I began with reference to Hopkins as a matrix of invention. He offers me many matrices. Because of his keen reactivity and receptivity, I am not surprised to see patterns of mind, or templates of personality, guiding what he sees and ordering his responses. To sketch briefly a prominent one: rising and falling. The material living world that we are part of is moved by incessant action of spring/rising and fall/falling. (The gerunds *rising* and *falling* convey a dynamic temporal sense; the substantives *spring* and *fall* are generally more useful because they are static abstractions.) In contrast to the material world is the immaterial living world that we (in faith) are part of, which moves through the same action transcendentally but in the opposite order: Fall/falling, then Spring / rising / anastasis / resurrectio. If there are two and if they are sequential, which of the two is truer to reality, or are they somehow both true? (I am tempted to ask: which one? is it each one?) Nature is ambiguous: Is the season of spring the *terminus a quo* or the *terminus ad quem*? Viewed reproductively, spring with "all this juice and all this joy" generates flowers which are fertilized for fruitfulness, a harvest of fruit which will fall in the Fall. Viewed aesthetically and morally, fall is "barbarous in beauty" filled with "rapturous love's greeting," and even though the world is "unleaving," "leaves" [are] "like the things of man" and grieving is utterly natural, even for a young child.

How much rising and falling there is in Hopkins. To name a few instances: the sestet of "God's Grandeur"—western darkness / eastern sunrise. Does the windhover fall or not fall as the plough falls functionally into the earth down sillion and as the embers give sign of life by their fall gall? The skylark rises and falls.

The Eurydice fell in mendacious Spring. Purcell fell, but, hopefully, "fair fallen," as the speaker virtually rises on the "air of angels" which "lift me, lay me!" as the great stormfowl makes ready to fly. Is this not the basic Christian paradox, as Donne put it in "Good Friday, 1613. Riding Westward": ". . . towards the East. / There I should see a Sun, by rising, set, / And by that setting endless day beget"? As with Donne, occasionally the complementary action is expressed in paradoxical terms, with rising and falling displaced from temporal sequence into spatial coexistence, in a state of latency, simultaneously rising and falling: "The dearest freshness deep down things." (When all is said and done, however, the feel of the fall is stronger and occurs in Hopkins' works more often. It is also rhetorically more convincing. The sonorities of the Fall are very powerful: "Felled, felled, are all felled," "feel the fell of night," "Have fair fallen," "cliffs of fall / Frightful." The antithetical sonority is grounded in the phoneme "ing" which in Hopkins' instrumentation becomes a morpheme of vitality, movement, renewal, hope, even optimism: "minion, king-", "riding," "striding," "wing," "swing," "gliding," "hiding," "the thing!" But paradox can be stronger than resolution: this melancholy, naturalist utterance deflects reply: "Sorrow's springs are the same.")

In calling Hopkins a medium for me, I lift from him the burden of being a wise person. I have no doubt that he was a good person, but I think he was not particularly wise. He was not a privileged embodiment of special wisdom, but he was a provident glass on the world that I would not see so well without his tuition. Glass Hopkins is at various times window, camera lens, binoculars, microscope, mirror, telescope, gunsight, transom, skylight, body of water surface or depth, even at times, shining transparent crystal. When he was called "a strange young man . . . a fair natural" by the Jesuit lay brother who saw him crouching down "to gaze at the crushed quartz glittering as the sun came out again," the characterization was true and fair and ultimately honorific. It takes a natural to make a naturalist. "Honour is flashed off exploit," he would write in impatient recognition of great deeds, subverting mere flashiness to catch the higher honor of one like himself, Alfonso who "watched the door." If it's all about looking and seeing, what did Alfonso see while he watched?

As Dante says, "And so I took up with him, but always a step / behind." Over Hopkins' shoulder, trying to keep up, I blurt, "What do you see? Tell me what you see." And if he were laconic, which he is not, he would reply as Howard Carter did to Carnarvon's similar question, "Wonderful things."

Hopkins' writings construct a coherent persona, and to my mind and for my purposes, coherence is preferable to consistency. The achievement of Hopkins' life as life was consistency. He reportedly died happy in that achievement. But a consistent life is not necessarily a coherent life. Consistency of faith, hope and charity were his aspirations as a Christian Catholic Jesuit. He is much admired for having lived out those aspirations, as many people live out their expressed ideals. But the interest in Hopkins as a living teacher is from another quarter. At the present moment, and since his death, he has become his writings. From those writings emanates challenging and inspiring coherence. And we should unequivocally acknowledge that without his gift of language, he would be nobody now. Hopkins was coherently true to his gifts, coping with the vagaries and vicissitudes of a difficult life, writing poems, journals, letters, essays, sermons and meditations that constitute a substantial *corpus vivens.*

I value Hopkins' gift of expression as he expresses, not the inexpressible but the supremely expressible. With the splendor of eloquence, his sharp words outline and adorn in custom inscapes the shapes and contours of my mind. I have never heard a better existential definition of my difficult-to-know, but intensely-aware <u>self</u> than "counter, original, spare, strange." These are Hopkins' words in his arrangement. Sequentially and collectively, each word in this microcosmic formulation enlightens me to myself. I am a little world made cunningly. If there is logos to the macrocosm of it all, however counter, original, spare, strange it may be, Hopkins provides a good line of sight on the quarry. If he is an enigma, I do not take umbrage but rather admire, and through his glass see somewhat less darkly.

MY ENCOUNTERS WITH HOPKINS

I want to make two very important points about Hopkins. First, Hopkins in the poems uses language with extraordinary energy. He knows that "this Victorian English is a bad business," citing Tennyson, Swinburne, and Morris; indeed an obvious contrast to the linguistic energy of Hopkins is the *vapid sound* of Swinburne. Hopkins' powerful use of language is all the more important at the present time, when so much verse is incredibly *slack*, is simply bad prose.

Second, Hopkins exhibits in the poems what Bakhtin calls the Dialogic Imagination. Since he is a Jesuit priest, there are, of course, official positions, and these are expounded in the prose. But in the poems, Hopkins is capable of questioning the official position, as in these opening lines of one of the sonnets of desolation: "Thou are indeed just, Lord, if I contend / With thee; but, sir, so what I plead is just." An analogue here is Yeats, who expounds his official positions in the prose of *A Vision*, but renders them problematic in the poems. This willingness on the part of Hopkins to explore the complexities of religious belief is again relevant to our contemporary situation; since in an increasingly secularised world naïve faith is no longer an option, we require religious art that is intellectually mature. That art is wonderfully provided by Hopkins.

About 1959, I had my first encounter with Hopkins in the Jesuit boarding school of Clongowes Wood College. With a brilliant English teacher, the writer Tom MacIntyre, we studied one poem—"Pied Beauty"—which was in the anthology prescribed for the then Intermediate Certificate in Ireland. I do not recall that "Pied Beauty" made any great impression on me, and certainly Hopkins' connection with Clongowes—he visited the school several times during his stint in Dublin—was not stressed. But neither, for that matter, was the fact that James

Joyce had attended Clongowes; indeed Joyce was viewed as a "heretic," *vir non nominandus inter Christianos.*

It was to be some three decades later before I had any serious encounter with Hopkins. During that time, I finished secondary school, got an M.A. in Classics and Ph.D. in Latin, taught in universities in Britain, Australia, and Ireland, and wrote books on Catullus and on Yeats. In 1990, Desmond Egan, the Director of the Hopkins International Summer School at Monasterevin in Co. Kildare, asked me to give a paper at the School. This required me to read through all of Hopkins, poetry and prose. Since my book on Yeats analysed Greek and Roman themes in that author, it seemed logical to attempt the same kind of thing for Hopkins. Hence my paper "Heraclitean Fire: Greek Themes in Hopkins," which was later published in the *International Journal of the Classical Tradition.* This paper examines Hopkins' study of Greek at Highgate School and at Balliol College, Oxford; the large number of research projects in Classics that he planned, but never completed; and the impact on his work of the Presocratic philosophers Parmenides and Heraclitus.

A second paper (1996), entitled "Style in the Poetry of Hopkins," concluded that Hopkins combined a highly Anglo-Saxon vocabulary with syntactic devices borrowed from Greek and Latin.

A third paper, "Representing the Material World: Hopkins and Others" (1998), argues that writers like George Russell (A.E.), Yeats, and Swinburne do not provide an adequate representation of the material world, whereas Hopkins, devoted to Scotist *haecceitas,* does.

A fourth paper, delivered at the Hopkins Summer School, was "Religious Themes in Hopkins" (2000); it concentrates on Hopkins' poetic depiction of the central doctrines of Christianity such as the Trinity, the Crucifixion, and the Resurrection, and regards these poems as presenting theological knowledge in a manner different from discursive prose.

While the papers presented at the Hopkins School in Monasterevin are a crucial part of the proceedings, the social side is also very important: meals together and drinks in that wonderful institution, the Irish pub. Since scholarly activity is, for the most part, such a private and indeed lonely affair, the opportunity to meet with others who share one's interests is very welcome. Among those I have met there are the indefatigable Director, Desmond Egan; Hopkins scholars Fr. Joe Feeney, S.J., Russell Murphy, and Norman White; and, from Italy, Franco Marucci, Giuseppe Serpillo, Francesco Marroni, and Renzo D'Agnillo.

It is worth noting that there are now some thirty Summer Schools held regularly in Ireland, many of which deal with a literary figure: Yeats, Joyce, Synge, Wilde, Hewitt, Stoker, Goldsmith, among others. Indeed, it would be possible to spend three or four months each summer going from one School to another (if your pocket and liver could stand it!).

WALTER J. ONG, S.J.

HOPKINS' ARTICULATE SELF

What Hopkins means to me—a question posed to me by the editors of *The Hopkins Quarterly*—can, I presume, be answered in several ways. In *Hopkins, the Self, and God,* the Alexander Lectures which I gave at the University of Toronto in 1982, I have in a way responded to this question, or at least laid out some grounds on which an answer may be worked out.

What Hopkins means to me is that he is the first writer who has fully and explicitly and with deliberate force responded to the articulate knowledge of the self which across the world human beings until fairly recent years have been unable directly to treat of or to write about or to speak about—or even to be articulately aware of explicitly. This sounds strange to us today. But that's the way it was. It takes time for human beings to lay hold of themselves reflectively. This is true in a great many ways.

For background, recall how long it is before a baby can even say "I" or "me." On the way to saying "I," a great-grandnephew of mine for a time used the term "my" for himself—less direct and less different from everything else than "I" or "me" would have been. "My a good boy." "He hit my." It doesn't make much sense to us, but to him it did and it came more easily than did our way (and his later way) of laying hold of the situation.

Hopkins' widely known attention to God's presence—in human consciousness and in the exterior world—hinges on the human being's, man's or woman's, ability to be articulate about the human self, an ability which comes late in the history of culture as of individuals. Only selves know other selves personally or explicitly. But until very recent times, although an individual woman or man was well aware of herself or himself, neither women nor men could be fully and explicitly articulate in speaking about this awareness.

In antiquity in the West, and, as it may appear, elsewhere in early human cultures, there is no straightforward attention to the self as self. There are no terms for the self in languages as far developed as classical Greek or Latin. From classical Latin, and from later Latin, the expression *egomet ipse* may be rendered by us today as "I myself." The *ego* means "I" but the *-met* has to be joined to another word and fortified by *ipse* to mean anything at all. It appears that in ancient Latin and Greek there was no way to talk directly about what we call the "self." No one talked about it directly. Ancient Latin and Greek were more interested in commonalities or in what we, following them, call—or used to call?—"universals."

In *Hopkins, the Self, and God* I have undertaken to treat in great detail the stages through which our present-day concern with the "self" developed. "Like all human beings, Gerard Manley Hopkins was the product of his own times," as Alison Sulloway in her *Gerard Manley Hopkins and the Victorian Temper* has detailed and, in different perspectives, as Wendell Stacy Johnson had earlier shown in *Gerard Manley Hopkins: The Poet as Victorian*. Introspection, not greatly developed in early human history, grew in the West through the Middle Ages and the Renaissance, and later clearly marks the thought of Descartes (1596-1650).

In *The Invention of the Self: The Hinges of Consciousness in the Eighteenth Century*, John O. Lyons shows how during the eighteenth century "consciousness" had achieved deeper inwardness in what it attended to, an inwardness which would be marked later by the emergence of the awarenesses found in depth psychology and eventually in phenomenological psychology, and later in Martin Buber's personalist existentialism explained in his *I and Thou* (*Ich und Du*, 1922).

All this interiorizing developed along with the weakening of the old rhetorical tradition, the art of persuading another or others, which from the beginning, until quelled by Aristotelian logic and scholasticism, had dominated formal study of discourse in the West (and perhaps in one or another way elsewhere). Rhetorical activity involved operations working on others—and often, through its common focus on public oratory, gave a public cast or twist to all education and thought from classical antiquity to recent generations.

Recently studies of consciousness have multiplied and are still multiplying. All those that I have been able to examine—including dozens of books and far more short studies—fail to attend directly to what Hopkins so much attends to: the fact that human consciousness always entails in some way self-consciousness, in which the self is utterly different for each person. When I say "I," I am quite aware that no one else can use this term to mean what it means to me. Referring to what I mean by this "I," others use the term "you." Self-consciousness is unique for every person, however hundreds of billions or billions of billions this "every" may include. Each of us knows this in his or her saying of "I." No matter how many billions of persons exist, none of the other can or could say "I" and refer to what I refer to when I say "I."

Few—almost no—treatments of human consciousness even advert to this absolutely central, unique and assertive feature of human consciousness. The one well-known author who does and of whom I am aware is William James, an M.D. with a bent to careful description of human activity. James published this in 1890, the year after Hopkins died:

> The altogether unique kind of interest which the human mind feels in those parts of creation which it calls me or mine may be a moral riddle, but it is a fundamental psychological fact. No mind can take the same interest in his neighbor's me as in his own. The neighbor's me falls together with all the rest of things in one foreign mass against which his own me stands out in startling relief.

Hopkins attends to the self not in terms of any discipline but directly in terms of the self that each and every normal human being is simply aware of when he or she thinks of herself or of himself—or, for that matter of anything else. You need no theory to have this awareness of yourself. Theory has nothing to do with it. Simple attention has everything to do with it.

Hopkins puts it this way: "We say that any two things however unlike are in something like. This is the one exception: when I compare my self, my being-myself, with anything else whatsoever, all things alike, all in the same degree, rebuff me with blank unlikeness."

As I have undertaken to show at great length in *Hopkins, the Self, and God,* Hopkins' thought, which is also characteristically in one way or another, clinical or based on direct and careful observation, was also characteristically and throughout sensitive to the self as such. This sensitivity was fostered in Hopkins' case by the "panegyric accuracy" that Ruskin demanded of all artists with which Victorians had learned to describe the world, an accuracy in earlier ages unknown but, after Gutenberg and his congeners, fostered by print and the exactly repeatable visual statement which print first made possible on a sizable scale. We are today seldom aware of the fact that, before print, exactly repeatable visual statement (that is, visual drawing representing exactly what the eye beheld) was unknown, and indeed hardly ambitioned. In the absence of printing, if you wanted several copies of a given visual display or drawing and therefore had one artist copy a drawing by another artist (or by himself or herself), the copy could reproduce the original, but always with some at least slight unconscious or conscious variation (which the culture of the time not only accepted, but even mandated). Any artist was *obligated* to be at least *somewhat* original. To imitate *exactly* was cheapness. In a print culture we today think readily of two or hundreds or more illustrations which are exactly the same. Before print, the realization of such total sameness in actuality was quite unthinkable and mostly undesirable.

Hopkins' prose descriptions are examples of "panegyric accuracy." For example, from his *Journal* for 11 July 1866:

> Oaks: the organisation of this tree is difficult. Speaking generally no doubt the determining planes are concentric, a system of brief contiguous and continuous tangents, whereas those of the cedar would roughly be called horizontals and those of the beech radiating but modified by droop and by a screw-set towards jutting points.

Try to find something like this "panegyric accuracy" in texts of Julius Caesar's day. "Hopkins typically treats of the self as face-to-face with itself, confrontationally."

Hopkins' typical self or "I" is not identifying itself with itself nor regarding itself à la Descartes as a starting point for anything. It is simply what one faces up to, experiences, "tastes," and expresses in each saying of "I" or "me."

In a way, Hopkins' sense of self needs no explaining. Although few persons are articulate about the uniqueness of the self, each of us knows this uniqueness intimately in his or her own consciousness. Of course Hopkins was aware of Walt Whitman's poetry and of Whitman's celebration of the "expansive, omnibus self," but he writes Bridges that Whitman "eats his [cake] offhand, I keep mine. It makes a great difference." Hopkins makes it clear that he by no means want to run down Whitman, whom he in many ways admires.

Hopkins is, in effect, just where we all are, although less effectively or articulately than Hopkins. Each of us feels and knows the uniqueness of his or her "I." But few could or can—or even want to—talk about self-consciousness with Hopkins' sensitivity and informed intensity. In this intensity, as Hopkins has it, we all relate to one another—as well as to God. In the self of each of us. This articulate sense and welcoming of each individual self in his or her total uniqueness is what makes Hopkins quite exceptional. It is at the heart of what Hopkins means to me.

MICHAEL MOORE

WHY HOPKINS MATTERS

I came to Hopkins by accident, reluctantly, and late. Prior to beginning Ph.D. studies in the early seventies at Queen's University, Canada, I knew the poetry of Hopkins only by reputation as something freakish, impenetrable, and pious—best avoided. Incidental glimpses, caught while turning the pages of anthologies on my way to more accessible fare, seemed to confirm that "Hopkins" was one tendentious verbal thicket after another. And although he was a great favourite of the only considerable writer I knew in those days, this testimony of one eccentric aesthete to another was hardly a recommendation to so pedestrian a sensibility as mine.

The presence on the Queen's faculty of the eminent Hopkins editor Norman H. MacKenzie made further avoidance difficult, especially after I found myself enrolled perforce in his graduate seminar. The rest is, as they say, history. Resigned to the reading, I was immediately astounded that so remarkable a voice could ever have been kept relegated to the margins of the English literary canon. Hopkins converted me "at a crash" to alterity and complexity of in-tension as the measure of poetic utterance. And so it came to pass that within four years of first grudgingly assailing a line of Hopkins, I completed a traditional historicist dissertation about him under Norman's patient direction, and have trod have trod have trod ever since the path less travelled by.

Of course Hopkins has been for me, as for others, much more than grist for the grinding academic mill. Indeed, I must confess now to appreciating his poetry *despite* its having turned out to be the bread and butter of merely professional study. And yet I'm aware of valuing Hopkins differently from most other aficionados. Unlike many, I like him best where he is most diacritical, least rhetorical. Most dramatic, least personal. Most unlike my own experiences and habits of thought, least comfortably "identified with." Most . . . different. I can't pretend to share in the intensely personal devotion or debt of gratitude some people say they owe to the example of Hopkins' courageous life or, more often, to the inspiring religiosity of his verse. Nor do his frequently admired "themes" or "ideas" strike me as remarkable in themselves, or as quintessential to his achievement. No other poet is so ill-served by paraphrase. No other poetry better embodies Coleridge's two defining literary axioms: untranslatability, and capacity for endlessly rewarding *re*-reading.

Rather, I'm inclined to believe that the essence of Hopkins' importance lies somehow in his conduct (and so to some extent his generative theory) of poetic language itself. It is here, if anywhere, that he makes a difference that matters, by making difference the difference that matters in literature. And I believe he did, or would, think so too. Here is his own oft-quoted, oft-ignored, testimony about how he would want his work understood and estimated: "Poetry is speech framed . . . to be heard for its own sake and interest even over and above its interest of meaning. Some matter and meaning is essential to it but . . . [p]oetry is in fact speech . . . for the inscape's sake—and therefore the inscape must be dwelt on." What then might be the inscape of Hopkins? What should we be dwelling on? What is most significant in his distinctiveness?

Well, I see Hopkins as the English nineteenth-century's only thoroughgoing antinominalist. A radical realist. Of all-dissolving abstraction the most defiant and veriest-veined unraveller. His energetic and intricate idiom makes a calculated case for what poetry is and, by implication, what it isn't. In poetry, words are not arbitrary names, not abstract gestures, not approximate signs or substitutions. In poetry, words are real, both in themselves (as material actions, as poesis) and in dramatic relation to (self-?) consciousness (what we abstractly call perceiving, knowing, meaning). Hence Hopkins' inclusive epistemology of inscape and instress, and his devotion to Duns Scotus, the scholastic archrival of the nominalist Occam. Hence his firmly Logos-centric vision of world and word as declaratory and incarnational. Hence the ultimately linguistic justification for his being a poet at all, i.e., for forswearing his vow of silence, allowing himself poesis only by relocating it within that vision and at the secret core of his religious vocation. And hence too the vivid immediacy and plenitude of his poetic language, refracting upon sustained reflection into multiple and polyvalent—not "ambiguous"—networks (he would say "strains") of implication.

Of course structuralist and post-structuralist linguists dismiss realism as impossible in theory and naive in practice. And it's true enough that most of Hopkins' own notes and letters on technical or historical semantics, per se, were mistaken (imaginative?) speculations. Yet his poetry itself often matters most, as poetry, where his performance improvises most daringly upon the aural and semantic resources of language, extending (wrenching?) and redeeming it from the dead and deadening "signifying practices" of conventional discourse, literary and non-literary alike.

In sum, I owe to Hopkins the crystallization of many of the fundamental questions I've spent my academic life asking about the nature and value of literature. No matter that his own answers, explicit or implicit, to those questions sometimes seem alien. Other. Hopkins is, after all, the poet of difference, of differing, of doing otherwise. And in any case we shouldn't be looking to literature for answers. As Sir Philip Sidney said, on behalf of all poets, in the teeth of moral philosophy, religion, and rhetoric alike, "The poet nothing affirmeth." To dwell on what Hopkins does paraphrasably affirm would be to foreground the moments when he is least a poet and most a fellow traveller daring (and daring us) to venture onward from even the most acute poesis (perception, imagination, expression) to pathos (moral feeling), ethos (moral principle), and praxis (moral action). Pathos, ethos, and praxis matter, but they are not why literature matters. Not why Hopkins matters.

So for me the poetry of Hopkins matters primarily because of (not in spite of) its extreme literariness, its intrinsicating dissonance, its calculated resistance to the in-difference of what his friend Bridges fastidiously called "the continuous literary decorum." Peculiarity is the life of it. And, as Hopkins freely acknowledged, queerness inevitably the vice of it. In using the word *queer* he could not, of course, have been anticipating either the opprobrium or the rehabilitation it would in time undergo. Yet in it he names and embraces the spirit (including the theology) of his strategic intervention in modern poetics. Far from freakish outlawry, it is his hard bright witness against the dimness of us, against the blurring, numbing unreality of a world fatally self-betrayed then and now to the normative, essentialist, and consonant conventionalities of despair.

PILGRIMAGE TO A TEXT

" . . . a dexterous and starlight order . . ."

NORMAN H. MACKENZIE

A Tale of Five Continents

My First Acquaintance with Poets

> "I am sweetly soothed by your saying that you cd. make any one understand my poem by reciting it well," wrote Gerard to his brother Everard Hopkins. "That is what I always hoped, thought, and said; it is my precise aim. . . . I must however add that to perform it quite satisfactorily is not at all easy, I do not say I could do it; but this is nothing against the truth of the principle maintained."

William Hazlitt, from whose memoir I borrowed my subheading, could look back on the immense privilege he had enjoyed as a young man of not only meeting Coleridge but hearing him perform poetry: they strolled along a wooded slope and while they sat side by side on a fallen ash-tree Hazlitt listened intently as Coleridge read pieces from the as-yet unpublished MS of the *Lyrical Ballads* in a "sonorous and musical voice . . . [and] the sense of a new style and a new spirit in poetry came over me."

In 1931 the poet whose acquaintance I made on a landmark occasion was Tennyson, and he in turn over the next unforgettable months introduced me to other poets. A large proportion of my intervening seventy years have been given to attempts to do for my students what Hopkins calls on all of us to undertake—loaning both voice and personality to poems lying dormant on the printed page, voiceless like the score of a symphony waiting for an orchestra to unprison its rhythms and harmonies.

Hopkins' letter to his brother Everard, dated November 5, 1885, was discovered by the researches of Fr. Tony Bischoff, S.J., and is happily included in Catherine Phillips' edition of his *Selected Letters.* Hopkins goes on to affirm his life-long conviction that the true nature of poetry is revealed only by its "performance": as the "darling child of speech . . . it must be spoken; . . . *till it is spoken it is not performed.*"

Professor Ernest Ferlita, S.J., a professor of drama and himself a practiced actor, in his own contribution to these essays, "Hopkins Gladly Performed," is able to add to speech the element of gesture. He has donated to Hopkins the posthumous gift of some brief passages for *St. Winefred's Well* so that he could present this fragmentary play on the stage. Those of us who like myself have limited experience on the boards may have to constrict our "performance" of verse to the voice only.

Unlike many Canadian children in recent decades, in South Africa from the earliest classes onwards I was given readers that included verse. In senior school our specialist teachers of English were well qualified in literature, yet somehow failed to ignite a flame in me. I recall our having to recite in turn portions of Tennyson's "Morte D'Arthur"—as members contributed their share towards concealing Excalibur in the bulrushes from the wounded King in tones varying from an uncomprehending sing-song to boredom and haste. Our English masters never provided us with a recital that fired our imagination.

Then in my final school year came a dramatic experience, as vivid and far-reaching as a second conversion. It happened in a Latin class conducted by our marvellous headmaster: coming across an allusion to the Judgment of Paris he suddenly stopped, and sent one of the boarders to his home beside the school to bring back his volume of *The Poems of Tennyson*. Quickly he turned to "Oenone," published just before Hopkins was born and I feel sure among the poems the Jesuit relished in his younger days.

"There lies a vale in Ida"

As Mr. Lang read the exquisite lines I closed my eyes, letting the cadences engulf me:

> There lies a vale in Ida, lovelier
> Than all the valleys of Ionian hills.
> The swimming vapour slopes athwart the glen,
> Puts forth an arm, and creeps from pine to pine,

And loiters, slowly drawn. On either hand
The lawns and meadow-ledges midway down
Hang rich in flowers, and far below them roars
The long brook falling through the cloven ravine
In cataract after cataract to the sea.

He read for perhaps twenty minutes, reluctant to stop. I was carried away into another world by the superb opulence of the descriptions, shut off from awareness of my mundane surroundings. That day I was inducted into a new realm, filled with a poetic elation that has never left me: I had been present at a *performance* of poetry. Though it was our matriculation year with university entrance at stake, for months I spent hours a day devouring hundreds of poems, by Tennyson first, then Keats and then Shelley, memorising striking passages. The following year, convalescing in hospital from surgery after peritonitis, I traversed Milton's *Paradise Lost*, rationing myself to one book a day.

Such pivotal experiences are more usually the result of private reading rather than listening—encountering a particular book at just the right juncture. With both sources of inspiration the timing is all-important. Returning to "Oenone" in later years I was unable to recapture my initial excitement. But the experience was so radical that ever since, in teaching, I have tended to obey any strong impulse to digress, guided by audience response.

It was not surprising that my illumination came through a poet other than Hopkins. The Bridges First Edition of 1918 had become slowly depleted in the lean post-war decade. In the three years preceding my initiation into poetry only four solitary copies of Hopkins remained for world-wide distribution—and we were six thousand miles away in Southern Africa in a strongly Protestant community.

This First Acquaintance with Poetry Performed set me a standard I have exerted myself to emulate. When after two degrees, in English and Classics, I entered an Education programme, we were given training in bringing life to the poems we read. Later in London, while completing a Ph. D. thesis on some Renaissance prose writers, I enrolled in a verse-speaking class in the London Polytechnic. In many successive visits to

Britain I had private tuition from a professor of speech in the Royal Academy of Dramatic Art: he despaired of my vowels, but was pleased with my improving sensitivity to mood and colour in verse and prose. The London stage of the late 1930s offered some of the greatest Shakespearian actors in history: John Gielgud, Ralph Richardson, Alec Guinness. I attended each classical play three times in the cheapest seats, and could then mark up a text showing the rise and fall of powerful inflexions in some crucial passages, as well as many other technical features of superb staging.

Our Responsibility for the Training of Students

I joined Queen's in 1966, just as the Gardner/MacKenzie edition of the *Poems* was on the slip-way. My responsibility for establishing our Ph.D. programme in English gave me a chance to emphasize with future lecturers in English the necessity of attaining their highest standards in speaking to classes, in the arresting delivery of poetry, and also in writing: I asked my own Hopkins groups to present their seminar pages from notes only, not from a starched script. Hopkins, in his letter already quoted, argues that "poetry is emphatically speech, speech purged of dross like gold in the furnace, so it must have emphatically the essential elements of speech." After each seminar performance I invited the speaker to my study to discuss matters of voice control and variety, and to practice reading other poems.

By rights this autobiographical ramble ought to be mentally attached to the busy pages of Acknowledgements in my edition of the *Poetical Works of Gerard Manley Hopkins.* Even there the names of Jesuit friends to whom by now I am most in debt remain incomplete. Campion Hall, Oxford, over many years infused relaxation time into my Sisyphean editorial "hill-climbing" in the Bodleian by always finding me a welcome and a guest-room whenever I revisited the MSS.

It was of course not Hopkins' fault that when at last we encountered each other in 1945 the meeting was less dramatic than happened with other writers in this book. World War II had bifurcated me into a part-time coastal-defence gunner on a scenic headland of Hong Kong, and a lecturer in English in her university. After the surrender of the Colony I had been among the more able-bodied POWs shipped via Nagasaki and Hiroshima (fateful names) to work as unskilled coolies in a Japanese naval shipbuilding yard. How much worse our fate might have been became obvious when at long last (it seemed like several decades) we were liberated by British troops: our train rumbled through the bombed-flat sites of such former populous cities as Kobe and Osaka—scarcely a building still standing. Yokohama Bay was jammed with enormous aircraft-carriers and battleships, on which, we were told, peace terms were being signed. We were packed into a small warship bound for Australia, the nearest country where we could recover health before being repatriated to our former homes for six months or more of quiet recuperation. The only place where I could find peace to complete my war-diary in the swarming ship was (by special permission from a bemused officer) the bomb-bay on the keel: I hoped our route had been swept clear of mines! The diary was pencilled on toilet-paper (occasionally in code) and hidden in a narrow-necked army canteen. I did not venture to re-read it till about 1970.

A Gamble that Paid Dividends

Unlike nearly all my friends the last thing I wanted was idle brooding time in a loving but over-protective religious atmosphere. A demanding post seemed a better cure for a headful of memories. Once on the mend I became exhilarated by Melbourne University's high academic standards, supported by excellent high schools. The new Head of the English Department, Ian Maxwell, had devised an inspiring experimental "modern" poetry bracket for First Year students: this included two of my prime favourites, W.B. Yeats and T.S. Eliot, along with an intriguing Jesuit writer I had never seriously confronted before. Like the other two poets, Hopkins was invitingly difficult, obviously worth exploring.

Melbourne University's attractions induced me to make what might well have proved a foolhardy decision: instead of following common sense and going home to regain weight—but risk losing the chance of joining the Melbourne staff—I applied for the only two vacancies in English in Australia: one in Melbourne and one in Perth. There were few rash competitors for these immediate ex-service posts. I got both. The runner-up for Perth who accepted the second lectureship, although not an ex-POW, had a nervous breakdown. That I escaped and even thrived was due to the support of professor Maxwell and the Master of Queen's College, Melbourne, Dr. Raynor Johnson. But it was an ordeal for a steel-yard labourer to find himself suddenly the local "Yeats Expert," with Maxwell and other senior English faculty occupying the front seats in a vast lecture-theatre.

All my books and lecture notes from two previous university posts having been lost in the fall of Hong Kong, I had to work at furious speed to prepare myself for a double position—lecturer in Melbourne University with its thousand students of English, and tutor in the residential Queen's College, to supplement lectures and seminars given in the university. Another tutor and I had to cover the whole curriculum for English pass and honours degrees: I claimed Hopkins for myself. For two years every segment of each week had to be plotted out in a diary for frantic rereading of novels, plays and poems. Along with this I had to adjust to a vigorously different culture—Australians are down-to-earth, impatient of affectation. I came to appreciate their openness and to feel accepted.

In the first long vacation, over Christmas, I sailed home on a cargo ship via Durban, Natal, with a volume of Hopkins' *Poems* (Second Edition) as my inseparable companion. I was lucky to find a copy. Post-war books were in such short supply that our English Department had to publish our own anthology of Hopkins, Yeats and Eliot under licence, ready for the revolutionary First Year poetry course beginning in March 1947. In preparing my tutorials on Hopkins, to assist me I had only the pioneer study by Fr. Gerald Lahey, S.J. (OUP 1930). This work, though pardonably astray on minor points, generated a widening audience for his poems through enthusiastic verse quotations along with liberal extracts from his diaries and other journals. I was soon a Hopkins addict.

A Flashback to Hopkins' Highgate

In pre-war days I had become usefully familiar with Hopkins' Highgate and his Anglican environment before I met any devotees of his verse. He was an Anglican for almost exactly half his brief life. While I was a Ph.D. student in London for two and a half years (from January 1938) I had the privilege of being among paying guests in a household run by a former Anglican missionary-explorer, Kenneth Grubb (Secretary of the World Council of Churches), who invited us to join Anglican family prayers each morning. Like Hopkins, I was often up too late. But in summer I could never sleep in, because to save money for visits to Continental Europe and make space for the family sons, home from boarding school, I gave up my room for a couch in the lounge where prayers were held. Our host, when he found time to relax after dinner, often chose Robert Bridges' *Testament of Beauty*: he richly earned a post-war Knighthood—at the expense of ruined health. (By coincidence, I later discovered that my mother had been born only a block away in 1889, the year of Hopkins' death, to an Anglican evangelist.) Every Sunday, along with some medicos, I had given Scripture lessons to boys from Hopkins' old Highgate School, and in summer helped to take them camping in Wales and Cornwall close to areas in which Hopkins had enjoyed reading parties from Oxford.

One of Hopkins' most animated letters to his mother, written from the Lamb Inn, Tiverton, 29 July 1865, tells of meeting some glamorous cousins from the Manley branch of his father's family. By a strange chance, the young son of Tiverton's vicar, just entering the Royal Academy of Music, had the room next to mine, and used to invite me down to happy spells in Devon. During a birthday party for him (John Burden was later one of Britain's chief horn-players) I met a group of his friends from all over the parish, who may well have included distant Hopkins relatives. Laying a treasure-trail from the vicarage to the hamlet of Manley and back, I made the blunder of assuming these sturdy rural youngsters would be at home in trees, and so I suspended the prize from the highest branch of a large hardwood in the vicarage garden. Chaos! Not a single one of them shared with me and (as I subsequently learned) Hopkins, a passion for tree-top retreats. Judging from several episodes in the poet's life, if he had been in the wrecked *Deutschland* himself, he would probably have been among those who quietly helped the less nimble into the rigging beyond the thrall of the waves.

In September 1939 I was with seventy Highgate School fellows under canvas in a Cornish field overlooking the English Channel when Britain declared war. I was the camp "adjutant" or general manager, as well as their unprofessional "music," and readily agreed with a worried deputation from the fishing village below that we ought to scatter our neatly lined-up tents to make them look less like an army target. But I can't recall Hopkins' name and poetry ever cropping up among my fellow organizers though they were themselves old Highgate School boys and must surely have heard of their past alumnus. My captivating introduction to the poet was transferred to the antipodes, and was postponed till after the devastations of the war in the Pacific. Yet coming to delight in Hopkins' Hampstead and the English countryside ten years before catching up with his poetry was far better than the reverse sequence would have been, owing to the later scars of bombing and of army defences left all over England. Moreover the calamitous sinking of ships in World War II made subsequent sea passages hard to obtain. Even when I was desperate to return from Cape Town to my second year of teaching in Melbourne in March 1947, I was at first offered only a ruinously expensive route across the Atlantic, over the Andes and then the breadth of the Pacific. How I wished I could spare the money for this exotic journey.

A Daunting Assignment

Hopkins often felt mercilessly overworked, whereas my own deans and principals constantly detected in me funds of untapped energy. By my third Melbourne year I was just beginning to be comfortable with my teaching responsibilities when the Council of Queen's College granted the Master (a physicist with two Oxford doctorates) six months of overdue leave—and asked me to take charge as Acting Master. I was appalled at the prospect. Of the hundred men in residence (we also had non-resident men and women in our seminars) two-thirds had seen action in the Pacific. There were twenty tutors to co-ordinate, covering all Faculties, and ten very senior Honorary Teaching Fellows (one resigned that year, modestly explaining that he had just been made founding Vice-Chancellor of the lavishly-funded embryonic University of New South Wales). I explained to my fiancée the folly of saying "Yes," only to be told "Of course you can do it!" I had grown to greatly like Australians (she was one), and wisely acted on Rita's vote of confidence.

Of my inaugural address to the men I suspect the part that clinched their approval was "Call me Norm!" They tested me out the first few days with amusing tricks, but at the third dinner, when I led the tutors to the high table in our panelled dining hall, we were greeted by a placard "Norman Conquest."

The men were good-humouredly co-operative. They had been accustomed to holding a complaints-meeting of the house-committee and sending their president to accost the Master with urgent requests. Instead they accepted my invitation for their full committee to meet in my comfortable sitting-room, with me present to offer friendly and experienced advice when consulted. Together we worked out the best affordable solutions, and arranged for improvements needed for the approaching celebration of the College's Sixtieth Anniversary.

On Sundays I conducted Methodist evening services in the lovely college chapel—until my M.A. year I had devoted all spare time every morning between lectures to theology and Bible-study, intending to enter Westminster College, Cambridge, as a candidate for the Presbyterian ministry. My recovery from Japan was accelerated by marriage to my life-partner Rita, who had served through the war in the RAAAF Signals, and who was then in her third year as violinist and coloratura soprano in the university's Conservatorium. She was also an artist with a full Art School training (see Frontispiece to my *Facsimiles*, Vol. i, for her portrait of Hopkins as she "reads" him).

A Deceptive Allurement

Meanwhile the embryonic University of Natal, which I had visited in 1947, had offered me a Senior Lectureship in Durban, and when I declined, happy in Australia, they doubled the salary and solved our financial and post-war housing problems by inviting me to take over their Men's Residence: though the men still occupied old army huts, there was, I was assured, money set aside for a large new building that I could help design. This seemed too good to refuse. I set about consulting colleges alongside Queen's to discover what features to include or avoid: the Rector of Newman College, the Very Rev. J.M. Murphy, S.J., was particularly helpful. Since Joe Feeney has recently tracked all the way to Melbourne the Murphy of Hopkins' exuberant "'Consule Jones,'" who made "sermons so fierce and hell-fiery,/ Mothers miscarry and spinsters go mad," I have speculated whether this sober rector had some fire-brand relative.

I shall never forget the ominous start of our six years in Natal in January 1949. The police, augmented by officers and soldiers from other provinces, were struggling to contain a murderous eight-day conflict between Zulus and Indians. As we were being driven from Durban station we were almost stunned by information the university had been afraid to disclose earlier: the Men's Residence was completely out of hand. My predecessor, an ex-army Major (I had been merely an artillery gunner), had lost control of the ex-servicemen, though he was a full Professor of Psychology. Persistent vandalism by drunken engineering students was rousing strong antagonisms against the new University of Natal that was due to be ceremoniously inaugurated in March. Financially also, the residence had been running at a disastrous loss, which simply could not continue. The senior matron had been winning popularity by undercutting all efforts to achieve discipline, but the Warden had not found the courage to dismiss her because she had ingratiated herself with the men. The Council had naturally refused to release the capital for a new residence until the men could be trusted not to sabotage it in periodic rampages.

My five-year stint as Warden or Dean of the Men's

Residence accordingly began with a trial of strength. As the new term approached the president of the student house-committee, who had outmanoeuvred my predecessor, arrived back, fresh from the ego-boosting exercise of drilling the combined recruits to the South African Defence Force from all over the Union. He was, of course, in his officer's uniform, swagger stick under his arm. He abruptly delivered his ultimatum: he was utterly opposed to my intention of expelling men whom I thought guilty of disgracing the university! He was courteously but firmly invited to come back in a week's time when he had worked out all the implications of his stand, but I assured him I had absolutely no intention of abandoning the only plan that offered any promise of curing the scandalous situation. He returned in a completely different frame of mind, pledging that he and the whole house-committee would support me to the full. The term was barely a month old when three men, celebrating their birthdays in the old style, daubed plumber's tar on the bathroom tiles of one of Durban's up-scale hotels. They found, in utter disbelief, that I kept my promises: they were suddenly not only ex-servicemen but ex-residents, with a list of alternative addresses to call upon. This put an instant end to orgies.

Rita laboriously checked all the food accounts for a year, wrecking what had developed into lucrative double-billing. However, when towards the close of the session it became known that the assiduously popular matron was to be replaced by a Domestic Bursar with book-keeping experience, all my allies deserted me, petitioning on her behalf. I had to soldier through six grim months until the obvious superiority of Mrs. Harle won back the deserters. There had been periodic problems also when the black staff enjoyed a binge, but the appointment of Prince Austin of the Royal Zulu House as ceremonial induna had a magical effect. The Council approved funds for a new Residence, and once that was built the men treated it with proud respect. Planning it cost me the equivalent of four months' full-time drafting, followed by weekly checking to catch incessant deviations during the construction process, missed by the Clerk of Works.

Unfortunately, to balance our books and improve the quality and variety of their meals I had to keep the Hall open eleven months of the year: paying guests from other universities were eager to enjoy Durban's famous beaches. I could never entirely relax even during vacations when I was trying to build up my notes on Hopkins.

The Risk of Pseudo-Degrees

As for the Department of English, in addition to full-time and evening classes from Monday to Friday, we had to lecture on Saturdays and Sundays (in Durban's steamy semi-tropical climate) to tired but eager Zulu and Indian school-teachers who travelled from as far as 80 miles away to win the crowning glory of a degree. But it was soon clear to me that mistaken kindness had allowed them to pass examinations on poems and novels they could not understand: they earnestly prepared from critical books in the library one comprehensive answer for each of their authors, and reproduced it from memory whatever question was asked. Although our teaching load was already heavy we had to add for all the week-end students Practical Criticism seminars such as other sections received during week-days, and every examination paper in future began with a test of comprehension that could not be evaded with a memorized essay. Without improvements in our training methods I could see that these teachers would never be able to produce pupils with an adequate command of English, or themselves be able to understand good fiction and prose. Meanwhile of the small final degree class, 70% had to repeat the year, but they were then able to spend their twenty-five or so further years as useful English teachers in the schools. By the end of my sixth year in Durban, week-end Part Timers had risen to the level of the week-day Part Timers, and could read with pleasure, e.g., some of Hopkins' sonnets.

In spite of such improvements Durban was never an auspicious place for me. I remained aware of divided loyalties, although some of the people I was fortunate enough to recruit for our Residence or inherit in the English Department gave magnificent service under adverse conditions. One major rift was between the Durban "drudges" and the Natal University staff in the lovely old educational inland town of Pietermaritzburg. They seldom visited the sauna-like coast, so I saw very little, e.g., of Will Gardner, the notable Hopkins specialist. Our Durban libraries were pathetic, and all the journals were reserved for Pietermaritzburg.

Escape

At last in 1954 six months' leave in Britain let me pursue my 17th-century studies, so successfully indeed that the London University Institute of Historical Research published forthwith a 55-page article in their *Bulletin*. More important, I was interviewed for a new post, and the next year escaped from my fractionary Durban employments by appointment to the chair of English in the newly created University College of Rhodesia and Nyasaland. This was a fully integrated inter-racial institution, under the benevolent aegis of the University of London, with Advanced Level entry as in England. It was situated in Salisbury, capital of Southern Rhodesia (now Harare, Zimbabwe), where I had been born in 1915, during World War I.

A Crucial Choice

Various contributors to this series have written with deep gratitude of the mentors who opened for them the opportunity of writing a thesis or a book on Hopkins. I hold the celebrated A. Norman Jeffares high on my list of those to thank. As our house guest in 1961 in Rhodesia he noticed the constellations of books by and about my favourite "modern" poets, Hopkins, T.S. Eliot and W.B. Yeats. He was about to launch a new series of literary studies, *Writers and Critics*, and generously offered me first pick out of the three.

With T.S. Eliot, on whose *Four Quartets* I had once planned a book, my lack of familiarity with the American background in which he had grown up made me hesitant: that *Writers and Critics* volume was entrusted to the late Northrop Frye, Canada's foremost literary critic. On W.B. Yeats I already had considerable material through my enthusiasm for Anglo-Irish literature. For

Hopkins, on the other hand, there was in 1961 a comparative dearth of scholarly studies, and my own research was relatively thin. But I had a sabbatical in England due the following year.

Long Leave 1962-63, and Manresa House

Remembering the priceless mental background to English literature I had myself received at the age of 12 from immersion in parts of England, Scotland and Ireland, I planned our family tour in 1962 carefully, not limiting it to Jesuit associations. The most important centres I reserved till later. One was Manresa House where Hopkins had three spells: as a novice, later as Professor of Rhetoric and finally as a tertian. It had recently been released by the Jesuits and renovated to suit an incoming Teachers' Training College. Special arrangements had to be made with a London County Council historiographer and Fr. Peter Low, S.J., to take me over the wonderful old vacant building. Fr. Tony Bischoff, S.J., had searched the house thoroughly after the war, hoping for documents bearing Hopkins' name or in his hand: he had even organized the excavation of areas in the grounds, under his own supervision, where papers had been hurriedly buried by wartime government orders to reduce fire risks during air raids. He found nothing.

We were completing our circuit when something made me turn back, and in the corner of the long room we had just passed through I caught sight of a pile of a dozen or so old note-books on top of a cupboard against a far wall—obviously found by carpenters during the refurbishing process. They were official record-books, kept by Jesuit novices, juniors or rhetoricians, going back to the 1860s. I was lent two to examine, overlapping periods when Hopkins was there. There was a panic years later when some could not be located—they were still at the Manresa Press, I believe—but they are all now safe in the Provincial Archives. Fr. Alfred Thomas, S.J., constructed from these, and other parallel journals he himself found, his greatly enlightening volume, *Hopkins the Jesuit* (OUP, 1969), preserving for us an intimate insider's account of the poet's years of training.

Admission to the Hopkins Repositories

Special treatment greeted me in the Writer's Library, Mount Street (or Farm Street), London, as also in Campion Hall, Oxford. I had made good Jesuit friends in three other continents, but with Fr. Basil Fitzgibbon, the Campion Hall librarian, I had an instant empathy: he possessed a Bollandist passion for reaching historical bedrock and wholeheartedly helped along my own researches. Only after his death did I read in his official obituary accounts of his war service, including daring solo missions in the enemy-infested jungles of Burma. The Master of Campion Hall, Fr. Deryck Hanshell, S.J., asked me to help during my London studies with restoring to the Hall Hopkins MSS that had been loaned in the mid-1950s for the use in London of editors working on the Oxford University Press volumes published in 1959: his *Journals and Papers* and his *Sermons and Devotional Writings*. Happily I was able to overcome the two difficulties that had delayed their return. I then spent several days checking all the Campion Hall MSS in detail against Fr. Tony Bischoff's catalogue.

Basil Fitzgibbon made proper boxes for all the MSS—and the Master during dinner on my final evening, before the Martyrology, expressed the thanks of the Hall, and announced that in future Hopkins MSS could not be borrowed by members except on a scholarly basis, nor shown to visitors without his express permission.

Correspondence, Meetings, with Fr. Tony Bischoff

At Basil Fitzgibbon's suggestion I also later wrote to Fr. Tony Bischoff, S.J., about our shared enthusiasms, inaugurating an active exchange of correspondence that lasted until his death in 1993 at the age of 82. My warm acknowledgements of his help in all my books were accompanied by detailed ascriptions whenever I used information derived from him.

When his progress with the biography of Hopkins became stalled, I interceded on his behalf both with his Oregon Provincial and with Fr. Martin D'Arcy, head of the English Province. His one year sabbatical eventually stretched till his retirement. He fortunately turned down my crazy scheme that he should move to a Catholic House in Kingston, where we would help each other to complete our endless labours by becoming co-authors of his projected biography, *Poet in Black*, and joint editors of my variorum edition of the *Poems*. Oxford University Press was apoplectic when they heard the idea, and the memory brings spinal shudders to me also. Fr. Tony's contributions to Hopkins studies, especially at Gonzaga University, were substantial, even though they did not result in the volume for which he had amassed so much material. He told me, naming names, that there was in his time a plot to destroy Hopkins' two tiny Oxford Note-books (C. i. and C. ii.), for which he had provided special protective boxes: the conspirators did not like the accessibility of the poet's Anglican Confession-notes. This slaughter might have deprived us of the autographs of a large percentage of his pre-Jesuit verse. Fr. Tony believed the collapse of this shocking plan was due to the sudden realisation that he had complete photocopies of both vest-pocket note-books.

Textual Explorations

While I was on sabbatical in Britain in 1962 I decided it was time to check on the accuracy of the Hopkins texts: some of the readings in Will Gardner's Third Edition struck me as decidedly suspect—in places such as "The Escorial" not included in Robert Bridges' First Edition. The collection of mainly autograph poems R.B. had assembled in MS A had by 1962 passed to his son Edward, the first Baronet. We were living quite close to his home, and my wish to ensure that no corruptions had developed since his father had been responsible for the Hopkins canon guaranteed an immediate welcome. For me this was a memorable and vital occasion, the prelude to his sustained generosity without which my future editing would have been twice as arduous. He arranged to deposit MS A in the London offices of the Historical Monuments Commission (of which he was the energetic chairman), right opposite the House of Lords where he was often in attendance. I had met him in the relaxation of his rural home, a scholar lovingly handling an album of priceless value. But the moment I stepped into the offices of the Commission the degree of static in the air told me if Lord Bridges was in or imminently expected. An incisively efficient man himself, he had great expectations of his assistants. During the war he had, inter alia, held the onerous post of Secretary to the British War Cabinet under that formidable Prime Minister, Winston Churchill, and he had been the Head of the whole Civil Service in Britain. Yet his personal interest in the creation and maintenance of a sound Hopkins text took priority over much more momentous affairs. Whenever I wrote to him from abroad asking him to check some minutiae in MS A, he nearly always replied by return mail. Later, for years during the editing of the *Poetical Works*, he and after his death Thomas, the second Lord Bridges, loaned the album to the Bodleian Library for my exclusive use.

The Registrar's Left-hand "Man in London"

I have sometimes described myself as often more administrative stooge than Hopkins scholar. Unfortunately my precious "sabbatical" fell victim to the same malady. As I had already served four years as Dean of the Faculty of Arts (on the English pattern that expects Deans, elected by their colleagues, to continue being active teachers), and also been a perpetual member of the Building Sub-committee, planning and inspecting laboratories and lecture-rooms for all Faculties, our Registrar in Rhodesia regarded my presence in London, though technically a sabbatical, as a gift to the administration straight from heaven. A fusillade of unwelcome cables, notes of appointments to keep as the college's representative in the University of London, documents, etc., battered my mind almost daily, hampering my progress. The weather did not help, lavishing upon Britain and parts of Europe intense frost that froze even buried water-mains, and heavy snow that closed highways for days on end. For London it was declared the worst winter in 122 years.

In spite of this, when my sabbatical came to an end I had a rich haul of material, and the *Writers and Critics* book on Hopkins was finished except for the final chapter. Written largely in the British Museum Library it was in longhand (I'm a two-finger-plus-thumb typist). The last pages were penned on board ship as I returned to Rhodesia via Cape Town, in advance of the rest of the family, with our bargain of a new car as deck cargo, still unluckily bearing international number plates. After the voyage ended I faced a drive of some 906 miles to Johannesburg, and a further 715 miles to the Rhodesian capital, 1621 miles in all. A lawyer friend accompanied me. The Peugeot station wagon was loaded with our heavy winter bedding and clothes, and just behind the driver's seat, where I could snatch it in the event of a collision or fire, was a large suitcase containing the sole MS of the book, along with all five volumes of Hopkins' prose, heavily annotated in pencil and cross-referenced. In addition to these there were many hundreds of cards (5" x 8") inscribed on both sides, representing my notes from contemporary records and my research discoveries not only during the sabbatical but in the interstices of fifteen years too much of which had been spent in crafting the structures of two new universities.

In Johannesburg we rushed into a good hotel to secure a lock-up garage. In the eight minutes we were away, a car window was forced: the only case taken was the vital one—not with the expected passports and currency, but with all my sabbatical harvest, the finished MS, and accumulated research notes. The effect was almost like a family bereavement.

During my sabbatical the previous liberal white government in Rhodesia had fallen, and on reaching Salisbury I discovered I would have to serve as Dean of Arts for a fifth year as the college negotiated approval for Rhodesia's first completely inter-racial hospital, where our future doctors, black or white, would examine patients irrespective of colour.

Wonderful support was given me by my family and by the Jesuits both in London and Campion Hall, at a juncture when I badly needed it. But the university college itself was navigating through uncharted reefs: the Principal and Deans met daily (I vividly recall fifteen hours a week with two chain-smokers). Only at week-ends could I disappear into an empty seminar room, away from phones, to knit together the skeleton of the stolen book. The simultaneous destruction of all my Hopkins material left blanks on every page, to be filled in Britain.

Africa's Lack of Great Libraries

The comparative poverty of library resources in Africa was proving increasingly burdensome. During my first six years in Rhodesia I had laboriously drawn on almost every university in the continent, from Ghana to Cape Town, for books and journals: it took months to cover what could be completed in a week in a major repository. Our family began to consider migrating yet again, this time to a country where libraries were given higher priority than anywhere in Africa. That our college in Rhodesia was able to assemble in ten years from absolute zero a hand-picked multi-faculty library of about 100,000 volumes was largely due to the support of two generous American foundations—the Carnegie and the Rockefeller.

My Dream of an Oxford English Texts Edition

During my sabbatical in 1962-63 I had for the first time handled the original autographs and other MSS of Hopkins' verse. Comparing them with the standard Oxford (Third) edition by W.H. Gardner, published in 1948 and frequently reprinted, I found that, isolated in South Africa from the year he became editor, he had simply adopted the transcriptions of people to whom he had printed an acknowledgement of "help." My stolen MS, however, avoided any reference to errors, though the range of imagery through which the drafts might run had caught my fancy (see, e.g., OET, p. 472). Discussing this with Graham Storey in Cambridge I accepted with alacrity his suggestion that my next book ought to be an Oxford English Texts *Hopkins* volume with variant readings.

On the way back to England in January 1964 to recover material needed for the *Writers and Critics* volume I called on the university in Ethiopia, then run by Canadian Jesuits: they made my visit delightfully memorable by speedily unbooking my hotel reservation as a "complete mistake," and transferring me to their House for personally conducted tours. In England my proposal for a major Oxford English Texts edition of Hopkins was well received by the Delegates of the Clarendon Press (confirmed in a letter 10 April 1964). I was then asked if the main body of my edition would reprint Will Gardner's text with variants from it in the footnotes, and when I had to reply that this would be impossible I was given a copy of his Third Edition in its latest version and asked to mark up overnight from my notes on the MSS what changes seemed necessary. In a sample of the first forty poems there were in the text and notes about 260 deviations (minor, medium or serious) from the particular MS of each poem he had named as his authority. They were horrified and called an editorial meeting immediately.

This precipitated me into an unfortunate situation. I wished to proceed as rapidly as possible with the OET edition, pleading that once it had been published Gardner could then adopt the readings he preferred for a new edition. But both John Bell and Derek Hudson refused to spend any more money printing a corrupt text. They asked me to cooperate with Gardner in correcting the errors, preferably as co-editor, if Gardner agreed. This was an understandable attitude, but it affected my future adversely for decades.

The Jointing of the Fourth Edition

In the forty-five years between Bridges' pioneer edition and my proposal of a Variorum Hopkins no one had followed him in building a firm MS foundation. Subsequent scholars had made slips in transcribing newly released pieces—Charles Williams, Humphry House, Tony Bischoff, etc.

When in 1948 Oxford appointed Will Gardner their official Hopkins editor he was, in Bloomfontein and Natal, separated from the MSS by three weeks' travel on land and sea: moreover it did not occur to him as necessary to scrutinize the originals. He had some very limited microfilms, and relied upon other scholars to alert him to any imperfections. He was lucky. In his edition's smooth sixteen-year run there had been only one pebbly patch— over a comma in "The Windhover." He had also in 1953 launched a strikingly successful Penguin edition, *Gerard Manley Hopkins: Poems and Prose*, a most useful anthology which many of us, myself included, prescribed for our students. By 1963 the paperback's circulation must have reached about 200,000, lending the editor confidence to assure readers in that year's reprint that all peculiarities in his poetry texts had "been correctly copied from the MSS of G.M. Hopkins, unless the contrary is stated in a note. WHG." (This was a certification I have never been able to offer for myself.) The texts of the poems included in the Penguin collection were identical with those in his Third Oxford Edition.

He had the following year (unknown to me) submitted to Oxford a Fourth Edition, with an extended Preface but a virtually identical text, and was deeply hurt to receive it back from Derek Hudson with a private letter saying that it could not be published until he had resolved with me the queries I had raised about a number of his readings. Hudson suggested that he might perhaps care to invite me to assist him as co-editor. Will Gardner was naturally shaken by this utterly unexpected news. The shock, however, would have been many times worse if the errors had been aired in a widely read journal by some graduate student with access to the MSS he had failed to use as his ground-work.

As already hinted, Will Gardner and I had been colleagues in the same university (though in separate cities) for six years but in 1955 we had lost touch when we both moved elsewhere to chairs of English. He did not realize how recent my discoveries were. He complained, "If only you could have intimated that you had found something wrong years ago, or at least as soon as you heard that I was preparing a Fourth Edition I would . . . have rechecked every part of the edition from first sources on the lines and in the directions indicated by your friendly criticism." On the contrary, he wrote, "Your remarks have always been kind, complimentary and encouraging." He appealed to me to give him all the help I could "in the true spirit of international scholarship."

I quickly sent him numerous examples of his deviations, but had to add that, "In view of last year's disastrous loss of Hopkins material . . . I am in no position to offer you the fruit of months of research in return for a line of thanks in a Foreword." In response came Will's letter "to acknowledge, with gratitude, your kind, just, and saddening letter of 21st April" [1964], and to invite me to become joint editor. I started work on his Fourth Edition master copy by checking through the texts and notes he had submitted to Oxford. I proposed about 500 changes, some of them only minutiae such as he had once announced (a comma in "The Windhover"), and some others due to Gardner's acceptance of my conviction that we ought to treat Hopkins' last known version of a line as the text instead of the one an editor might like best.

Transmigration to Canada

The three-year editorial process (1964-67) was complicated by overlapping with three other loads on top of teaching and administration—the rewriting of the stolen *Writers and Critics Hopkins* (my notes record weeks of 90-100 working hours) and two uprootings of our family. The first was from Rhodesia (just before the white government unilaterally declared independence from Britain) to Ontario in 1965, a major upheaval, but one that brought me within easy range of the giant libraries of Harvard, Yale, Columbia and Princeton. Our first Canadian university was new, isolated, and fractious with French/English rivalries; but after a year I accepted a drop in salary to join Queen's University in Kingston, Ontario. Established in 1841, the Queen's library had acquired during the Victorian age most of the journals and books that had influenced Hopkins. Shortly after my arrival two unselfish colleagues responsible for library orders came to ask me what works not already in Queen's I most needed for my research. I immediately named the Jesuit journal *The Month*, founded in 1864 (a full century earlier), but remarked that complete runs would be very costly. Not till long afterwards did I hear that they had spent all that was left of the annual departmental allocation to form a splendid start on obtaining for me this valuable resource. Our holdings of *The Month* are now virtually complete, and I have personally subscribed to it for about forty years. It is the one journal I made a point of opening the day it arrived: its rare editorial integrity has commanded deep respect. Its cessation with the April 2001 issue leaves a gap very hard to fill.

Our Fourth Edition Becomes a Paperback

Looking through the thick folders of letters Gardner and I exchanged, with others from Oxford University Press, I am unpleasantly reminded of the fantastic amount of detail that we had to discuss and agree upon.

The Fourth Edition was published in 1967, and reissued as an Oxford paperback in 1970. Catherine Carver, formerly in OUP's New York division, was responsible for the witty cover showing "Gerard Hopkins reflected in a lake." I tried to win this inspiring woman as my OET editor (which would have greatly accelerated my progress), but she had been relegated to the computer section. John Bell had been a congenial Oxford editor for the hardback.

Since Gardner's death in 1969 the modest royalties (at one time about a twopence a copy) have been split equally between the Gardner estate (including his son Colin, who succeeded him as professor) and me. I had sole responsibility for improvements, and Oxford is still reprinting the edition on its own initiative. The total circulation since 1967 must now be around 70,000—a mere handful compared with Gardner's Penguin edition.

Bodley's August Librarian

Thanks largely to Lord Bridges I came to be on very good terms with the Bodleian Library. The librarian himself is a sacrosanct figure never seen by even senior researchers, but Lord Bridges had placed his precious MS A in the Bodleian on loan for my exclusive use for some years, and promised to let the library have Robert Bridges' extensive MSS and books in a loan collection once he had set them all in order. This is one of the ways in which a fabulous national treasury is created, so the library was particularly anxious to please him. One day it occurred to Lord Bridges that I might be able to help him over a vexatious problem he was having with the Berg Library in New York, so he phoned the Bodleian Librarian (Lord Bridges always went straight to the top) and said, "Oh, Shackleton, I believe Norman MacKenzie is working on one of my MSS in Duke Humphrey's. Do you think you could call him to your 'phone for me please?" I can imagine what sort of response anybody else would have received for trying *that* one on Bodley's librarian! Presently I felt a tap on my shoulder and there was Robert Shackleton himself, inviting me to descend several floors to his sanctum to take a phone call. He must have been surprised to find me so young and unimpressive.

After this happy event (though I could do nothing for Lord Bridges with the Berg) I was, quite undeservedly, treated by the librarians as an ally, and was even able to arrange with the head of Scotland Yard's Forensic Document Examination Department to receive a senior research librarian, Dr. David Rogers, and me carrying the priceless Hopkins MS B (normally on permanent exhibit under glass) for examination by their purpose-made Infrared Image Converter. I needed scientific aid to differentiate between Bridges' transcripts of a poem and Hopkins' all-too-neat emendations. Details are related in the Introduction to *Poetical Works*, xxxix, ff. An instrument was even engineered at great expense for the Bodleian. I used it extensively in editing MS B, but it became progressively unreliable.

Where There's Smoke

As the Bodleian Library owns three albums of Hopkins' verse, most of my time was spent there. The most valuable Humanities books and MSS have to be read in the beautiful Duke Humphrey's gallery, surrounded by ancient volumes which used to be chained. Its disadvantage is that the centuries-old windows are comparatively small. I aimed at being the first reader to arrive every morning (just as the cleaners were leaving), so as to claim the seat with the best natural light. One evening, while the building was undergoing a very costly renovation, I was, as usual, the last reader left, surrounded by the four albums of Hopkins MSS on stands. Suddenly I became aware of smoke seeping in from the corrugated iron where a window was being rebuilt. I handed in the MSS quickly, asking the assistant what he had been cooking? He told me that the Fire Department had been summoned. As I reached the front of the building a huge fire engine arrived and in no time had its extension ladder on a library roof—unfortunately on the Radcliffe Camera, instead of Bodley. Meanwhile a swift library assistant with a hand extinguisher had dealt with the fire. Some workmen, it seems, feeling cold, had carried a charcoal burner up to the top floor and it had set some timbers alight. Next morning a furious Keeper of Western MSS summoned the contractor, only to be met with his pained protest: "But it was only a very small fire, Dr. Hunt!" Within fifty feet were some Incunabula (of which only a few copies exist in the world), other numerous rarities, and reference books, many with MSS additions, of incalculable value. And four Hopkins volumes!

The Instituting of Secret Juries

The three years expended upon the reshaping of the Fourth Edition proved an almost fatal delay for my Oxford English Texts project. The Clarendon Press Delegates, perturbed by the harsh reception of several volumes in the OET series, instituted what many authors found to be an exasperating and tedious screening process. The Clarendon editor of each title had to select a secret jury to advise him. The author was called upon for a sample which was slowly circulated, mainly around tutors' studies (a circuit apparently equivalent to a sizable segment of the earth's annual orbit, occupying four to six months), then back to the press's editor, who gathered—often purely negative—comments together to assist—or assail—the author.

Having waited all summer for the verdict, I was by then usually deep in a new teaching term. Not once did the reports show evidence that a juryman had ventured into the Bodleian to spend half-an-hour on the Hopkins MSS. By the following year the Clarendon Press editor might well have left for pastures new, and a fresh sample would be required. The crucial problem with Hopkins was the best method of displaying his abundant early versions. The alternatives we explored are summarized in *Facsimiles* i, Appendix A, and *Poetical Works*, Introduction, lxv ff. One senior editor did not help by repeatedly maintaining that "Anybody can read Hopkins' writing," but he always declined to let me test him, or some of the best Oxford students, on a sample passage with several successive layers of contributions: identifying *who* was responsible for *what* was the problem I was tackling.

Queen's Students

Queen's students have been the most rewarding I have ever had the pleasure of teaching, because of their responsiveness and the rigour with which they are selected. Our congenial Head of Department, John Stedmond, gave me the task of establishing a doctoral programme in English. During my six years as Director our graduate numbers rose to about ninety, drawn from around the world. Of these about a dozen were generally under my personal supervision, with theses ranging from Milton to T.S. Eliot. There were always some Hopkinsians among them: Michael Moore and Lesley Higgins made outstanding contributions. Summers were even busier than the rest of the year.

Our Daughter's Apprenticeship

My progress with the complicated edition was in competition with my duties at Queen's—as usual these had a strong administrative component. During a culmination of responsibility, when I was Chairman of Queen's Council for Graduate Studies and Research, covering all faculties, in addition to my busy teaching and supervising schedule, I had the absolutely invaluable help of our daughter Catherine (now Mrs.Phillips) in not only marshalling my sprawling material into shape but carrying out an exacting analysis of the evolution of Hopkins' handwriting that required intense concentration, along with an artist's eye and memory. This has enabled her to suggest probable places in the poet's chronology for pieces that he had neither troubled to date nor entrusted to Robert Bridges. She has herself described some of her many other investigations. It was a delight one summer to have her assistance in Oxford on the MSS themselves. Campion Hall welcomed her warmly, but when the next-door residence proved full almost to the rafters Cathy gladly accepted a bed in an attic cubby-hole that was part of the emergency exit onto the roof. Together we met some of the OUP senior editors—for whom she has long since sailed under her own flag. Her ability to decipher tangled script is best shown by her immaculate edition for Cornell of Yeats's *The Hour-Glass: Manuscript Materials* (1994), where plate after plate of what appears to be shorthand hieroglyphics is transformed on the facing page—by some process of divination—into plain English.

"Errors"—Regrettable or Just Costly

In retrospect I can recognize many errors of judgement that I regret. Other decisions have proved costly to me, but beneficial to my students, and sometimes to Hopkins also. While I was Director of English graduates, students often complained of frustration because thesis instalments they had given their supervisor a month or more earlier had still not been evaluated—just my problem with the Hopkins jurors. I became over-conscientious in trying to be prompt. And my fear of losing another slice of my life if MSS were lost during a sabbatical overseas induced me to spend much of my research time in Kingston, remaining accessible to worried (though apologetic) students.

The worst instance came with the award of a Killam Fellowship (1979-81) that could have released me entirely for two years from Queen's responsibilities. I did not accept the full amount because some graduates might have been stranded with no substitute to replace me. They all justified my care. Miyo Takano, e.g., published her Hopkins thesis and later translated into Japanese Hopkins' *Letters to Bridges*. David Levy completed an M.A. on Hopkins and Astronomy, and became famous for discovering or helping to uncover marauding comets (including one that crashed into Jupiter): in his lectures across North America he always quotes Hopkins, and his many publications have helped him to earn two Hon. D.Scs. Manzoor Islam, on a strictly limited leave from the University of Bangladesh, not only speedily finished his dissertation on Yeats and Swedenborg but is now giving papers with fresh research to Swedenborg conferences in Sweden and elsewhere. All of them have come back to Kingston to visit me.

The reduction in lecturing enabled me to produce *A Reader's Guide to Hopkins* (1981) for Thames and Hudson, with

Cornell University Press. My patience with Oxford had been crushed by an eighteen-month delay in the adjudication of a special consultant. After a headlong collision I had simply disappeared underground and completed this other project. I have been recently flattered by the invitation from Saint Joseph's University Press in Philadelphia to make some updatings in the Guide for a second edition.

I "retired" in 1981, and began to relax a little. But two years later I was galvanized into activity by the sudden death of our celebrated Coleridge scholar, George Whalley, a man with an immense opulence of recondite knowledge, who had donated two sheaves of his research life to Queen's English Department as head, and who was still in perpetual demand as a problem-solver across Canada. We were exactly the same age, 68. His contributions to the multi-volume definitive edition of Coleridge were far from complete, and his fellow-editors were all engrossed with their own assignments. George's passing terminated my brief indulgence in a normal time-table. I settled into an editing year of forty-nine to fifty-two weeks, week-ends included, until three more labour-intensive volumes were out.

Garland to the Rescue

As for the OET, eventually the Clarendon agreed to allow me an entire second volume, to consist of facsimile reproductions, a concession for which I know no precedent in the series. But at the eleventh hour Thomas Collins, general editor of Garland Publishing's poetic autographs in large-page facsimile, invited me to produce two volumes for his series. I had an excellent New York editor, Elspeth Hart, and the *Early* and *Later* poetic facsimiles appeared in 1989 and 1991. I hope that these publications may result in reduced wear and fading among the original MSS, some of which show distressing signs of deterioration.

The final stages of preparing the OET for publication, though arduous for us all because of its complicated material, were lightened for me by two stalwart Oxford editors, John Bell and Frances Whistler.

Jesuit Affiliations

This record of interactions with Hopkins has mentioned only a few of my many debts to the Society. These started in my freshman year when in 1932 Jesuits on the staff of St. Aidan's College, Grahamstown, South Africa, found me a copy of the Latin Vulgate I had been searching for: dated 1868, the year the poet became a novice, the volume has survived all my peregrinations. When I lectured in Hong Kong (1940-41) and in Rhodesia (1955-65) I had Jesuit colleagues on the faculty. In North America Saint Joseph's University in Philadelphia, with Fr. Joe Feeney as navigator, greatly stimulated me by making me an honorary alumnus with a D. Litt., and they hosted the largest and most inspiring Hopkins Conference in which I have ever had the privilege of participating.

Martin D'Arcy Lecturer

A major stimulus in preventing me from abandoning the OET has been the constant encouragement of the Fellows of Campion Hall, under the successive Masters specifically thanked in that volume. The peak of my lecturing career was contrived for me by Fr. Peter Hackett, S.J., when he was Master of Campion Hall: in celebration of the 1989 Hopkins centenary, and with the support of Oxford's Faculty of English, he arranged for the annual Martin D'Arcy lectures for Michaelmas 1988 to be on Gerard Manley Hopkins, and invited me to deliver them—the first non-Jesuit to be so honoured. Tutors strenuously discourage students from dissipating their concentration across the endlessly varied lectures available, so attendance is completely unpredictable: I hoped to reach and maintain double digits. But Hopkins' poetry touches an amazing range of people, both religious and secular. Though Hopkins was not then on any Oxford reading list, the first lecture, before college seminars began, drew some ninety students, dons and townsfolk. Later numbers varied from fifty to seventy, of whom a regular core of about forty attended every lecture. I was cheered by their readiness to carry out investigations to fill in gaps in my knowledge, and welcomed the staunch attendance of a Bodleian group of senior research staff. In between lectures I was busy correcting proofs of the *Poetical Works*.

The Demise of the Infrared Image Converter

During the final lecture I announced a happy agreement I had been able to achieve between Bodley's librarian, David Vasey, and the Director of Oxford's Research Laboratory for Archaeology and Art History, Dr. Edward Hall, to avoid the further deterioration of the Infrared Image Converter. In the Bodleian library there was no special cubicle available to shield it from the blaze of light that was injuring its sensitive screens. The librarian agreed in future to transfer MSS for infrared examination to the Art Laboratory, where it would soon be housed and cared for by an expert technician. This ideal remedy was also mentioned in the Introduction to the *Poetical Works* (xliii). To my deep disappointment I subsequently heard from Ted Hall that when his technicians brought back various scattered remnants of this costly machine from the Bodleian, he found they had been damaged beyond repair.

A New Book

My Martin D'Arcy lectures have now been much revised and regenerated along multi-disciplinary lines. For thirty-three years in Kingston I have benefited from a lecture club founded in 1897 that meets in private living-rooms and is therefore limited to thirty members elected for their breadth of interests. From 1977 to 1997 I was the Saturday Club's sole organizer and secretary, summarizing papers in science, medicine, engineering, art, the humanities, music, politics, law, etc., for our minutes and the Archives. Some of my Hopkins lectures were first tried out on my colleagues, experts in other areas. As secretary I was able to pry open the club into the admission of women, inexcusably excluded for eighty-five years. I end my over-lengthy notes on my Hopkins studies and my tributes to many friends with mention of this stimulating but time-devouring service.

I have enjoyed (or endured) a far more adventurous life than Hopkins did, sprawled over five continents and nearly double his in length. I have taught many hundreds more (and more varied) students than he tried to instruct. Yet in so far as I am remembered at all in future years it will be as an editor of the man whose verse I have attempted to preserve and expound.

Some Reflections on Hopkins the Man

My response to Hopkins has been basically linguistic, through admiration for his incomparable capacity to touch our minds and emotions in ways no other English poet seems quite able to do. Though he is likely to outlast all of us put together, he was not a teacher I would gladly have seen appointed to any of the eight universities with which I have been associated. I have much sympathy with the Dublin registrar impatiently waiting for his examination scores, while Hopkins sat into the small hours turbaned in wet towels trying to weigh as on a goldsmith's balance one dull script against another, though their scrawled ink-tracks were certainly no gilded rivers. Meanwhile his inspirations for the completion of *St. Winefred's Well* (that he had failed to commit to paper though he had enjoyed leisure enough during his holiday in Wales to do so) were chased from his mind by petty niceties of Latin and Greek.

At what point did his upbringing fail him?—though of course its very limitations might have helped to provoke him into irrepressible verse. He certainly suffered from an inelastic schooling, the infliction of an outmoded classical training that was being lambasted (mostly in vain) by official Commissions of Inquiry that included "barbarian" men of science. It is simple for us, knowing him as the poet not recognized even in his obituaries, to enumerate ways in which he could have been better nurtured. In Highgate's school under a bullying head he may have lost some of the resilience he badly needed in later life. If only he could instead have gone to Eton—but that would probably have been beyond the reach of his family. Eton might have developed his musical talents as an adolescent when he could most easily have learned to read a score and attain some fluency on the piano. They also exerted less bullying pressure on their boys to attain perfection in the classics: Eton's relaxing custom of marking some of the Anglican calendar's numerous saints' days with a half-holiday rendered the school less pious but more humane.

At Oxford he felt guilty over "wasting time" in the Oxford Union where men from all the colleges could meet, and whose library offered the only readily accessible collection of books and journals not on his too-focussed reading lists. His already supersensitive moral ammeter was recalibrated to swing towards "danger" in what we would call normal and even desirable circumstances, to some extent through the excessive influence of Liddon and Pusey: their High church repressiveness led, I believe, to his missing many opportunities that would have made him a better dramatist as well as a wiser model for us to follow.

On the biographical side Norman White and Robert Bernard Martin have greatly enriched us with the first highly detailed studies of Hopkins' life. There remain, however, two funds of information about him that seem to me to invite further careful examination. The first consists of his surviving Anglican confession notes (March 1865 to January 1866), released by the Jesuits for publication in my Facsimiles of his *Early Poetic Manuscripts and Note-books* (New York: Garland, 1989). These contemporary jottings catch his passing moods much more precisely than do the blurred and touched-up memories thrown off in his letters twenty years later. Our concepts of his sexual orientation, however, generally built up slowly, need time to modify, and cannot be gauged without reference to the trivialities in his non-sexual actions over which he agonized. Any general shift in opinion is liable to be a gradual one.

Robert Martin in *A Very Private Life* has voiced major misgivings over the second source of biographical information that calls for deeper study, Fr. Joseph Darlington, S.J., for whose many anecdotes about Hopkins in Dublin he is himself often the only witness. Although Martin modestly consigns these doubts to his Appendix (pp. 417-20), he points to various inaccuracies and to the progressively negative slant of Darlington's recollections. I would like to hear of a scholarly reassessment of Darlington, preferably by a Jesuit with full access to the records of University College, Dublin. Darlington made a remarkable contribution to its success. There are about thirty references to him in *A Page of Irish History: Story of University College, Dublin, 1883-1909* (Dublin: Talbot Press, 1930). James Joyce (*A Portrait of the Artist*) and Stanislaus Joyce are other writers with views of Darlington to be consulted. Fr. Joe Feeney's remarkable assemblage of all surviving impressions of Hopkins expressed by his fellow Jesuits (in the Allsopp/Downes volume of 1994, *Saving Beauty*) provides a solid foundation, but we need additional light on how Darlington himself was appraised in his relationship with other colleagues.

Not a solitary one of us in this volume, though several Jesuits or ex-Jesuits are included, has probably shared his religious pilgrimage or endured his limitations. But then none of us could have enriched the English world with the greatest marine ode in our literature, or have put into unmatchable form the acute distress caught in his "Sonnets of Desolation."

DRAMATIZING THE TEXT

". . . rash-fresh re-winded new-skeinèd score . . ."

My Beautiful Persian Carpet

In 1912, Ruth Draper was approaching thirty. For many years she had been entertaining audiences at private parties with her dramatic monologues. Should she turn professional? Was she good enough? She sought the advice of a fellow American, none other than the great novelist Henry James, a devoted friend and admirer. His reply was delightfully characteristic. "My dear child, you have woven your own very beautiful Persian carpet. Stand on it."

In 1983, I was reminded of that exchange for several reasons. I had written and performed a one-man play called *Hopkins!* based on the life and poetry of the Victorian poet. But the idea for it had come to me in a rather strange way. After two years of scouring libraries for a suitable subject, I was still empty-handed, so I gave up looking. Some months later, I was acting on the stage of St. George's Theatre in north London, when the name Hopkins sounded loudly and unexpectedly inside my head. I almost jumped. I knew immediately that I had found the subject I was looking for—a Victorian poet/priest. I call this "strange" because that theatre was originally a Victorian church. Not being a Christian, I was presented with a big challenge, but, being spiritually conscious, I responded sympathetically to Gerard's passionately devout nature. In fact, I believe that my not being a Catholic gave me an artistic advantage—objectivity. I was neither preaching nor proselytising.

"What you look hard at, seems to look hard at you . . . ." Never was this more true than while I was researching and writing *Hopkins!* In fact, I gave up several times in despair. I could feel him leaning over my shoulder wincing at possible errors and misrepresentations. My aim was ambitious—not simply a poetry recital but a drama in which I would portray Gerard from the age of 17 to 44. That is why, for example, I included a couple of dirty limericks from the 1860s to represent the kind of robust humour he must have encountered during his student days at Oxford and probably enjoyed in spite of his more scrupulous self. I called the play *Hopkins!* even though the director Trevor Nunn once scorned the use of the exclamation mark as a cheap way of heating up titles of shows—e.g., *Oklahoma! Oliver!* However, Gerard was no stranger to the exclamation mark—there are thirteen in his sonnet "Starlight Night"!—so I felt fully justified in employing it.

My flying carpet eventually took me to places as far away from London as New Orleans and Spokane. (During an interview with the film director Steven Spielberg, I mentioned that I was about to perform my play there and he looked at me incredulously and said, "What do you want to go to *Spokane* for?" as if it were the back of beyond.) It even took me to Los Angeles, where I was a guest of the Jesuits at Loyola University. They told me that a visitor to their dining room, remembering the vows of poverty, chastity and obedience which Jesuits had to take in Gerard's day, looked at the delicious food, the choice of wines and spirits, and the twinkling lights of Santa Monica Bay through the window, and said, "If this is poverty, show me chastity!"

But it wasn't a ride without bumps. In order to market my play, I needed to quote mouth-watering reviews. And for some reason, critical praise at the Edinburgh Festival carries great weight. So I girded my loins and booked eight performances for myself at the Cannongate Lodge just off the Royal Mile. But how to compete for customers against nearly a thousand other Fringe companies, apart from the "official" Festival productions? Edinburgh was awash with handbills being thrust at passers by on every street. I needed an eye-catching gimmick.

Here's what I did. At the ripe old age of 42, I became my own sandwich-man. Yes, on two white sheets of hardboard, I painted **SEE "HOPKINS!"** in bold black lettering, plus details of the time and place. With white boot laces, I tied the boards over my shoulders, one hanging on my chest, the other on my back. For maximum impact, I wore a white cricket umpire's hat and a white tee-shirt. I looked like a pint of milk. There was a certain amount of chiacking from scaffolding workers as I trudged up and down the crowded Royal Mile but I was eye-catching if nothing else.

So what if my dignity was a bit dented? I had worked too hard on my play to act to rows of empty seats. It had taken two years to research and write it, two months to learn it and six weeks to rehearse it. I had made the furniture specifically to fold up in the boot of my car. I'd designed and printed all the posters, leaflets and programmes. From an old bed sheet, I had even devised a big banner to hang above the door of the theatre, announcing my play. Each morning, having slept on the floor of someone's flat (I was lucky!—digs are as scarce as hens' teeth during the festival), I tidied away my sleeping bag, went for a run, rattled through the text, made lunch, donned the sandwich boards and paraded up and down the Royal Mile, then collected unsold tickets from the Fringe Office, took them to my theatre's box office and returned to my digs for my costume, make-up and wig. They couldn't be left in the dressing room because they would have been stolen. Oh the glamour of it all. I then returned to the theatre, dressed, made up and set out my furniture and props. I performed the play and then cleared the stage for the next show. After changing, I collected my box-office receipts and took my costume back to my digs where I collapsed.

On the fourth sweltering hot August day, I was outside the Fringe Festival Office wearing the sandwich board and handing out leaflets to passers by, hoping the box office queue would spot my advertisement and book seats. Nearby, a fresh-faced quartet dressed in Victorian garb were singing songs with all the enthusiasm of youth. Suddenly feeling very old, I sank dog-tired onto a sand-bin for a few moments' rest. A solid wall of people shuffled past me. A man paused, looked down at me and my sandwich board, smiled and said, "That's an easy way to make money." He must have thought I was half-witted because my mouth opened and shut like a goldfish but nothing came out. How could I begin to describe the train of events that had landed me on that sand-bin wearing that thing? How could he know what I would be doing at 2:30 that afternoon? I grinned weakly at his disappearing figure.

Mercifully, it was the last time I would have to drum up customers. *The Scotsman* gave me a wonderful review and all remaining performances quickly sold out. I was to perform the play in every conceivable kind of venue, including a college lecture hall where the only lighting was directed onto the blackboard behind me, and even a Portakabin annexed to a girls' school. In the latter case, I don't know which of us was more glad when it was over—those fourteen-year-old girls or me. I can only hope at least one of them was infected with a lifelong enthusiasm for his bewitching poetry. The actress Patricia Routledge commiserated with me over the rigours of such touring, calling it missionary work, not in the religious sense but because one is taking live theatre to places other commercial ventures can't reach.

Two months after appearing at the Edinburgh Festival, and with no warning, I suffered a devastating bereavement and entered the land of grief, with its manic insights and agonies. I was booked to perform *Hopkins!* in Manresa House, Roehampton, only five days after the funeral. This was where Gerard began his noviciate. Work of the right kind is wonderfully therapeutic, and Gerard demanded the best I was capable of. His spirit felt very close. Far from having to make something of second-rate material, my own modest homespun Persian carpet was woven of the finest coloured silks and it carried me over a terrible chasm. My love for Gerard's poetry, and my gratitude to him, remain unbounded.

BRASS-BOLD: AN ACTOR AND G.M. HOPKINS

In 1970 I chose the audience for which I wanted to perform Hopkins and that choice governed a number of subsequent decisions I had to make as an actor. I wanted to share him with a public that included those who had never heard of him, and those who had only read him. I felt this meant that I had to favor, through all the glorious chiming, sprung rhythm and counterpointed cadences, the lines of thought. I had to get completed images where they were going without resorting to an express delivery that robbed those images of their powerful inscape and muscled tracery. Even an audience acquainted with poetry, one that is at least slightly partial to its habitual linguistic distillation and calisthenics, has a very powerful dependency on syntax, even implied syntax: "This is a subject or verb, or a modifier of one or the other, and somehow, sometime, this guy's gotta get the subject and its retinue connected with the verb and its."

Deprive any audience of those connections too many times during an hour's performance, and you deprive yourself of that audience's attention. In "'As kingfishers catch fire,'" for instance, this means an actor has to survive the flames of kingfishers and dragonflies, ringing stones and swung bell bows to get to the key that holds all of these examples together:

> Each mortal thing does one thing and the same:
> Deals out that being indoors each one dwells

But, in this example, too hasty a pass over the four previous orchestral, image-laden lines and there is no emotional reason for what follows. A compromise is necessary: an increase in tempo beginning with the second line, and elemental pantomimic gestures for "wells," "tucked string," and "fling out." Performed words must always be heard perfectly, and with a tempo increase an actor must overstress diction. Besides insuring clarity, overstressing diction retains the charge of alliterative and assonantal magnetism. I have always sensed that the objective music so characteristic of Hopkins' voice stands on its own if phrased and stressed as indicated and pronounced efficiently. His insistence on the aural experience of his verse testifies to his confidence in the objective strength of the sounds and their rhythmic textures. But I do not think he ever imagined a kind of declamation that hovers on the units of his sound. For me such emphases weaken relationships between those units, and cloud the thought-lines they should illumine. Besides, such dwelling on the musical components seems unnecessarily to slow down the personal urgency that drives so much of the poetry.

What I refer to as pantomimic gestures are brief and descriptive hand-signs defining objects ("roundy wells," "tucked string," "bell's / Bow") or specific actions ("fling out"). They are distinct in style from the registrations of emphasis and broad indices of direction or space I use in the sestet: highlighting "the just man justices," and contrasting "the Father" in a place generally above "men's faces" which are in the audience in front of me.

Another governing choice was to work without the text onstage. I cannot deny that there are brilliant recitals of these works by performers holding the book or relying on a lectern. But in my view, standing alone and speaking to the audience is direct. Holding a book or sharing the stage with a lectern holding the book (and I have tried this approach) renders the actor only a conduit. The author is present and the audience is consciously or unconsciously relating to both the actor and his author. The actor's most basic illusion, that *he* has a story to tell, that this material is spontaneously welling up from his *own* soul, is undercut by the symbolic presence of the author.

The absence of a text onstage frees the actor because all the space is rendered neutral, usable. With a lectern, a portion of the territory is compromised. If the book is in the actor's hand, his gestures are compromised. In the section of "The Wreck of the Deutschland" that I perform (II, 12-19), I need all the space available to be neutral so that I can, in fact, conjure the sea, the ship, "whirlwind-swivellèd snow," "canvass and compass, the whorl and the wheel." Wherever one addresses any of these images on the stage, the audience will follow in the assignation. And when the personal drama begins to unfold on the vertical axis between the crew in the rigging and the nun on deck, a three-dimensional scale emerges for which the actor must be able to stage-manage a very busy scenario without the inanimate dead weight of a lectern anywhere in sight.

In my view, the broader these scenes are played, the more emphatic the soliloquy of stanza 18 becomes. From the wide-open narrative of the storm and the passengers, the actor can almost coil into the heart he chides in his breast. Full-front exposition yields to this private, even embarrassing surprise that might effectively tempt him to turn slightly away from his audience into a profile posture.

Less general choices are demanded with work on individual poems. Each one must be given an atmosphere its own. The sun is shining for "Spring"; it's nighttime in "The Lantern out of Doors." It's windy in "That Nature is a Heraclitean Fire and of the comfort of the Resurrection" and "Hurrahing in Harvest." Most of "Felix Randal" is somber memory; "Pied Beauty" is prayerful, playful charm. From before the first syllable of each poem the actor must project its tone, even when the subject is more conceptual. "Henry Purcell" opens with a prayer, "The Leaden Echo and the Golden Echo" with a problem. One's entire body registers these attitudes. Tension in the shoulders and upper body can register conflict much more effectively than strained facial features. A stance turned partially away from the front with the actor looking at the audience over his shoulder projects a question or uncertainty. How much breath is taken before the first syllables can determine how open and lightsome the upper body feels as one begins a piece. I would never think of playing "Cloud-puffball, torn tufts, tossed pillows" without lots of wind in my sails, my chest and spirit high and open. Whereas I am quieter, less expansive when I ask my question of Margaret in the opening of "Spring and Fall."

And speaking of Margaret, there is the question of speaking to

Margaret—and Felix, and Henry, Christ, Earth sweet Earth, Despair. So much of the repertoire is soliloquy: the actor/poet talking to himself for all to hear (usually staring at a space above the heads of the audience). When lines are directly addressed to a particular character, there are blocking choices to be made: the addressee has to be somewhere on the stage. I find this a very challenging problem of focus and concentration. But it is worth solving because even a projected imaginary character produces tangible dramatic tension for the actor and the audience. Props need their stage places as well, and even the inventive constellations in "The Starlight Night" call for some detailed mapping.

Happily, Hopkins was meticulous about stress and rhythm. What he feared we wouldn't get he so often marked, and those marks are part of an actor's memory load until they become habit. Then fragile dualities such as "fawn"and "froth" illuminate with equal valence and larks fill out their measures in new-skeinèd scores.

But there are still choices to be made from line to line and word to word: whether to caress a line's internal rhymes or over-attack an alliterative series; how long to dwell on the last rhyming syllable of a line whose sense drives on to the next line or even the next tercet; how to pronounce "bow" in "each hung bell's / Bow swung," or "dauphin"; how (or whether) to divide fairly a single "Oh," between "the black West" and "morning"; what a parenthesis sounds like "(my God!)" and how its contents differ from what follows: "my God"; what Hopkins was hearing when he suggested that "Spelt from Sibyl's Leaves" should "be almost sung."

Stage techniques and the decision to favor the delivery of meaning can speak to only some of these questions. Blessedly, the scholars help me with the other decisions. Theirs is a generous and persistent concern that all of us who love Hopkins approach his insights faithfully. And their care and wise sleuthing of the evidences yield more than illumination. They sometimes force me to gasp, to inhale in the same deep "ah!" that celebrates the presence of a certain pair of beloved "bright wings."

ERNEST J. FERLITA, S.J.

Hopkins Gladly Performed

Some of Hopkins' poems are difficult to perform, but I must say I have delighted in performing several of them. By performing I obviously mean something more than merely reading aloud; I mean becoming the speaker in the poem and expressing thought and feeling by the shaping of every word according to the rhythm of every line, occasionally accompanying word with gesture, the visual enhancing the aural, sometimes even clarifying it.

Much of Hopkins' verse, because of its distinctive rhythm, actually invites performance: "Sprung rhythm gives back to poetry its true soul and self." But as he says in connection with his "Loss of the Eurydice," to perform it "quite satisfactorily" is not at all easy: "I do not say I could do it." After all, a composer "need not be able to play his violin music or sing his song." Indeed, he adds, "the higher wrought the art, clearly the wider severance between the parts of the author and the performer."

Though all this is pertinent to Hopkins' poems, it becomes all the more evident in reference to the poetic drama he was working on in his later years but never finished, *St. Winefred's Well*. One of the first things a performer discovers in Hopkins' dramatic language is its power to express passion. "Sprung rhythm," Hopkins says, "lends itself to expressing passion." He does not say why but he certainly demonstrates it, especially in Caradoc's soliloquy after he has murdered Winefred. No doubt it is partly due to the fact that it is "the most . . . emphatic of all possible rhythms" and partly to that *abruptness* which is what he understands by *sprung*, strictly speaking, "where one stress follows another running, without syllable between," as in this line and a half in which there are two such instances and three others where the syllable between is very slight (all six stresses are marked by Hopkins himself):

> What I have done violent
> I have líke a líon dóne, | líonlíke dóne.

The gestural dimension of his language is yet another quality discovered in performance. Not every poem of his demands gesture—some can be performed without even one—but others bring hands, face, body into play. The gestures are sometimes very obvious, as in the first soliloquy of *St. Winefred's Well*. Teryth gazes after his daughter with great fondness. But even as his heart expands with love, he feels it constrict with fear and hears "some tongue" cry:

> . . . What, Teryth! | what, thou poor fond father!
> How when this bloom, this honeysuckle, | that rides the air
>   so rich about thee,
> Is all, all sheared away, | thus!

The word "thus" demands a gesture: the left hand shaping the bloom in the air and the right hand slashing down from above the left shoulder. This is a foreshadowing of what actually happens. Caradoc, having murdered Winefred (Gwenvrewi in Welsh), cries out:

> Down this darksome world | cómfort whére can I find
> When 'ts light I quenched; its rose, | time's one rich rose,
>   my hand,
> By her bloom, fast by | her fresh, her fleecèd bloom,
> Hideous dáshed dówn, leaving | earth a winter withering
> With no now, no Gwenvrewi.

The syntactical difficulty of these lines disappears when the gesture they demand is seen. Just as Teryth's in the first soliloquy, Caradoc's left hand shapes the rose richly blooming in the air, which is then hideously dashed down by the right as it swings past the fresh, the "fleecèd" bloom.

    How to perform "The Windhover." This sonnet, which Hopkins said at the time was the best thing he had ever written, is perhaps the most challenging. For the simple reason that a performer must understand, on a poem's first level of meaning, every word, and if there is dispute about a word, must decide what interpretation to perform. In "The Windhover," the word most disputed is, of course, "buckle." That word demands a gesture, but what will it be?

I am not suggesting there is only one way of gesturing, but when one says "I caught this morning morning's minion," it seems to me that one is called to look outward; and then, on "king- / dom of daylight's dauphin," to raise one's right hand in that direction, and then begin moving it slowly and steadily towards the left as one follows with the eyes the "dapple-dawn-drawn Falcon, in his riding / Of the rolling level underneath him steady air"; and then pushing out with the left hand on "striding / High there" and pushing again on "rung" and "rein" and turning it up and out, fingers quivering, on "wimpling wing"; then following the Falcon again with the right hand, still raised, moving from left to right on "then off, off forth on swing" and turning it to shape in the air "a skate's heel" sweeping "smooth on a bow-bend"; and finally, with both hands indicating how "the hurl and gliding / Rebuffed the big wind." Does Hopkins end here the description of what he saw? It would seem so, because he ends the octave by saying that his "heart in hiding / Stirred for a bird,—the achieve of, the mastery of the thing!"

Yet there are those who insist that the first lines of the sestet tell us unequivocally that the Falcon is now seen diving, swooping, plunging down. That is what the word "buckle" is taken to mean. I must say that up till now, in performing the poem, I have gone along with this interpretation, looking out and suddenly seeing the bird dive and opening the arms high and wide on "Brute beauty and valour and act, oh, air, pride, plume" and letting them swoop down and the hands coming together on "here / Buckle!" This gesture can also suggest that brute beauty and all those other things "buckle together" in the dive.

But I am now among those who, like Norman H. MacKenzie, "doubt whether the stoop is implied anywhere in the sonnet," and he refers us to a very convincing essay by R.A. Jayantha, "Does the Falcon in 'The Windhover' Really Dive?" If Hopkins had intended "to present the windhover as diving down, because he regarded it as the most exciting and significant of its movements, then the most appropriate moment for it would have been before his heart 'stirred' in response to it, and the most appropriate place for it in the poem, the octave itself in which the bird is 'inscaped.'" So what does "buckle" mean? It is not easy to say. Following other commentators, such as Robert Boyle, S.J., Jayantha prefers "to take 'buckle' as referring to the poet's heart, and as meaning 'to put on.'" But according to MacKenzie, Elisabeth Schneider "plausibly interprets 'Buckle!' as meaning 'This world of natural beauty and power . . . collapses—and *the fire* of the spiritual world, . . . of Christ, *breaks* through.'" I lean towards Schneider's interpretation, and in performing it I would make some appropriate gesture.

By choosing one interpretation am I delimiting what Hopkins intends? Perhaps, "considering Hopkins' deliberate use of ambiguity in his poems." But I do feel that some choice has to be made as to a word's first level of meaning in order to perform it in context. That would not necessarily exclude other levels of meaning.

Hopkins matters to me because performance matters to me, and performing his works is a challenge I gladly accept.

How I Became a Hopkins Performer

Hopkins was the poet for my "A" Level examinations and so I first read him when I was sixteen years old. I found the poems almost impenetrable at that time, but enough of the magic of the words got through to let me know that there was something there worth going back for later.

As I grew into my twenties and thirties, I had repeated experiences of meeting new situations in which I felt more or less out of my depth: a man walked in front of my car and was killed. Feeling myself awakened spiritually and called to service as a healer, I was torn between this call and my desire to continue exercising my creativity as an actor. My marriage failed and I found myself alone; I plunged down into the depths of a depression from which I feared I would never surface. I travelled to beautiful places and felt my soul soar with the majesty of the natural world. I felt a strong sense of horror at the destruction and pollution of the Earth.

In each and every one of these situations I found words from Hopkins reaching out to me like messages from a guide who had gone on ahead to check out the way, or like signposts left for a lost man to cling to:

Flesh falls within sight of us . . .

. . . and dost thou touch me afresh? . . .

This to hoard unheard,
Heard unheeded, leaves me a lonely began. . . .

Selfyeast of spirit a dull dough sours. . . .

. . . mind has mountains; cliffs of fall
Frightful, sheer, no-man-fathomed. . . .

. . . the azurous hung hills are his world-wielding shoulder . . .

What is all this juice and all this joy? . . .

O if we but knew what we do
When we delve or hew—

It is immensely comforting in times of distress to know that someone has been there before and has felt the same way. Hopkins became and remains a dear companion on my journey.

Hopkins' life and work are like a rushing river which, constrained on either side by rough rocks, has not the luxury of lateral spread to meander the broad plain but cuts instead a deep canyon. His worldly experience was narrow and the restrictions he placed upon himself severe, but this has served only to deepen and magnify the cutting power of his legacy. It is precisely because he explored this vertical and inward axis that his work has such intense relevance—he has cut through the strata of human experience and his poetry resonates at every level.

When I have been troubled by relationship issues, either within my self, with another, or with God, Hopkins has been there with his words and the deep thoughts they represent. When I have felt anger towards the stupidity and selfishness of humanity in relation to the natural world no one expresses it better. In times of isolation or depression I have found him standing by my side. Whenever I have needed words to convey my sense of awe and wonder at the majesty of creation his words are those that have been whispered in my ear.

In short I feel that I have developed a strong personal relationship with this poet which is of immense value in my life— as deep as any I have with anyone currently living. Then I read in his letters and journals that he considered his work to be only partially complete without a voice to sound it aloud: "till it is spoken it is not performed, it does not perform, it is not itself." I realised that perhaps there was something that I could do for him in return for all that he has given me. Perhaps by performing his poetry I could enable his work to live as he always intended and wished that it would do ("it is my precise aim") and at the same time perhaps the work would become more accessible and be able to reach a wider audience.

That is how I became a Hopkins performer.

PERSONAL RESPONSES

". . . the rehearsal / Of own, of abrupt self . . ."

A L I S O N   G .   S U L L O W A Y

Hopkins and His Canonical Preservation

If brevity is the soul of wit in the young and intellectually frolicsome, in the elderly, such as myself, it is the soul of common sense. And so, as Polonius did not say, or do, I shall be brief.

I first encountered Hopkins as a mere schoolgirl, where there was an extraordinarily well trained teacher of English literature. Miss Punderson, or "Pundy," as she was called behind her back, had cheerfully allowed herself to be swept into the Hopkinsian fervor of the 1930s. She introduced us to Hopkins as though she wished to share an extraordinary "find" with us, as of course she did.

Miss Punderson's "archeological find" must have impressed me deeply, because decades later, I chose Hopkins as a dissertation topic. It won me an Ansley Publication Prize, which eventually, after some sad wandering in the wilderness, brought me to Virginia Polytechnic Institute, Virginia's fine state university, where I have been ever since. My chairman here was kind enough to award me an "Emerita," when I retired, and understandably I attribute this award to Hopkins himself, and I must frankly tell you why.

I had left graduate school and embarked upon my first teaching job. The chairman of the department had warned me that his colleagues tended to treat newcomers like felons who needed to be kept in their felonious place at all times. Some of these colleagues demanded that I babysit their infants or pets whenever they wished, and when I politely refused, I was placed in purdah by both students and faculty. It was as though Hopkins had never lived, nor I in need of a dissertation topic. When my contract was up, I left this place and went back to New York to see what other appointments were open to my felonious kind of scholar.

This first full-time appointment had been a deeply scaring experience, for which the noisy and self-important gouging of the ground to prepare for the new science building—in such a tiny place—seemed to be an ominous metaphor. On the way back to New York, I heard these rhyming words composing themselves in my mind:

> This spring here
> Is a sweet, trite thing
> As springs are everywhere.
> Then why this wild new wound in the earth,
> This spring here?

I always thought of Hopkins himself as having won any honors bestowed on me, and I will frankly tell you why.

One night, at the crucial moment when the night's blackness is conquered by tinges of color, I heard a little rustle next to my bed. I turned on the light and *there* was my poet, Hopkins. I felt no fear of him; in fact, I asked him several interpretive questions, to which he put his head on one side, and then answered my questions with an up and down gesture of the head, signifying, I supposed, that he agreed with my interpretations. Then he slowly and simply disappeared.

As a pragmatic person, I welcomed Hopkins' apparition with considerable pleasure. He had answered several crucial problems which allowed me to finish the dissertation and fly to New York for the customary defense of it. And I must admit that without Hopkins' appearance in that cold cruel place, I might possibly have given up the search for an academic way to honor him, and those who also honored him, and have settled for truly menial work at a truly menial wage.

The "habitual Hopkinsians," as we are called, who have consistently supported Hopkins, are obviously first in importance to his survival. Joseph Feeney, S.J., is very dear to me, but his greatest gift to Hopkins was his co-editorship, with Joaquin Kuhn, of *The Hopkins Quarterly*. Run with skill and devotion, this journal offers an obvious place for scholars attracted to Hopkins, to place essays on the poet's life and works. One of the most notable scholars in this Hopkinsian "industry" is Norman White, whose love-hate relationship with the poet has resulted in one insightful work after the other. For example, White's great book *Hopkins: A Literary Biography* is a study of where Hopkins was and what he thought and said to various friends and relatives throughout his life.

My latest "Hopkinsian" friend is Cary Plotkin of Columbia University, whom I met at conferences on Hopkins. I was rightly bemused by this man's brilliance; for example, he was asked to offer a "wrap-up" essay on the conference I was attending. He did so without disturbing a single mental muscle. His capacity as a philologist should open all our eyes to new ways of looking at Hopkins afresh.

I should also like to thank the Jesuit professors at Saint Joseph's University in Philadelphia for their invariably cheerful kindness to me when I visited the Jesuit house during a conference at the University. These friends and affectionate acquaintances have kept an elderly woman convinced all over again that, in choosing Hopkins to celebrate so often, she has made the soundest choice possible for her academic life. This is so, not only for Hopkins' indisputable merits, but also for the merits of those to whom Hopkins has introduced her.

JEFFREY B. LOOMIS

A POET WHO RESURRECTS COMFORT

Teachers of neophyte undergraduates often must deal with the excessive subjectivity of the youths in their charge. Students far too frequently seem to sense, sketched within published literary fiction, the key traits of their Uncle Otto. Then the narratives they weave about Otto, while supposedly explaining the other writer's fiction, spin them moon rotations away from wise literary explication.

Many times, when revolting against such student subjectivism, I have wanted to turn staunchly absolutist about appropriate literary critical practice—as absolutist as was Mark Schorer, in the January 1948 *Hudson Review*: "Modern criticism," Schorer there pronounced, "has shown that to speak of content as such is not to speak of art at all, but of experience; and . . . it is only when we speak of the *achieved* content, the work of art as a work of art, that we speak as critics."

Not for long can I remain as formally purist as Schorer. On the other hand, upon rereading his dicta, I do become glad that I long ago discovered and declared, concerning Gerard Manley Hopkins' personal appeal to me, that it contained both formal and experience-reflective components. I wrote, in my 1988 book *Dayspring in Darkness: Sacrament in Hopkins*, that my "awestruck pleasure in his lyrics' lustrous music" was what had at first attracted me to his poems, even before I responded to them with "awestruck curiosity about [his] defamiliarized semantics and the shocking spiritual experience that they suggest."

I am surely glad, as a teacher, for Hopkins' formal intricacy and vitality. Even if some students spurn his religiosity, they still usually enjoy, and extremely so, the integrated technique and ideas of his amazing poems. To works so lexically robust that they inspire vital porings through the *Oxford English Dictionary*, Hopkins adds rich Biblicism and theology, powerfully invigorating a reader's mind. But, even more, as formal features of the writing which also centrally help to delineate its content, his themes repeatedly quicken our attention to many of life's most meaningful experiences, including (for me) the spiritual ones.

I am, after all, still somewhat like my experience-oriented students. I care about the window that Hopkins opens on experience, especially spiritual experience. Granted, perhaps I may sometimes have thus oversimplified him—tending to see his most affirmative statements, uttered in poems, fully conquer his frettings, which abound in his prose. Yet today, guided by the cautious theorist of biography Boris Tomashevsky, I would only dare to say that Hopkins hints, in his poems' autobiographical *personae*, at spiritual resolutions he would always *like* to have enjoyed.

But, of course, such resolutions of spirit are the goal for all conscious religious meditation. Probably the most vital information I ever learned about Hopkins was that he made functional, in his poems, the common patterns of Ignatian devotional meditation. Composition of place, moral reasoning, and colloquy do appear to combine, although in diverse ways, in all his poems. And the ability to trace such structural subsections helps me both better to analyze and to teach the poems.

But, more importantly, the continuity between Ignatian meditative structure and Hopkins' poetic designs helps reveal to me the depth of spiritual self-probing which Hopkins could himself achieve, within poetic praxis as well as within standard devotional meditation. In 1987 I heard Michael Wyatt give an extraordinary sermon, at San Francisco's Grace Episcopal Cathedral. He told us that within the human psyche—but located even deeper than the Freudian "personal unconscious" and the Jungian "collective unconscious"—one could find mysterious caverns stirred by the Holy Ghost. Immediately upon hearing Wyatt's analysis, I thought that for Hopkins, as for few others, the poetic process had led as far as even those deep caves.

Yet none of this might matter to me at all—if Hopkins' meditative practice had not, without my knowing it, helped prepare me to find a revelatory meditative practice of my own. Forced, through a spate of short-term academic appointments, to move between four different states in four different years, I seemed engaged, during the late 1980s, in "fortune's football[ing]," or in my own nomadic *imitatio* of Hopkins' own numerous geographical relocations. Yet the Jesuit poet's lessons upheld me, throughout these sad seasons, and thus helped create, in me, what seems like a dazzlingly *positive* personal literary response.

To be sure, I also could, during that trying period, have learned much about the therapeutic values of poetry from such writers as Sexton, Roethke, Kumin, Levertov, Stafford, and Kinnell. Indeed I did so, having read many of their poems during those very months of "fortune's football" wandering. I could also—as a specifically Episcopalian Christian writer—have then learned even more about my specific sort of spiritual engagement with literary art from George Herbert. And indeed, it was during this very dark personal era when influence from Hopkins, a great admirer of Herbert, finally led me, even though I had always been the birth-son of *Gerald Hubert* Loomis, to read amply from the author of *The Temple*, who seems my other *spiritual* father besides Hopkins.

But, in any case, my own, although quasi-Hopkinsian, "inspirations unbidden" pursued me (experientially, psychically, and intellectually) across several states and through a difficult cycle of years. Constantly, too, unsought "inspirations" led me from meditative journaling into the drafting of poems. On one occasion, for instance, I transcribed onto paper (as composition of place?) a scene of my raging at God from atop a hill in Minneapolis. But only minutes later, I was spiritually chastened— and, indeed, moving the pen towards quiet colloquy, as if against my will. I suspect that I may have felt much as Hopkins felt, when he was completing the closing couplet in the Dark Sonnet "'I wake and feel'": the couplet where he admitted that, for a despondent recent while, he had seemed allied with the damned. My ultimate declarations, in the cathartic release which culminated *my* day's sobering effort at a poem, were that "I am just a reed, in need of air, / And only able to breathe, at all, / Because of You [God]."

It surely wasn't true that I consciously planned, a dozen years ago or so, to live (albeit with limited formal scribal talent) a meditational life in the Ignatian tradition of Hopkins. Frankly, at that period I was so personally frustrated that I often could forget (at least for hours at a time) that I ever had sensed any inklings of personal faith. But, when meditational self-transcending praxis trenchantly enforced itself upon my jagged existence, previous learning about Hopkins helped suggest spiritual meanings behind events.

I surely cannot write, as can others, about how my Hopkinsian work has fit me neatly into the professoriate. Like so many others of my academic generation (but, of course, like Gerard Manley Hopkins, too), I have passed through many a way-station on the bumpy roads of nomadic professional adulthood. Due to specific employment opportunities which *did* come my way, I have turned to dramatic literature, and not to poetry, for much of my active scholarly emphasis today. Only rarely, in truth, and then only fairly recently, have I ever been able to use much Hopkins material in the courses that I was assigned. Still, I have, since 1994, been granted the chance to write the "Year's Work in Hopkins Studies" column for *Victorian Poetry*. And that task allows me to keep following the many issues, both content-oriented and formalistic, which constitute Hopkinsian research and reaction today.

Gerard Manley Hopkins, my favorite poet, indeed was (despite maybe an occasional overwrought rhyme) a great master-technician of form. Nonetheless, I love Hopkins most of all for his poems' (and for his partly revealed self's) experiential content. My book about him argues, finally, that the Holy Spirit sacramentally infused itself into all the sacramentally committed living that Hopkins knew—albeit that some of that living stung Hopkins with lashed welts of human psychic pain. And it must be the Spirit's presence, both in Hopkins' words and in the inner being at which those words hint, which makes me feel, from my distant but intense contact with Hopkins, a "comfort" he could not always hosanna. If I may adapt (I hope not too brazenly) the famous words which Hopkins himself used in describing Christ, I would say that Hopkins, through the gifts of Trinitarian grace, "set," for me, "the example." And the Paraclete used it—raising me to new life.

A VIGOROUS DISCIPLINE

> You have been good enough to call that "supreme poet" a "solemn master" for me. These are not empty words. . . . The reading of Dante is a vigorous discipline for the heart, the intellect, the whole man. In the school of Dante I have learned a great part of that mental provision (however insignificant it may be) which has served to make the journey of my life.
>
> William Gladstone, 1883

For the last thirty-five years reading Hopkins has been for me what reading Dante was for Gladstone: a vigorous discipline for my heart, my intellect, my whole being. Hopkins has helped me define and sustain the journey of my life. He has been my constant companion ever since I began thinking about a dissertation at Berkeley in 1968. My primary interest at the time was the poetry of nature, and my period of specialization was English literature from 1789 to 1940. Naturally, I thought of Wordsworth. However, I was daunted by all the books on his nature poetry. Checking out the Hopkins scholarship, I was astonished to discover no book and very few articles on him as a poet of nature.

I realized that writing about Hopkins also offered me a chance to tap the religious training I had received in Catholic grade school. Though I had lost my faith in eighth grade, I knew that I had an advantage over some Hopkins critics, even over his friend Robert Bridges, in not being repulsed by the focus on Mary and other peculiarly Catholic ideas. Unconsciously, perhaps even then I knew I was hoping to salvage some of my spirituality. Deeper still in my unconscious, I may have heard his "terrible sonnets" calling me to confront my own bouts of melancholy. However, I was not really conscious of these opportunities Hopkins presented to deal with my melancholy and my spirituality, for my college education had split my heart off from my mind.

When I was awarded a Fellowship from the National Endowment for the Humanities to study Hopkins in Oxford during 1974-75, my love of nature led me to live in those hills west of Oxford that Hopkins and so many other students hiked and memorialized in words. I was haunted especially by Hopkins' comment, in "Hurrahing in Harvest," that "the azurous hung hills are his world-wielding shoulder."

Those words made me think of Jesus' statement, "This is my body," when he held up the bread at Passover. Hopkins' love of the Eucharist kept reminding me of my epiphany when I made my first communion at age seven. I remember how ecstatic I was, as the presence of God filled my being to overflowing. I never forgot that long-lost experience of Eden. Though as an adult I had only what Newman would call "a notional assent" to the possibility of such an experience, I kept searching for it in nature.

I was reminded of that epiphany again when I researched the connection between nature and Eucharistic symbolism in Pusey's *Lectures on Types and Prophecies of the Old Testament* at Oxford. Nevertheless, all this remained merely intellectual. In my quest for tenure I followed the rules and left out the personal in my writing, saying nothing directly about Hopkins' effect on me. I did know from my experience in Freshman English that autobiographical writing was often the best writing, and I was uncomfortable with the pretense that "scholarship" in the humanities is as "objective" as that in the sciences, but I did not know how to challenge that assumption in my own writing.

When I wrote reviews of Ruth Seelhammer's "Memoir" for *The Hopkins Quarterly* and of W.A.M. Peters' *Gerard Manley Hopkins: A Tribute* for my annual review of Hopkins scholarship for *Victorian Poetry*, I learned how to write more personally about Hopkins. I was especially struck by Peters' assertion that Hopkins "was neither a romantic, nor a religious, nor a nature poet, but a man of love."

Nevertheless, I did not follow their example until I prepared an essay for *Renascence* for the Hopkins centenary. By then I had familiarized myself with a literary theory that supported more personal accounts of literature: reader-centered criticism. I cited Thomas Merton's conversion upon reading Hopkins and his desire to write his dissertation on Hopkins; I also noted the powerful impact "The Wreck of the Deutschland" had on John Powell, S.J., as recounted in his *He Touched Me: My Pilgrimage of Prayer*, and I discussed my own experience of Catholicism and of psychotherapy.

Around this time, I had a second epiphany which deeply affected my response to Hopkins. During a psychotherapy session on rebirthing, I saw in my mind's eye rays of love coming out from a heart of a loving mother, an image like that of Mary seen in many Catholic churches. In the "daydream" I stood and walked to her and felt the loving arms, the support, and the comfort. I knew that I was a child of God. Indeed in my mind's ear, I heard a female voice say, "This is my son, in whom I am well pleased." I realized that my emotions were the language of the soul, God's way of guiding me on my path.

My newly emerging spirituality found an outlet in the local Center for Attitudinal Healing, one of over a hundred such centers throughout the world founded by Gerald Jampolsky, a Jewish psychiatrist who sought a way to help cancer patients and their friends and relatives. His first book, entitled *Love Is Letting Go of Fear*, was to my mind the essence of Christianity. Throughout my ten years as a volunteer at the Center, facilitating groups primarily for friends and relatives of very sick people, I recalled Peters' description of Hopkins as a man of love and was inspired by Hopkins' "Felix Randal" and his ministry in general.

I began to change my attitude toward English, and I became aware of some of the reasons I switched my allegiance from botany to literature in high school. First of all, I realized that it was primarily the emotional content of literature that had attracted me, though that is not very evident in all the "criticism" I have produced as professional literary scholar. Secondly, I became aware that I had sensed a potential therapeutic power in literature.

The next stage in my reading of Hopkins occurred in 1997 when I became a visiting professor at the University of Paris at

Nanterre and I found myself living in a Catholic country for the first time. The medievalism that, following Hopkins, I encountered at Oxford was now supplemented by a living faith and ritual. I was astonished, for example, by the extraordinary emphasis on the Real Presence throughout the city, not only at Sacré Coeur, where It is displayed twenty-four hours a day, but in every parish church on Thursday nights when groups of people could be seen staring for hours with rapt attention at the Host. I felt I fully understood Hopkins' distinction between a "mere return to middle age forms" and a true "medievalism in *feeling* through medieval subjects."

My apartment was about a mile and a half from Notre Dame. My "reading" of this famous medieval building was much different from my traditional intellectual book learning. The latter was an experience of an isolated, puritan reader, suspicious of icons and theatricality, clutching a text stripped of almost all the expressivity that graphics, fonts, typography, layout, and color could provide. In Notre Dame, I saw "the book"—not just enshrined but performed in a group setting, supported by hauntingly beautiful music, dazzling art, sculpture, stained glass, and architecture. Confronted by this magnificent structure, I sensed that I was completing the journey from my head to my heart.

However, I still feel Hopkins' presence most strongly when nature itself elicits my spirituality. I now live where I can see azurous hung hills all around me. I love to walk out in the meadow behind my house and watch the sun rise above those hills. When that glowing disk appears above the trees, for me it is a natural Eucharist, and I respond with "Pied Beauty" and "'As kingfishers catch fire.'" "'As kingfishers catch fire'" especially has become for me a powerful tool for building self-esteem and a sense of personal spirituality.

As I write this now, Hopkins has the reader-response he no doubt sought. I have returned to Church, as they say, and his poems led me there, but, remembering Peters' description of him as a man of love, my focus remains on learning that "love is letting go of fear." I take to my heart everything in the Church which supports that essential statement, and leave the rest.

MARIA LICHTMANN

WHAT HOPKINS MEANS TO ME

Nearly twenty years ago, as a graduate student in Religious Studies at Yale, I began a dissertation on Hopkins' poetics and spirituality. Even before my graduate studies, however, I was preparing myself, unawares, for this work. As a life-long Catholic, I may not have felt the convert's fervor as Hopkins did, but I knew firsthand the sacramental view of life—that everything that is is holy—which so deeply influenced everything Hopkins wrote and lived. Even so, I was not completely prepared for the extent of his Christocentrism and incarnationalism—his view that Christ became incarnate not just once in human form, but even in primordial matter: "the azurous hung hills *are* his world-wielding shoulder / Majestic." Hopkins had to *teach* me here, as in so many other ways. As a member of a Jesuit lay organization in high school and college, I had been somewhat Jesuit-trained, and had attended retreats based in the *Spiritual Exercises.* During my freshman and sophomore years of college, a French professor had given me the pocket Penguin edition of Hopkins' poetry, which I carried around as a treasure though I did not understand it at all. One poem, though, "Spring and Fall," surprised me with its honesty because it subverted the usual pious commonplaces about suffering and death. From that point on, I was alert to a new dimension in reading this poet. My later discovery of the "Terrible Sonnets" confirmed the sense that this poet, like the psalmists, had dared to describe rather than deflect his pain. But it was only as a member of a contemplative religious order that I first began to drink in the poetry of Gerard Manley Hopkins like new wine. I remember actually sneaking down to the convent library after the Grand Silence to memorize whole sections of "The Wreck of the Deutschland" so that my spirit could be nourished by the power and beauty of his words.

When I first set out to do a Ph.D. in religion and literature at Yale, I was told that no such program actually existed, but if my professors would not really "hold my hands" they would stand on the side and cheer me on. And so they did. It was exactly what I needed in creating a fairly innovative and enriching experience there. Before coming to Yale, I had already done a degree and university teaching in English literature, but now I was prompted by a search for meaning that led me into philosophical and religious studies. As it turned out, my studies in biblical poetry, philosophy of religion, and the history of spirituality became an unplanned, and utterly fortuitous, preparation for the study of Hopkins.

That time of concentrated research into the letters, undergraduate essays, and spiritual writings of this fine poet and complex man ushered in one of the happiest years of my life. If my advisors in religious studies did not exactly encourage me to work on Hopkins, they did not discourage me either, and so I went my way, working independently and submitting a chapter a month for review by my principal advisor, Peter Hawkins. Peter's lack of in-depth knowledge of the poet proved to be a blessing in disguise, since he continually asked questions that forced me to confront issues I would otherwise have taken for granted. I knew then that in selecting Hopkins as the subject of the dissertation, I was taking on a "poet's poet." I did not know how integrated I would find the writings of this poet who had experienced so much conflict in his life. But, wherever I turned in Hopkins' writings, I found direct lines that led back to the poetry. I discovered that this poet's life and poetry—in its agonies and its ecstasies—were all of a piece. His aesthetic, spiritual, and personal dimensions were disparate threads woven into an intricate fabric of lights and darks. The effect on me of encountering this integrity was profound. Instead of the almost inevitable disillusionment and cynicism in scholarship today, I saw in this man's public and private expressions an utter sincerity and honesty that challenged me to "go and do likewise," especially in regard to my work on him and his poetry.

The integrity that he left behind—embodied in his family motto "*Esse quam videri*" ("to be rather than to seem")—was so much greater than he knew within himself, torn as he was between his gifts as a poet and his sense of failure as a priest, compounded by the disintegrating effects of his many short assignments and his long tenure in a place where he felt useless. Like the Christ to whom he gave his life, he too was "doomed to succeed by failure." Like the things of nature he so admired, who cry "What I do is me: for that I came," he too had been spelling himself in his poems, "deal[ing] out that being indoors each one dwells."

These studies and personal experiences culminated in a dissertation that I was moved, a few years later, to turn into a book which became *The Contemplative Poetry of Gerard Manley Hopkins*. The further I went into a study of Hopkins' poetry, the more grateful I became to Hopkins scholars who had gone before. Their guidance was indispensable, even though eventually, like Hopkins whose tendency was "to admire and do otherwise," I went my own way in emphasizing the importance of biblical parallelism, the contemplative over the meditative construal of the poems, pre-Socratic philosophers, anti-Romantic poetics, and even the dark night of the soul far more than other scholars had before.

A summer's trip to the annual International Hopkins Summer School in Monasterevin, Ireland, took me from Oxford to Wales to Dublin—three places that were formative in Hopkins' development as a person and as a poet. On my way from Oxford to Ireland, I retraced the steps of the poet by visiting St. Beuno's in North Wales, where Hopkins wrote arguably the best, and certainly the most exuberant, of his poems. As I stood behind St. Beuno's on the hill of Moel Maenefa overlooking the expansive green patchwork of the Vale of the Clwyd and watched huge white clouds fill the dome of sky, I saw a little of the "pied beauty" that this poet had so beautifully inscribed.

This year I have undertaken to write another book on Hopkins, this one on poetry and prayer, a fitting subject for this poet whose poems were prayers. Now that I am engaged in writing about Hopkins again, but in a less scholarly vein, I have become even more aware of the poignancy of his life. In his heroic effort to love even in the face of his own darkness, Hopkins is a hero who "watched the door," looking with love into the most ordinary places until they opened onto beauty and grace. The poignancy of his life turns out to be a dominant piece of its own "piedness," its integrity and beauty, yes, its inscape. What is left when I assess this poet's inscape, his rare combination of artistic, intellectual, and spiritual genius, is gratitude. I am grateful for the great gift of knowing him.

How I Came, by Others' Wisdom and Kindness, to Be a (Novice) Hopkins Scholar

> I say that we are wound
> With mercy round and round
> As if with air.

"Poetry will save the world." When I heard Desmond Egan make this statement in Ireland a few years ago, I smiled. For, while Henry Lawson and Patrick White are respected figures in Australia's cultural history, Ned Kelly (Australia's greatest folk-hero), Dawn Fraser (Australia's greatest swimmer), and Sir William Slim (Australia's greatest soldier) are the people whom Australians most admire. As well, I teach biomedical ethics; my closest colleagues work in biochemistry, physics, chemistry, moral theology. Further, I was educated at a time when Neo-Thomism reigned supreme, admired because of its Cartesian clarity, its emphasis on objective truth and natural law. My college years were the 1960s, with their furious debates about unions, Vietnam, Vatican II, Germaine Greer's *The Female Eunuch*, apartheid in South Africa, the environment, the Cuban missile crisis. However, as a graduate student with plans to work in marriage counseling or youth ministry, I toiled to find the gems of *useful* knowledge in the thick tomes of metaphysics, dogmatic and moral theology, as well as the Bible—all too quickly setting aside (as I now know) the authors' styles, voices, metaphors, and literary forms, even when reading Genesis or John's Gospel.

Hardly the best background to complete a European doctoral dissertation on "The Meaning of Human Life in the Writings of Gerard Manley Hopkins, S.J. (1844-1889)."

However, some of us are fortunate to meet a wise guide at a critical moment in life's swift course. And, as I began my doctoral program in Rome at the age of 33, thinking I would spend four years on the morality of divorce or the history of abortion, I was twice-blessed because I was mentored by two "arch-especial" spirits who changed my life's orientation.

The first was an unassuming scholar of St. Paul's moral teaching, a French-Canadian humanist who admired Paul Valéry, and who took Thursdays off from preparing his ethics lectures to study Roman art and architecture; he was the dean of the Faculty of Theology at the Gregorian University when I arrived there in 1975, Édouard Hamel, S.J. The second (we met a year later when research on Hopkins began in earnest) was the curator of the Hopkins Collection at Gonzaga University in Spokane, the most insightful interpreter of English, French, and Japanese literature and cinema I have ever known: Ruth Seelhammer.

"Find out where your sources are, and go there," Édouard Hamel told me. "I have a student studying Julien Green in Paris, another working on Karl Rahner in Freiburg-im-Breisgau. I will help you locate the best place to complete your research." The search led not to Oxford as originally thought, but to Spokane. "Read Hopkins' published work, then the best studies on his life and thought, for instance, Alfred Thomas, *Hopkins the Jesuit: The Years of Training* (1969), John Pick, *Gerard Manley Hopkins: Priest and Poet* (1942), the books by Todd Bender, David Downes, W.H. Gardner, and Peter Milward. I will introduce you to some of the Jesuits here who teach Ignatian spirituality, philosophy, and literature. Their graduate courses will help you," Ruth Seelhammer said as I began to become familiar with the contents of the polished birch bookcases in Crosby Library's Hopkins Room.

Thus I entered Hopkins' world. The reading and courses led to tentative essays: "Hopkins at Oxford (1863-1867): His Formal Studies" (*HQ*, 1977-78); "Hopkins at Highgate: Biographical Fragments" (*HQ*, 1979); a comment on Elisabeth Schneider's reading of the climax of "The Wreck of the Deutschland" (*Explicator*, 1980). I had the good fortune to visit Roehampton, Campion Hall in Oxford, the British Museum, the grave of the sisters drowned on the Deutschland. I was invited to participate in an MLA seminar on Hopkins organized by Richard Giles in

1977, and blessed to be brought further into this world of "forged" features through meeting scholars (American, Canadian, Irish, Japanese, Korean, Welsh, English) who left lasting impressions on me because of their faith and sincerity, their passionate love of literature and humanity, their knowledge of Hopkins.

In spite of gracious comments that state the contrary, I am a "novice" Hopkins scholar—and will always remain one. I have not written a book like Franco Marucci's *The Fine Delight That Fathers Thought: Rhetoric and Medievalism in Gerard Manley Hopkins* (1994), or Norman White's *Hopkins: A Literary Biography* (1994). I have neither the knowledge nor the opportunity to complete such studies, in part because I do not teach Ph.D. courses in Victorian literature, but undergraduate courses in biomedical ethics, and because I am engaged in organizing conferences on "Religious Perspectives in Medical Ethics," writing essays on physician-assisted suicide, completing *Christian Ethics and The New Catechism*, and *Models of Christian Ethics*. To date, I have not written a major essay on Hopkins either, although I have been pleased with "Peter Gallwey and Gerard Manley Hopkins: An Unrecorded Influence" (*Studies*, 1983); "G.M. Hopkins, Narrative, and the Heart of Morality: Exposition & Critique" (*Irish Theological Quarterly*, 1994), and "Gerard Manley Hopkins: The Oxford Years" (*Gregorianum*, 1990), and my latest short study on "Hopkins' European Mentors" (*Studies*, 1997). My main work has been to co-edit *Gerard Manley Hopkins: His Life, Writing, and Place in English Literature* (1989), *John Henry Newman: Theology & Reform* (1992), and *Saving Beauty: Further Studies in Hopkins* (1994).

Novice that I am, it has been an undeserved pleasure to have been invited to make small research contributions to Hopkins conferences over the years at the University of Nebraska, Saint Joseph's University, Baylor University, Rockhurst College, University of South Dakota, and most recently at the University of Arkansas. It was also an unexpected honor to be asked to preach the sermon at St. Bartholomew's Church, Haslemere, Surrey, in 1994, on the occasion of the parish's memorial service to celebrate Hopkins' birth. My most satisfying work has been to write essay-reviews for *Christianity and Literature*, *Studies*, and *Nineteenth-Century Prose*.

Hopkins' cut-short, over-stressed life, his striking images, and self-sacrificing spirituality, have held my interest for twenty-five years—and I know that I will continue to be moved by his retreat-notes, informed by his letters, and lifted up by his ever-fresh sonnets. Through Hopkins I have come to know Newman's sermons, Walker Percy's novels, and Flannery O'Connor's short stories; the writings of Ignatius Loyola and Teilhard de Chardin hold more significance now. Hopkins has given me some otherwise-unseen insights into life's meaning and deep mystery. Now as "narrative ethics" forces ethicists to acknowledge that moral philosophy is a genre of literature and to better appreciate a text's limits and discontinuities, the time spent on Hopkins' passionate poetry will bear greater fruit—and I should meet fewer colleagues who are puzzled by the association of ethics and poetry, the arts and health.

Thus, as "nature's bonfire burns on," welcome activities will keep me in touch with Hopkins: visiting Oxford to take part in ethics conferences (a few minutes in St. Aloysius Church with its aging green-marble holy water font given in Hopkins' memory); seeing photos in my office that I took during the Hopkins memorial service held in Glasnevin Cemetery on June 8, 1989; reading faxes from Desmond Egan, newsletters from the Hopkins Society in Wales, issues of *The Hopkins Quarterly*. Most of all, I will be kept close to Hopkins' world by assisting friends who shoulder the annual G.M. Hopkins Summer School in Monasterevin, Ireland, and by looking forward to participating occasionally.

These, plus the bright memories of kind people and lovely places, the racing clouds above Miami, the rose-red sunsets over Florida's Gulf Coast, the occasional surprise, for instance, of hearing the Welsh baritone Bryn Terfel announce during a recent recital that he would sing "Who Is Sylvia?"—each "heaven's sweet gift"—will let me remain a novice Hopkins scholar as He continues to "easter in us," and "be a dayspring to the dimness of us."

"STRIDING HIGH THERE":
HOPKINS' POETIC ACHIEVEMENTS

I came across Hopkins' poetry when I began to study for my doctorate. My tutor, Professor Francesco Marroni, noticed my fondness for Christina Rossetti and the Tractarians, on whom I had given a paper at a conference, and encouraged me to specialize in Victorian religious poetry. "We are chosen by the authors and the topics we like better," he said to convince me to keep to a path that was still largely untrodden in the Italian domain of English studies. I well remember my perplexed reaction to his words. On one side, I wished to continue my research on a subject that I found congenial and captivating. On the other side, I was afraid of a serious challenge that I would have to accept: that of confronting the *monstre sacré* of English poetry, Gerard Manley Hopkins.

Little I knew about Hopkins' poetic achievements at that time. As an undergraduate student, I had never been required to study his poems, since his linguistic experiments were considered too hard for young non-native readers. I had once skimmed through his verse on my own initiative to get an idea of his notorious "particularity." The result had been puzzlement and frustration. Unable to decipher his intricate syntax and abstruse coinages, I had soon given up the idea and concentrated on "more useful" topics. But now the spectre of Hopkins was looming in my mind again.

I decided to meet the challenge. I first chose some sonnets and shorter lyrics, which I strove to read in English rather than translating them into Italian. Later on, my attention was devoted to longer and more complex works, such as "The Wreck of the Deutschland." To catch the overall design of the poems that resisted my interpretation, I used to hang them on the wall and establish a closer relation with their verse, which I watched and read aloud many times a day. Slowly and patiently, I overcame the interpretative barriers. Delight and joy replaced weariness when I learnt to make sense of Hopkins' daring combinations of sounds and words. The better I became at disclosing hidden nuances, the more I enjoyed the verbal magic, the uneven associations, and the powerful pictures of his poems.

What I felt was that, in a strange and inexplicable way, I had been chosen by an author who deserved being ranged with the greatest. In addition to proving a bold experimenter and a poet-enchanter, Hopkins appeared to me as an intellectual fighter for meaning and order. He was an artist who had struggled to accomplish a grandiose worldview without ever reaching a balance but who had, nonetheless, managed to perceive and convey some glimpses of eternity. The depth of his poetic visions became even clearer when I started to investigate the many intertextual echoes of his oeuvre. Contrary to my first idea of him as an isolated and quite eccentric figure, I sensed his wish to establish and maintain a spiritual correspondence with previous and contemporary artists who, exactly like him, had dealt with the unsolvable mysteries of existence. And it is this very poetic dialogue, this courageous confrontation with different viewpoints and painful dilemmas, that, in my opinion, adds to Hopkins' greatness.

To better illustrate this point, I will mention a parallelism with Shakespeare that I have recently found out. Some months ago I was reading *Macbeth*, when I suddenly realized that the unnatural events described in Act II were strongly remindful of "The Windhover." In particular, I noticed that the animal imagery of Scene 4 (the falcon and the horse) was the same used in Hopkins' sonnet:

> *Old Man*
>
> A falcon, towering in her pride of place,
> Was by a mousing owl hawk'd at, and kill'd.
>
> *Ross*
>
> And Duncan's horses—a thing most strange and certain—
> Beauteous and swift, the minions of their race,
> Turned wild in nature, broke their stalls, flung out,

> Contending 'gainst obedience, as they would make
> War with mankind.
>
> *Old Man*
>
>   'Tis said they ate each other.

What the quotation makes clear is that Hopkins revitalizes some tropes of *Macbeth* to voice the anxiety of his age, which was likewise ridden by doubts and insecurity. Differently from Shakespeare, however, he reconfigures the animal metaphors in new terms, thus offering his own contribution to the human search for meaning and expression. Let us now compare the two texts in detail.

In *Macbeth* the proud falcon and the beautiful horses, "minions of their race," are the emblems of a natural and social system that is menaced by an impending disaster. Unable to foresee a new order that might replace the old one, Shakespeare connotes transition in frightful terms: the owl's killing of the falcon and the rebellion of the horses against mankind are two images of collapse and degeneration which pave the way to further horrors (such as the cannibal feast mentioned). Roughly the reverse is true of "The Windhover," in which Hopkins tries to check chaos by envisaging a cohesive spiritual force. Instead of being turned upside-down, the hierarchy of being is preserved by a divine essence which infuses the world and keeps its many layers together. The falcon "striding high there" like a magnificent but tame horse, is the pivot of a social and ontological order (i.e., the medieval scale *king – dauphin – chevalier -* [*ploughman*], symbol of class union, and the coalescence of matter and spirit represented by Christ), which can resist the anomic forces of anarchy and degradation.

This "corrective" response to *Macbeth* is a proof of Hopkins' sensitivity to the problems of his age, in which the belief in progress was questioned by underlying fears of a breakdown. Without ever silencing his uncertainties, which are implicit in the speaker's hermeneutic quest ("the achieve of, the mastery of the thing!"), the poet breaks the dangerous impasse which trapped many Victorians. The solution he proposes is a mysterious but spiritually-imbued model of reality, which tempers the negativity of a well-known archetype (the apocalyptic world of *Macbeth*) to foster a more hopeful future.

In choosing to converse with Shakespeare, Hopkins shows the vast potentialities of an artistic sodality which is akin to Forster's view of all the great novelists writing together in one room. His ability to keep the dialogue alive through the centuries is another sign of his utmost poetic endowments. Apart from being a linguistic magician and a committed intellectual, he is also a member of the little cenacle of eminent poets who have contributed to perfect the literary medium in order to achieve truth and beauty.

This very picture is what I present to my students nowadays. After becoming a teacher at my university, I have tried to raise interest in a poet who is too often excluded from academic curricula. And I am glad to say that the students' response is encouraging.

EWA BORKOWSKA

HOPKINS AND GOD'S GRANDEUR

My interest in Hopkins started in 1985 when I had to make a decision about my research for a Ph.D. dissertation. I took to English poetry earlier than that, as a student of English when I was writing my thesis on William Blake. Interestingly, I learnt then that Thomas Merton also studied Blake for his first dissertation and then he turned to Hopkins. It was a pure coincidence because I learnt about Merton's choice during my research on Hopkins, and Merton's writing was not an incentive to my studies. I always wished to do research on English Christian poetry but in the European context which would also include German and Spanish poems. I added the poetry of John Donne to my studies of Hopkins in what was published as a book in 1995 (my *Habilitationschrift* which is a requirement at a Polish university to become Associate Professor and then full Professor). The mystical writing of John of the Cross conducted me to the darkest regions of Christian mysticism which helped me later on to interpret Hopkins' "dark sonnets" and other religious poems. My reading of Meister Eckhart, Hildegard of Bingen and Jacob Boehme directed me to German poetry but, perhaps subversively, towards the poetry of Rainer Maria Rilke which, despite its controversial points, seems to be very deeply Christian. Rilke does not write directly of God but his poetry bristles with references to God, often explicitly, frequently as *sous-entendu*. It was on my trips to England, especially to Oxford, Scotland and Lancashire, that I could find Hopkins' traces and see the places marked by his presence in the nineteenth century.

In the difficult years in Poland, before the collapse of Communism in 1989, access to Hopkins' writings was very limited as was access to all books written in English. It was then that my American friends in California and Texas (where a long time after, in 1995, I met Jerome Bump during my stay at

Southwest Texas State University) and New York helped me greatly to get not only Hopkins' poems and prose but also critical works on Hopkins. The materials for my research were mailed to me and thanks to them I could write my dissertation on Hopkins which was later published as a book. I received a volume of Hopkins' poems (fourth edition) from Professor Norman H. MacKenzie himself in 1985 with his own inscription. This was a most generous gesture which I would never forget. In the same year I also received, on my request, *Landscape and Inscape: Visions and Inspirations in Hopkins' Poetry* from Raymond Schoder, S.J., the book I would always enjoy reading and looking through for its most inspiring texts and beautiful illustrations of Hopkins' places of living and spiritual contemplating. I cannot forget about Donald Walhout whose book *Send My Roots Rain* was sent to me by the author himself in 1987 (two copies) with the letter wishing me success in my studies of Hopkins. There were also books from Walter J. Ong, S.J., who sent me, among others, his *Hopkins, the Self and God* with best wishes for my research. For all this my gratitude will always remain unstinted— "Glory be to God for dappled things."

My ontotheological and logotheological interpretation of Hopkins' poems through the philosophy of Merleau-Ponty, Heidegger (even if controversial), J. Hillis Miller and even Paul de Man and Nietzsche, was articulated in my two books in which I demonstrated a more modernist if not postmodernist vision of the poetry which I tried to *inscape*. I was much interested in the musical aspects of Hopkins' poems especially because of the poet's own concern with music which was tellingly expressed in "Floris in Italy," "Henry Purcell" and additional poetic works intressed by sprung rhythm and other interesting rhythmical patterns. This coincided with my own musical interests as once a student of piano music at the School of Music in Poland. Hopkins' aesthetics of *diatonism* and *chromaticism* allowed me to look at his poetry from the perspective of a "counterpoint of dissonance" supported by Michael Sprinker's critical work which I read with great interest and enthusiasm despite the fact that not all ideas of his philosophical criticism fit my own. What fascinated me most was not only the philosophical but also the philological interpretation of Hopkins as a Victorian poet whose linguistic exercises and command of the English language supported by classical studies allowed me to draw a portrait of an artist as a "goldsmith of (linguistic) art" and a "connoisseur of words" (this is Nietzsche's definition of philology).

Though at first visually minded, Hopkins underwent a metamorphosis in the course of which he found out that it was the sound which made the true nature (*instress*) of poetry to be "read with the ears." What helped me much in the musical interpretation of Hopkins was the definition of *inscape* in which the word "melody" appeared on a par with "design," an auxiliary issue for a construction of a very idiosyncratic architectural aesthetics. Besides most expressive acoustic elements, the visual imagery in Hopkins figured out as most prominent but it was always subsumed by the sound which obliged the reader to inscape his poems with the "sonorous eyes." My fascination with "The Windhover" and "The Wreck of the Deutschland" and other poems brought it about that I learnt them by heart so that I could "ingest" them, as George Steiner suggests in his *Real Presences.* What we read in Steiner is that the "private reader or listener can become an executant of felt meaning when he learns the poem or the musical passage by heart" since "what we know by heart becomes an agency in our consciousness, a 'pace-maker' in the growth and vital complication of our identity." Walter Pater's formula that "all art aspires to the condition of music" can be fully supported by Hopkins' art of poetic music, his artistic ideal of "perfect identification of matter and form."

Finally, thanks to the great generosity and kindness of *The Hopkins Quarterly* editors I have been receiving the issues and even back copies (from 1977) of this most prestigious Hopkins journal. It was the articles and essays of the most prominent Hopkins scholars that *instressed* me most and I found in them the inspiration for my further research. A variety of themes raised by the authors of the essays in *HQ* seems to proclaim an essential idea of man's unique self, his self-scape, and the "self steeped and pashed," as Hopkins himself put it in "Spelt from Sibyl's Leaves."

The issues of *HQ* which I received and read with enthusiasm confirmed my belief in the truth on which I grew up at home (since the state ideology then was anti-religious) that "the world is charged with the grandeur of God" and that

> Each mortal thing does one thing and the same:
> Deals out that being indoors each one dwells;
> Selves—goes itself; *myself* it speaks and spells,
> Crying *What I do is me: for that I came.*

Thus expressed, dedication to God as well as the respect for man's "self-independent selving" are the most fundamental premises of Christian faith which helped us survive through the dark night of the totalitarian regime—the centenary of Hopkins' death coincided with the collapse of the regime in East European countries in 1989.

JUDE V. NIXON

BIRTH OF A BRAIN:
FINDING HOPKINS FINDING SELF

I discovered Hopkins in fall 1978, late, I think, considering that I had just taken a degree in Protestant theology in one college and had been commuting across town studying for an English degree in another. One would have thought that these disciplines and the diverse institutions represented would have acquainted me sooner with Hopkins. But even in the mid-1970s, Hopkins was still not a familiar name. He was not heavily anthologized, and the seminal studies we now cite with great frequency were yet to be written. We did have most of the primary material, the fourth edition of the poems by Gardner and MacKenzie, and important early studies: Sulloway's *Gerard Manley Hopkins and the Victorian Temper*, Cotter's *Inscape*, Gardner's two-volume *Gerard Manley Hopkins*, Johnson's *The Poet as Victorian*, Bergonzi's *Gerard Manley Hopkins*, and Robinson's *In Extremity*. There were also the Pick and Lahey biographies, a handful of pioneering essays, and not much else. The decades of the 1980s and 1990s witnessed exponential growth in Hopkins scholarship, bringing him well into the mainstream of late Victorian thought.

My introduction to Hopkins came in a graduate seminar on late Victorian literature, taught by Dr. John Huzzard. John, as I recall, had not published on Hopkins, but nonetheless exuded a passion for him that was infectious. John always felt that Hopkins was more satisfying and more earnest than his fellow Victorians. Hopkins, quite simply, could be believed. Not a Tennyson or a Hardy, finessing faith and doubt, Hopkins either experienced them or didn't, and admitted it unashamedly. In many ways, his poetry is his confession, and his readers sacred ministrants. There is no doubt that my attraction to Hopkins grew out of John's passion for him. That appeal, however, was not to be some brief flirtation, which graduate students regularly experience—falling in with one author and falling out with another. It was, perhaps, a "blowpipe flame" which "[b]reathes once and, quenchèd faster than it came," but it left me wearing, bearing, caring, and combing the same now for almost two decades.

There is no doubt that Hopkins appeared all the more conspicuous because of the company he kept. Young and optimistic as I was, I found the other writers under consideration—Hardy, Swinburne, Thompson, Wilde, FitzGerald, and DeQuincey—utterly dark and depressing. The image of them that came to mind was from the American poet, Robinson Jeffers, who pictured protest as "a bubble in the molten mass, [which] pops and sighs out, and the mass hardens" ("Shine, Perishing Republic"). Hopkins, to me, was that bubble, the sole vestige of life in that asphyxiating mass. I had also just come through a two-year study of Greek, and was ready to tackle anything difficult, to undo any knot. Clearly, Hopkins' challenging versification attracted me, and I found trying to disentangle him addictive.

I did my formal presentation and wrote my paper on Hopkins. When the seminar ended with John's usual slides of England (of which I was duly warned) and a party at his house, he thrust into my hands a gift which, when unwrapped, contained the "dearest prizèd and pricèd": the *Letters* to Bridges, the *Correspondence* with Dixon, the *Further Letters*, the *Journals and Papers*, and the *Poems* (the fourth edition in hardcover). The only missing piece was the *Sermons and Devotional Writings*, not surprising really, considering John's skepticism of the institution of religion though never of spiritual things. I wished I had caught then some of that healthy religious skepticism as I did John's passion for Hopkins—"It wad frae monie a blunder free [me] / An' foolish notion" (Burns, "To a Louse"). This generous gift was the beginning of an affair with Hopkins, a matchmaking I owe to John, whom I memorialized in the acknowledgment pages of my *Gerard Manley Hopkins and His Contemporaries*. Given the curricular requirements, I do not believe that I returned to Hopkins in any formal way during the remaining years of the M.A.

My re-introduction came shortly after I took the M.A. I thought I was on my way to law school until a professor friend invited me to teach the unit on Hopkins to his junior British literature class. After that experience, I was clearly "else-minded." I immediately enrolled in a Ph.D. program, knowing that my study and doctoral work would in some way involve Hopkins. One of the first classes I took in the fall of 1981 was an introduction to graduate-studies courses, which required, among other things, a thirty-page bibliographical essay. This became my real introduction to Hopkins, because the project demanded a focus on the biographies, bibliographies, primary text, and critical body. I soon became acquainted with the extant scholarship on Hopkins and where it was tending.

In the fall of 1982, my interest in Hopkins was rekindled when I enrolled in a Victorian seminar taught by Dr. Donald Rackin, a Lewis Carroll scholar who had published on Hopkins. Don's essay, "'God's Grandeur': Hopkins' Sermon to Wordsworth," had appeared two years earlier. His opening remark in the seminar, perhaps influenced by that recent article, began with the claim, "If I had to choose from our selection of writers one author who best represents everything that is quintessentially Victorian, it would be Hopkins." Obviously, I did not comprehend the full extent of Don's stunning declaration. But in hearing it, I knew that I had found it, and felt "My heart . . . dovewinged, I can tell, / Carrier-witted, I am bold to boast." The works under consideration comprised *Sartor Resartus* and other Carlyle prominent pieces like "Characteristics" and "Chartism," quite a bit of Tennyson including *In Memoriam*, much on Browning including *The Ring and the Book*, Arnold's poetry and *Culture and Anarchy*, Pater's *The Renaissance* along with a few miscellaneous essays, and selections from Swinburne, Wilde, and Meredith. The Hopkins selection included "The Wreck of the Deutschland," the nature sonnets, "Spring and Fall," "'As kingfishers catch fire,'" "Heraclitean Fire," and the dark sonnets. My seminar paper explored the transformations in nature in "Heraclitean Fire" in light of the theory of flux in Pater's "Conclusion" to *The Renaissance*.

While I took quite a few Victorian seminars in the next three years, most of them on the novel, I did not again formally engage Hopkins until early spring 1984 when I began my dissertation prospectus. There was, however, a brief struggle, for I had become interested in D.H. Lawrence and Virginia Woolf, and briefly entertained the thought of a dissertation on them. Hopkins, however, soon claimed the day, and I proceeded on a prospectus linking Hopkins to the Romantic tradition. In the summer of that year, I secured a grant that afforded me six uninterrupted weeks of research at Oxford. I was able to scour through the Hopkins material in the Bodleian, and other sources at the British Library, Russell Square. I did not then visit Balliol's library or Campion Hall. Daily trips from my apartment to the Bodleian meant crossing the street at the War Memorial, adjacent to Balliol. I felt in touch with Hopkins, and even more so when I visited St. Aloysius', the little parish church on Woodstock Road, where Hopkins served briefly from 1878 to 1879, and where a baptismal font (then cracked) stood at the entrance as a memorial from the Paravicinis.

Oxford, to me, was two towns—a place teeming with life (university, industrial, and tourist) during the day, and a quiet, sleepy town in the evening, attracting only dinner guests and theatergoers. I took evening walks around Oxford, visited the colleges and quads, the Sheldonian, the Carfax Tower, Christ Church gardens, the various coffee and tea shops, and sauntered up to the park and cricket ground. A cricketer myself, I recalled Hopkins' employment of cricket, along with Darwinism, as metaphor for life's generalities. Later I discovered his other observation of cricket made in the context of the force of lightning, striking a tree near the boys' cricketfield at Stonyhurst. From all accounts, I gathered that Hopkins was poor at cricket but Bridges was quite competent. I got a sense of what Hopkins meant when he observed "nature and the many things which make Oxford attractive." A scholar-gipsy, if not an Oxonian, I fell in love with "sweet city with her dreaming spires," as Arnold referred to Oxford in "Thyrsis," "that landscape the charm of Oxford, green shouldering grey" for Hopkins, that "Towery city and branchy between towers; / Cuckoo-echoing, bell-swarmèd, lark-charmèd, rook-racked, river-rounded." Approaching the city by train, as I have often done, I am always reminded of Newman's 1864 post-exilic view of the city which he left in 1846: "I have never seen Oxford since, excepting its spires, as they are seen from the railway."

I completed my dissertation, defended it in the spring of 1986, and commenced a career in teaching; but in every sense I was a neophyte Hopkinsian. Return trips to Oxford led me to archival material on Hopkins, which acquainted me more with his work. During one of those summer trips, Norman White and I spent a day touring London, then took the Northern Line up to Hampstead. We explored the approximate vicinity where the Hopkins family house stood, the family church (in whose churchyard Turner is buried), and a pub, the Four Horseshoes, where a photograph of Hopkins, along with other Hampstead notables (Blake, Keats, Woolf, among others), hangs on the wall. On another trip, I wanted to discover more about the ecological disaster elegized in "Binsey Poplars," the results of which were subsequently published in two issues of *The Hopkins Quarterly*. What could not be captured was the delight I had in retracing Hopkins' walk from Balliol along Binsey Lane and the Towpath. I meandered along the slow-moving Isis where the poplars had gracefully lined the river, later took a bus up to Godstow, and rummaged through the archives at Christ Church College, owner of the Binsey estate, to discover an 1842 plan of the Estates at Binsey. It shows the aspens in soldierly formation ("following folded rank") on the Binsey, rather than on the Port Meadow side of the Isis before the trees were "Áll félled, félled . . . / Not spared, not one."

Thus far, my work on Hopkins had been done in relative isolation. I was not yet part of the community of Hopkins scholars. That all changed in 1987 when I contacted Professor Joe Feeney about co-hosting a 1989 Hopkins Centenary Conference. Joe was thrilled with the idea. The conference at Saint Joseph's University drew major Hopkins scholars, and was for me an incarnation of sorts. Here, bodily, were those very scholars who for years had influenced my appreciation of and work on Hopkins. What struck me as remarkable among this *riot of a rout*, this *bevy* of scholars, was not just the genuine fellow feelings all had, but how *dappled* they were, how *each tucked string tells, each hung bell's / Bow swung finds tongue to fling out broad its name.* Of the many Hopkins centennial celebrations that year (I attended three), the Philadelphia conference was easily the largest assembled body of Hopkins scholars.

In the decade since, my scholarship has taken me deeper into Hopkins but also away from him and the conversation with other Victorians and affiliations with other scholarly communities. But the Hopkins fellowship of scholars will always be home. I frequently make excursions, border crossings if you will, into foreign territory. And while other projects continue to compete with that prior claim, I am still *fastened* to that *world's splendour and wonder*. I can always find Hopkins in *bright boroughs* and *circle-citadels*, discover *the dearest freshness deep down*, and catch *Comforting smell breathed at very entering*. For a poet so possessed by natural beauty (whether *noise of falls*, the *lovely behaviour / Of silk-sack clouds*, all varieties of *dappled things*, and Harry's *Wind-lilylocks-laced*), it is inward beauty, the beauty of heart, attitude, and inspiration, that eclipses the outward: *Heart mánnerly / is more than handsome face, / Beauty's bearing or / muse of mounting vein*. For in *that* beauty, *God's better beauty, grace*, one is able to *glean our Saviour*.

PAUL MARIANI

HOPKINS AS LIFELINE

I greet him the days I meet him, and bless when I understand.

If I had not discovered Hopkins, I would have had to invent him. It was the spring of 1962, my last semester at Manhattan College, that cluster of buildings that rises on the hill above the 7th Avenue IRT at its Bronx terminal. On the other side of the elevated, beyond the four bars and two bookstores, Van Cortland Park slumbered. There were trees. I lived thirty miles away—an hour and fifteen as they say in New York—out in suburban Long Island, and was given a ride each weekday morning and evening in a hearsegray '57 Ford driven cautiously by my friend John Monahan. Back home, I gulped down dinner, then drove my father's truck to my job each night, working from six until ten, stacking shelves in one or another of the local A&Ps. Usually, I studied until two in the morning, then rose at 6:30 to begin another day. Weary of watching rats run about in mazes and writing up statistics which most of us jerryrigged anyway, I transferred over to English from Psychology at the last possible moment because even I had to admit to myself that I loved literature—especially English literature—and needed it the way one needs air or water.

Even without the prospect of a job after college, I was not to be deterred, any more than I'd been deterred at sixteen from attending Marianist Prep with the idea of someday becoming a priest. All I knew was that nothing else touched me the way a book did: not only Shakespeare, Dickens, and Melville, but Homer, Aeschylus, Aristophanes, and Dante. My father, who had seen his dream of running a gas station go under several years earlier, and who wanted his seven kids to become self-sufficient as soon as possible, scratched his head. What business did I as the oldest have taking English, he grumbled, though—thanks to my mother—he did not stop me.

Manhattan College is run by Christian Brothers whose mission is to teach, and they taught splendidly. We had a core curriculum in those days, perhaps too exclusively based on the Western classics, but a wonderful education for all that. A small group of us—perhaps a hundred Humanities students surrounded by a sea of more practical Engineers and Business Majors—lined up the Civilizations one after the other and let them wash over us: the Egyptians, Babylonians, Persians and Jews, the Greeks and the Romans (Freshman year), the Early and Later Middle Ages, with a heavy dose of Thomist Philosophy (Sophomore), the Renaissance, Reformation, and the Enlightenment (Junior), Romanticism and the Age of Revolution, followed by the later nineteenth and early twentieth centuries (Senior Year).

These we pursued with a four and sometimes five-pronged assault: history, literature, philosophy, the arts—visual and aural. What was lacking were great swatches of Africa, South America, most of the Asian rim. Still, it was a foundation, though one soon to be dismantled because most students found it too demanding. Then too there were the social upheavals of the 60s: the Civil Rights Movement, Viet Nam, the Women's Movement. Indeed, the demographics at Manhattan, like New York itself, were changing. Soon women would be admitted to the all-male domain of Manhattan, and the Irish would give way in part to a new generation of Spanish-speaking students.

But there was another thing as well. As a young Catholic I missed the presence in much of English literature of modern Catholic writers. What had happened to the tradition I had studied which included the New Testament, the early Church Fathers, Augustine, Francis of Assisi, the Medieval Philosophers of Light, Dante, Chaucer, Villon, Shakespeare, Cervantes, the English Metaphysicals, Pascal? Yes, there were Waugh and Morris West, and of course James Joyce, that apostate whose portrait of Irish Catholicism seemed so cold, so aloof, so analytical. And there were the heady English and American Moderns—Yeats, Eliot (at least an Anglo-Catholic), Pound, Dylan Thomas, Auden (another Anglo-Catholic).

But who—this is the way I framed it then—who spoke for what was dearest to me? Yes, I knew the Protestant Reformation in England had won the day—there was Edmund Spenser and John Milton to remind me of that—but were there no Catholic representatives? Had the great Catholic literary tradition in English—the world's lingua franca—simply disappeared? And yet I was surrounded by Catholics. Italian Catholics, Polish Catholics, especially Irish Catholics, young men from Manhattan and Brooklyn and the Bronx whose fathers and mothers lived in modest attached houses or tenements, labored in tall offices or on the subways or as police officers and teachers and postal workers, and proudly displayed portraits of Padraig Pearse and the Post Office on O'Connell Street framed in their foyers. Sundays year in and year out I was surrounded by Catholics at Mass—the age-old Latin responses about to give way to the transformations undertaken by an interim Pope who had called for a council to get some fresh air in the churches and had in the process changed the world.

Then, in my final semester at Manhattan, Dr. Paul Cortissoz assigned me—randomly—the poetry of W.B. Yeats to fathom and then present to my classmates. Jim Blake, my Beta Sigma fraternity brother, who affected a kind of Irish agnostic world-weariness, had been assigned some damnable Jesuit named Hopkins. Did I want to swap with him, he dared me, over a styrofoam cup of tepid coffee in Plato's Cave. American astronauts—John Glenn among them—were preparing to take heaven by storm. Without knowing it, so was I. I looked away from Blake at a poem called "The Wreck of the Deutschland." It was long, and I cannot say I understood it. But the language. The language! "Thou hast bound bones and veins in me," the words sang,

> . . . fastened me flesh,
> And after it almost unmade, what with dread,
> Thy doing: and dost thou touch me afresh?
> Over again I feel thy finger and find thee.

I felt like someone who has just picked up four aces in a hand of poker. I clutched the words to my chest. Yes, I told him, I'd swap him my Yeats for this. In truth, I had just fallen in love. Done, Blake slammed his hand down on the formica table top, glinting with that crooked smile of his. Done.

And so it began. The more I read the more I fell in love with the language, the explosive syntax, the passion. But it was not just how Hopkins sang. After all, Dylan Thomas had exploited that same Welsh richness in *Under Milkwood*, which I'd seen performed in the Village the year before. More important was the sense of the man that flashed from the page, his way of making the spirit speak.

Everywhere I felt a kind of subtext—what Hopkins I later learned called a poem's underthought—sustaining and deepening the poem's meaning. Poem after poem seemed irradiated with a kind of sacramentality. More, there was an intelligence about the lines, a formal intelligence which refused to dissolve no matter how closely I scrutinized the words or the silences between the words. Atoms whirred in those spaces, creating a kind of intense inner light.

This and other immensities I tried sharing with my classmates when it came my turn to address them. Of the actual presentation I remember nothing beyond a sense of delight I found it difficult to transmit to a group of men like me in their early twenties whose preoccupations were anywhere but this gray classroom on a gray day in March. That I remember, and a sort of pounding in my ears which the professor put down charitably to enthusiasm, but which Blake read as a sort of Italo-American lunacy. "Felix Randal the farrier, O is he dead then, my duty all ended." That was one line which played inside my head day after day. And here was another: "So some great stormfowl, whenever he has walked his while / The thunder-purple seabeach, plumèd purple-of-thunder." Rich, variegated, a poetry striving to be heard among the angelic choirs. But so too the sparer, starker pitch of "No worst, there is none. Pitched past pitch of grief," or the final lines of that other sonnet writ in blood:

> I see
> The lost are like this, and their scourge to be
> As I am mine, their sweating selves; but worse.

In the years to come I would discover that Wallace Stevens too had picked out the line from the Purcell sonnet to breathe in like some exquisite nosegay. And once—when I was teaching at Bread Loaf—Donald Justice quoted the lines from "I wake and feel the fell of dark," quoted just above, with a long pause before the final two words, as if to stress that, yes, this was what hell must feel like, Hopkins adding almost as an afterthought that whatever he was going through, hell itself was worse. But all that was later. For now Hopkins was mine and mine alone. No one else among my classmates, for most of whom poetry was at best a chore to be endured on the road to getting the B.A., seemed much to care about my discovery. Well, all right, I thought. It was like finding a wallet on the sidewalk flush with bills that no one else seemed interested in claiming.

Then graduation, then an M.A. at Colgate, and marriage, and the pursuit of a Ph.D. at the City University of New York, with classes on the tenth floor of Hunter at 68th and Third. More studies—Latin, Greek, German, French, Old English, Middle English, Linguistics, Dante with Allen Mandelbaum, Chaucer with Helaine Newstead, the Victorian Novel with Irving Howe, Victorian Poetry with Wendell Stacy Johnson, Modern Poetry with Norman Friedman. I taught radical students at Lehmann College in the Bronx amid demonstrations and protests, then took the subway downtown to 23rd Street to teach police officers—Frank Serpico among them—the two groups like the *Titanic* and its iceberg finally meeting at Columbia, one side, taunted, at last pummeling the other side with their nightsticks. And my own sons coming—Paul in 1965, then Mark in 1966, then John in 1968, Eileen giving birth to the last just a week before I donned my exquisite medieval garb to receive my diploma.

What would I do my dissertation on, Helaine Newstead, the no-nonsense Director of the Graduate Program in English, demanded to know. My mind buzzed. I had affected the style of *Sartor Resartus* much to the puzzlement of everyone. Carlyle, I said. Carlyle and the French Revolution. But Newstead sensed a hesitancy in me I myself had not yet registered. She had read my prose. Carlyle and I a good match did not make. I retreated, regrouped, returned a month later with another brilliant idea. Cardinal Newman, I said. *The Idea of a University*. Again she discerned an inner conflict. No, she said, addressing me like some Zen Master. I had yet to find my double. Again I retreated.

What did I really wish to do, I kept asking myself. Finally, it dawned on me. Hopkins. I would undertake to write a commentary on the spiritual and aesthetic development of Hopkins' sonnets, which in his case came to the bulk of his work. The project was manageable, though for someone a lot older than I was then. Newstead listened. Yes, she said, do it. She would help me get food on the table while I toiled daily in the library stacks unraveling Hopkins' poems. I was 26, ready to take on the world, to bulldoze my way in where angels . . .

Steadily, from nine to five, in a small carrel at Queens College, for a whole year, I wrote. After dinner and putting the kids to bed, I wrote some more. Regularly, I sent off the accumulating chapters to my readers. Word came back from on high. Continue. Finally, in November 1967, I turned in a 400-page typescript and managed to defend my thesis successfully. To celebrate, Allen Mandelbaum took Eileen and me out to see *Bonnie and Clyde*. I smiled. I had been through worse. Months later I met with Bernie Kendler, an editor at Cornell University Press. In the cafeteria at Hunter, between the classes I was teaching, we spoke. Revise the book, he offered, include all of Hopkins' poetry, and we'll consider publishing your manuscript.

Later that year, in a farmhouse in Hadley, Massachusetts, I worked assiduously on my commentary while two of my sons ran about the room knocking each other over, and the other, placidly, looked on from his crib, smiling as only Buddha smiles. "The Wreck," "The Loss of the Eurydice," "The Blessed Virgin," "The Leaden Echo and the Golden Echo," "Brothers," "The Bugler's First Communion." Each of these in due time was scrutinized, analyzed, entered. Meanwhile I taught Modern Poetry, the Classics, and Composition to undergrads at U. Mass, Amherst. The war in Viet Nam dragged on. Johnson refused to run for reelection, Martin Luther King and Bobby Kennedy were gunned down. In February 1970, just short of my thirtieth birthday, *A Commentary on the Complete Poems of Gerard Manley Hopkins* was published to almost total silence. I waited for *The New York Times* to announce the presence of a bright young luminary and waited in vain.

I turned to other things. Raising a family. Writing biographies of Williams, Berryman, Lowell, Hart Crane. Criticism, essays, reviews, five volumes of poetry. But in all these years—thirty-six of them since I first opened and read him—I have never been very far from Father Hopkins. I think of him daily, so that he's everywhere in my own poems. There are also the essays and reviews, and there are mentions of him as a touchstone in each of my biographies, for he figures strongly in all but the Williams, Williams somehow not hearing or being unwilling to hear Hopkins' richness as against his own plainer New Jersey speech.

But there's more. There's the fact that Hopkins has entered into my blood in even deeper ways, at the level of the spirit. The truth is that I've learned as much from him in terms of the Real Presence in the Eucharist, the midnight watches, the dark night, the small steady joys, the essential innocence underlying life to which we are called to witness. My oldest son is himself a Jesuit in the California Province, who taught Mandarin Chinese at Bellarmine Prep in San Jose, getting ready to move on to theology. It took me two and a half years to make the Long Retreat with my parish priest directing me—a man who had trained with the Jesuits—and I've made my share of modified eight-day retreats. Each morning now I rise and drive up the country roads to make the 7:00 a.m. Mass. Sometimes I lector, sometimes I distribute Eucharist. In short, I am blessed. And there is another thing I have been wanting to do. Go back now, towards evening, to write the life of Father Hopkins, and get what the lives I've read—informative as they are—all seem to miss: the Real Presence that sustained Father Hopkins through all his years as a Jesuit and did what he said fidelity did for another saint, Alphonsus Rodriguez:

> . . . crowd career with conquest while there went
> Those years and years by of world without event
> That in Majorca Alfonso watched the door.

Those lines, written in the last year of Hopkins' life, speak as much of my sense of Hopkins as they do of the humble Jesuit saint he was celebrating.

GODLY RESPONSES

". . . charged with the grandeur . . ."

HOPKINS, SACRIFICE AND GOD

My liking of Hopkins is intensely physical: I know of no other poet whose mastery of the auditory texture of words affects me so much, and this, linked to his capacity to structure a dense pattern of relationships among words and phrases, hits me every time I read him. I don't find him, at his best, easy to memorise precisely because the verbal and auditory pattern that he constructs is a deliberately constructed artistic form whose presence stands over against me, pressing me to construe it (with difficulty) and experience it. When I read them, I don't feel that I master the poems: they, rather, as chiselled shapes, simply seem to be there, before and after I read them. In a strange way, they make me feel redundant: whether I read them or not, they're there, unchanged and thick, and they don't need me meddling with them. It is purifying to be made by a work of art to feel contingent, because then the work of art acts as a sacrament of God's perfection as *Ipsum Esse*.

I also like him because he is so good on God. I feel a repugnance for an undulant spiritual rhetoric whose eloquence colonises the divine mystery. I'd much rather engage with the practices of popular devotion, with their modest signals of purpose and meaning, than read spiritual prose aimed at inducing hyper-ventilation of the soul. Speaking about God should be hard if it's to be done well; it should always have a sense of being impossible; it should be jagged and incomplete and give the reader the sense that God is not to be found in these words but that God begins when these words end. I've learned to trust Hopkins to get God right.

Others have written better than I can of the architectonic integration of creation, grace and incarnation in the first part of the "Deutschland," where Hopkins evokes the majesty of God and the chiaroscuro that encompasses a person standing under and in this mystery, and the Christic sacramentality ("Christ plays in ten thousand places") evident elsewhere in his treatment of nature. I want to focus on what seems to me his miniature religious masterpiece in prose, his treatment of God and sacrifice in his 1881 Long Retreat notes on "the Great Sacrifice":

> The first intention then of God outside himself or, as they say, ad extra, outwards, the first outstress of God's power was Christ; and we must believe that the next was the Blessed Virgin. Why did the Son of God go forth from the Father not only in the eternal and intrinsic procession of the Trinity but also by an extrinsic and less than eternal, let us say aeonian one?—To give God glory and that by sacrifice, sacrifice offered in the barren wilderness outside of God, as the children of Israel were led into the wilderness to offer sacrifice. This sacrifice and this outward procession is a consequence and shadow of the procession of the Trinity, from which mystery sacrifice takes its rise; but of this I do not mean to write here. It is as if the blissful agony or stress of selving in God had forced out drops of sweat or blood, which drops were the world, or as if the lights lit at the festival of the "peaceful Trinity" through some little cranny striking out lit up into being one "cleave" out of the world of possible creatures.

Theologically, this is an astonishing piece of writing, virtually impossible to paraphrase because of its concision, density and originality. Nowhere else does Hopkins develop this *idée maîtresse* of the sacrificial Trinity, and we can only regret this. While his sermons, such as that given on the humanity of Christ ("Christ as Hero"), come across as characteristically Victorian in their conception and expression, this passage is like a Barthian thunderbolt in a mid-Victorian sky, anticipating the great themes of Trinitarian theology which under Karl Barth's influence will come to dominate orthodox theology in the twentieth century. Barth's influence spreads into recent Catholic tradition through Hans Urs von Balthasar.

Barth, the Swiss Calvinist, taught that the determinative act of God's being, which precedes every other act of God and is the act simply of "being God," is God's decision to be "God for us as

Jesus." And so the movement towards Incarnation and self-sacrifice on the Cross is not an additional feature, but is the very actuality of God and, although it comes to expression at a point in our time, it is antecedent to everything else that God does. Incarnation is, we might say, God's way of being God. In this primal movement ("in God's pre-temporal eternity," Barth repeats), a self-sacrificing condescension is inscribed in God's being so that the glorification of the Father by the self-sacrificing Son on the cross is how God freely wills to be. The idea of Christ's sacrifice thrusts its roots deep into the abyss of the Trinity.

Now this Barthian teaching is what Hopkins anticipates when he writes that Christ's sacrifice is "a consequence and shadow of the procession of the Trinity, from which mystery sacrifice takes its rise," but the puzzle is how he came to write it. It is customary to argue, as does Christopher Devlin, S.J., Hopkins' editor, that the usual suspects, Duns Scotus and Marie Lataste, were in the background of its composition, but I cannot see how Hopkins moved from reading Scotus and Lataste (a rather tame religious thinker) to writing this primary text of immense imaginative and religious power. To my knowledge, no medieval theologian identifies the movement outwards towards sacrifice as the original, foundational movement of the life of the Blessed Trinity in the way in which Hopkins does: Scotus does not take you there, and he did not take Hopkins there.

The passage may well have sprung, Athena-like, from Hopkins' own mind in a highly original piece of theological writing, but it is outside his normal range of Trinitarian interpretation which, in the poems, tends to be formulaic, rather than adventurous. But here, in this passage written purely for his own edification, Hopkins' poetic imagination surfaces: how wonderful to watch him switch from formal theological exposition to speak of "the blissful agony or stress of selving in God" forcing out "drops of sweat or blood."

The original feature here is that Hopkins describes the stress of selving in God, which leads to the world's creation ("which drops were the world"), in ways that evoke Gethsemane, the place of Christ's *agonia* (struggle) where drops of sweat and blood are forced out of the body of Christ as he faces his death (Lk 22.44). In the remarkable stereoscopic vision which this text asks of us, we are to imagine the "blissful agony" by which the world flows from the "selving" of God as analogous to Christ's in Gethsemane when sweat and blood flow from him. The world is "pressed" from God as sweat and blood are pressed from the body of Christ. I know of no parallel to this astonishing suggestion: it seems to be entirely original.

In his phrase about the "stress of selving in God," Hopkins, of course, is speaking analogically, moving from the created to the divine order: just as there is a dynamic within creatures to express their natures and thereby fulfil themselves, so too God's being is subject to a "stress" from within that leads to creation and sacrifice. What Barth will refer to as the "determinative act of God's being," Hopkins crisply calls the "selving" in God, but in spite of the difference in linguistic register, both think of this as the movement in God which impels the divine Son towards sacrifice on Golgotha.

In these dense sentences, Hopkins muses that God's selving (already an *agonia* in eternity, and how interesting that phrase is) leads first of all to creation—hence the depth of God's immanent presence ("the dearest freshness deep down things") attested to in his great nature poems—and culminates in the Son's self-sacrifice in the barren wilderness of Golgotha. Although this latter theme receives no explicit treatment in his poems, it is surely enacted in his sonnets of desolation ("I am gall, I am heartburn. God's most deep decree / Bitter would have me taste") in the barren wilderness outside of God. What, we are led to ask, if all this—the very existence of the creation, the redemptive sacrifice of Christ and our share in the bitterness of that offering—flows from the selving of God and is grounded in that divine *agonia*? At that point, words and theology should cease and prayer begin.

READING HOPKINS:
A DIALOGUE BETWEEN TWO TRADITIONS

How did I come to work on Hopkins? The origins hardly reveal the complications. I had recently finished my doctoral dissertation on typological symbolism and the poetics of Henry James and had published a few articles which attempted to uncover the source and nature of the religious aura of James' apparently secular works. I returned to my mentor, Allen Grossman—himself a distinguished poet, teacher and scholar, later a MacArthur Fellow—with the idea of working on a religious poet. He suggested Milton, and gave me an exercise on the language of *Samson Agonistes.* The results were disappointing to both of us, and did not justify a similar venture into *Paradise Lost.* Despite the overtly biblical thematics and Milton's renowned Hebraism, I did not find in his language what I then so vaguely sought. A further search became necessary.

At this point, I chanced to visit an old friend, Ruth Miller (a coincidence overcame considerable geographical barriers, since we were then separated by continents and not, as now, by a few Jerusalem neighborhoods). Among other things, she had done considerable scholarly work on Emily Dickinson, and was interested in moving me in that direction. However, my gut feeling was that I was looking for something else—for a poet firmly entrenched within a recognized religious tradition, about whose orthodoxy there could be no question—not a spiritual individualist. I did not yet know my reasons for this predilection. The name that came to Ruth immediately was Gerard Manley Hopkins. Amazingly, the only poem of his I seemed to know at all was "God's Grandeur" (which we assigned as an exercise to first year students), and I felt skeptical. I remember the feeling, but not the reason. Perhaps there was not a clear one; perhaps I was bedazzled by all the talk over "foil"; perhaps I felt the poem yielded itself up too easily, a poem without shadows. But skeptical as I was, I took the Fourth Edition off the library shelf the next day and began to read.

The aura of that day is still with me. Although my attention span is not always what it should be, I read and I read all that cold cloudy day. From the start, I knew that I had found what I was looking for, even though I had no knowledge whatsoever of Hopkins—either as man or poet. I did not even know that he had been a priest. By twilight I knew where I wanted to begin. If, in the past, I had often lost patience in the midst of long poems, "The Wreck of the Deutschland" held me fast to the end, and over and over again from beginning to end.

I returned to Allen Grossman and he was pleased—surprised also, I think, that he had not thought of the idea himself. He then instructed me in a method for starting—one which I try in abridged form to pass on to my students. I was to take a large-size loose-leaf notebook for recording the results of the slowest "reading" imaginable—over a month for "The Wreck of the Deutschland," one stanza every full work day. I was to write down every possible observation, analyze every poetic detail starting with rhyme and rhythm, using different color pencils to mark up the stanza transcribed at the top of the page semantically and syntactically. By the end of the month there was a rather thick notebook and a thoroughly overwhelmed reader. I had produced much more data than I could ever dream of using. Grossman then explained the rationale behind the exercise: to prevent me from reducing the poem too quickly to "meaning," to place a barrier of sense impressions in the way of any too easy making of "sense."

My first article on Hopkins (published in *The Hopkins Quarterly*) took a very long time to write and is perhaps overburdened with minutiae. Today I wonder how readable it is, but it certainly served to inundate me in Hopkins' voice. Perhaps it was this experience of the plethora of detail, the complexity of relations and the multiplicity of potential readings which eventually led me to hope for, and then strive to realize, a connection with my other central concern.

My two major areas of publication had been hitherto unrelated: Hopkins, on one hand, and connections between Jewish hermeneutics (Midrash and classical biblical commentary) and literary theory, on the other. Just as one wishes to make one's good friends acquainted, I had vague hopes and vaguer designs for some sort of a meeting between these two subjects of personal interest and commitment. But there was no obvious meeting-ground. For something to come of those hopes and designs, a long incubation period was needed. Since my training had taught me that scholarship should be an impersonal, objective endeavor and since the questions I needed to ask were quite personal, perhaps even eccentric and idiosyncratic, my progress was stymied by doubts. I had no idea of the form in which such issues could be made explicit within my work. To feel so significant an attraction, even a bond, which continues to defy understanding is to be constantly goaded to explain, at least to oneself. Surely my motivation is not of the sort which many Hopkins readers and scholars can share (or even perhaps sympathize with) in its specific form, but it may open a way for thinking about different kinds of writer/reader relations.

What was a person like myself doing entranced by Hopkins? First there is an apparent religious conflict; I could not possibly be Hopkins' "implied reader." Born into a totally assimilated secularist family which identified itself first as American and only later (quite last) as Jewish, I had in early adulthood chosen to become a religiously observant Jew. I went to live in Israel, where I felt that my beliefs and culture stood a chance of establishing some sort of meaningful relationship with each other. There I insistently raised my children in the Hebrew language (in which I was only partially literate), so that the images and metaphors of their infancy would be those of the Hebrew Bible. Despite an early lack which can never be completely overcome, I set about studying the classical texts of Judaism. But I also became a university teacher of English literature with a strong interest in literary theory. Apparently this was a life on two sides of a sharp divide—certainly not a path which would seem to lead to Hopkins.

Nevertheless, the utter seriousness and centrality of Hopkins' religious commitment and concerns spoke immediately and directly to my own sense of life. The structural analogy was clear enough, but what about the content matter? And is there not a question of morality here? Hopkins himself would surely not have approved of what I was up to! He would, of necessity, have viewed my way of life as benighted (at the very least); he would have had to count me among the damned—no easy matter to understand and swallow, but also not a matter to be ignored. I, for my part, while not obliged (fortunately!) so to condemn him, must nevertheless take my stand as one of those who consciously and consistently have rejected his central theological tenets: the very possibility of physical incarnation and the view of adequation essential for the forgiveness of human sinfulness which it mediates. For Hopkins, the "Law" to which I am committed could be seen only as an anathema, a veil hiding the truth and banishing me from the Kingdom. Perhaps most relevant of all, the Letter—for me the only possible container of holiness—is, for his theology, just what counteracts and undermines Spirit. Thus our very notions of language—what it can and cannot do—are at odds.

In a time when a "hermeneutics of suspicion" has become the rule, it is acceptable, even required, for readers and critics to position themselves. If there is no absolute, universally correct reading, we must know where an interpretation is coming from in order to understand its evolution and its usefulness. Most interpreters of Hopkins assume the hermeneutic naturalness of a Christian frame of reference: meditative, contemplative, typological, mystical, liturgical, etc. On the whole they speak from a position which they share with Hopkins, and they accept its elucidatory power as a given. I have no intention of contesting the claim, or denigrating their impressive contribution to our understanding of the poetry. By contrast, the sort of "positioning" done within the framework of gender and ethnic studies tends to be oppositional, to assume a resisting reader. Certainly it would be easy enough to pit Jewish and Christian hermeneutics against each other; such an exercise has a long enough history. That, however, is not what I seek, nor could it offer an answer to my query about the hold that Hopkins' poetry has upon me.

After much rethinking of the work I had done on Hopkins and on Jewish hermeneutics, I began to imagine a different kind of structural relationship. In retrospect, I see that Paul Ricoeur's terms "distantiation" and "appropriation" may help me to explain. Distantiation is the realization that we are dealing with the text of an Other, one who is non-coincidental with the reader in time, space and orientation. For Ricoeur, there is always distantiation. He would reject any view of textuality as a transparent medium that can function as the source of the sort of direct communication of minds in which the reader's interpretation can be adequate (even theoretically) to the author's intention or to the "inherent" meaning of a text. The inevitability of distantiation is synonymous with the impossibility of total appropriation, and appears to bear a positive valence for Ricoeur. Yet one reads, Ricoeur insists, in order to make the mind of another part of one's own to some extent. This is why reading is consequential, why it has an ethical impetus and a significance for the way one leads one's life. Partial "appropriation" is, for Ricoeur, a non-narcissistic process of self-enlargement, a creative activity; both reader and text are to some extent made anew in the hermeneutic moment.

Ricoeur's model sits easily within the framework of a Jewish approach to texts (in which atemporal adequation is never a real option) and allows me to pose my personal question in terms that may be generally comprehensible. What might the reading of Christian religious poetry contribute to a Jewish reader who rejects its basic theological premises? What might a reading from within a Jewish perspective contribute to a Christian reader's experience of Hopkins? This is Ricoeur's dialogue between distantiation and appropriation taken to an extreme.

It seems to me that we are considering not only two religions which have had a significant historical relationship, but also two traditions which have taken up and developed contrary positions in respect to language. There is no such comfortable and continuous thing as a Judaeo-Christian tradition; instead, we have a sort of hermeneutic dichotomy (which, of course, is never as polarized in practice as it seems to be in theory). Christianity describes itself as the religion of the Spirit of the Law, in order to differentiate itself from the Judaism which it characterizes as the religion of the Letter of the Law. For the Christian reader, the letter of the text is a veil which covers truth. It is necessary to go behind the letter in order to discover its meaning; words are poor instruments which may nevertheless serve to lead their readers beyond themselves to true being (Spirit). Although Christian readings of Scripture may function on various figurative levels (i.e., historical, anagogic, allegorical, eschatological) or link Old and New Testament texts typologically, the meaning of those texts is learned not from the words but from the hypostatization of Being and Truth in the Incarnation. In order to read the words at all, one must know ahead of time that they all point to the Word. Only prior faith in the Word ensures the meaning and makes it possible correctly to read the words. Ironically, one knows that one has found the spiritual meaning because one already knows the true meaning (the Incarnation) before one reads at all. Multivocal language refers always to its univocal source. This is the Western logocentricity which Derrida has so diligently sought to deconstruct. It was "deconstructed" by midrashic and halachic procedures even before it was definitively established in the Christian/Western world.

Both the sacramentalist and deconstructionist critics of Hopkins accept the Christian presupposition that language fell with the Fall of man and is now inadequate to Spirit. The former insist that Hopkins succeeded in overcoming the shiftiness of words in respect to reference and time, thus enabling his poems to perform what they aspire to: a reabsorption into the Word as a silent, eternal mode of Being. The latter use the binary opposition between word and Word to explain why Hopkins must necessarily have failed in his aim at such an atemporal absorption: he could not make words equal the Word; they must fall back incessantly upon yet further words. The sacramentalists and the deconstructionists agree as to Hopkins' aim; they disagree only in respect to his achievement. Deconstructionist critics thus have an explanation to proffer in respect to Hopkins' qualms of conscience about the writing and publishing of poetry: they claim that he recognized on some level, or at least acted out, the futility of an endeavor to make words become the Word.

The traditional Jewish way of reading yields a hermeneutic which is neither sacramentalist nor deconstructionist in any thoroughgoing sense (despite the attempts of some scholars to claim that it is the latter). This is because language itself is seen as performing a different function. In the Jewish tradition, G-d reveals himself only in words. There is no revelation outside of language; there is nothing that is exempt from the need for interpretation. Even the lightning on Mt. Sinai is accompanied by voices which become words. The Spirit of G-d, uncontainable in being, nevertheless suffuses language. But it must be interpreted from the start, and interpretation is always multiple, never co-equal with what it is interpreting. Even when G-d speaks directly to a human person, hermeneutic activity is necessary. Words are not transparent, self-illuminating or univocal, but they yield what is needed: sufficient knowledge for true service and holiness. Neither man nor language is irrevocably fallen; both remain free to function in fulfillment of G-d's will.

Indeed, the Derridean deconstruction of the dichotomy between speech and writing was performed already (albeit with a difference) by the talmudic sages. They claim that both the Written Torah (revealed word by word by G-d to Moses and recorded exactly) and the Oral Torah (all the interpretations of the Written Torah and the interpretations of the interpretations) were revealed simultaneously on Mt. Sinai; "everything a wise scholar (or the student of a wise scholar) will reveal in the future, has already been revealed to Moses on Sinai." The Midrash goes on to supply a lovely anecdote in which Moses, hearing the words of such a scholar and failing to understand them, takes comfort in the thought that he himself conveyed them. Such a mind-boggling hermeneutic situation needs unpacking. First, the Written Torah is held to contain everything that has ever been revealed or ever will be revealed; second, the Written Torah can hardly be said to exist (at least in the way that the Western world is accustomed to thinking about texts). The Written Torah is what is inscribed on a specified parchment with specified instruments and is read aloud in a specified manner, on specified occasions, in specified places. All this specification is made by the Oral Torah (that is, it is the outcome of interpretation). In addition, the moment anything is understood from the ritual recitation of the Written Torah, we are already located within the Oral Torah, which includes all interpretation. Written and Oral Torah are thus intertwined in an inextricable manner, a model for the relationship between G-d and man, which is mediated through language. The Written Torah is "spoken," the Oral Torah is "read" (in the sense of "studied"). Revelation is in language alone; there is nothing known outside of language to indicate what the words mean. They can therefore, theoretically, be read in every way possible, and frequently the talmudic sages appear to be occupied in producing all the potential meanings, including those which are quite counter-intuitive. Neither is there anything inside of language which can limit interpretation; only the tradition of interpretation can limit itself according to the criteria derived from itself. On the midrashic (interpretation of meaning) level the bounds are quite far-flung; on the halachic (normative behavior) level interpretation is also quite unimpeded, but there are institutional constraints in respect to operative decisions. This play between innovation and continuity is tradition.

I find this primacy of language in the poetry of Hopkins. It expresses itself in his semantic and syntactical eccentricity which gives rise to multiple, sometimes even contradictory, readings that do not appear to privilege univocality. The words of Hopkins' poems do not meld into a reference which transcends them; they stay stubbornly in place in our consciousness and experience. Their force and energy are so insistent, that they may be said nearly to enable us to understand how—in the words of the Midrash—G-d created the world through the letters of the Torah. I suggest that what is predominant in Jewish hermeneutics, and repressed in Christian theological and ritual modes, comes to the fore in much Christian religious poetry (a study of Metaphysical poetry and modern religious poetry would also be instructive). The life and spirit of the letter, which contains more than any reader at any particular moment can know, and which can be said to encompass all of its potentiality, become evident in the way that such poetry can work upon its reader. Its meaning need not be assumed to precede it; it need not be read in terms of what is already known (doctrine), but can be seen as acting, creating, opening as yet unrealized possibilities. The poetic words are not absorbed in a single Word; they retain their substantiality, they keep our attention riveted upon them. Thus the reading of Christian religious poetry can provide that very experience of the autonomous "letter" which Christian hermeneutics undermines. That which has been repressed, has been repressed because of its power. Undemonized, it can revitalize and enhance what it previously seemed to threaten.

The reverse is true as well. Jewish mysticism exhibits some of the desire for unity and completion which mainstream rabbinical Judaism has always largely resisted. Overt in Christianity, such needs and desires are suppressed in normative Judaism, and perhaps even in Jewish readings of Jewish mystical texts. Therefore, reading across cultures need not be oppositional. It can provide an experience of that which is submerged, perhaps unrecognized, within one's own tradition. Such a reading can illuminate both one's own and the other tradition in a way not anticipated by the "appropriate" cultural contexts. In such a case, historical contextualization comes not (as in scholarship generally) to locate and define the text in the terms of its origin, but rather to describe its performative potential in the context within which it is being read. This is a way to view the language of poetry as at least as generative as it is mimetic. The stress moves, then, from the referential to the performative. At present, I am working with a colleague, Kinereth Meyer, on a book-length study of Hopkins and Eliot within such a framework.

KAZUYOSHI ENOZAWA

WHY DOES HOPKINS' POETRY
MEAN SO MUCH TO THE JAPANESE?

"Memory is a deceitful jade," says Gerald Roberts in his essay "Coming to Hopkins." My own memory is deceitful, too. I do not remember the exact date at which I encountered Hopkins, but at least three things occur readily to my mind—first, that I presented my M.A. thesis on "Gerard Manley Hopkins" to my alma mater, Tokyo Kyoiku University in 1962; second, that I was received into the Catholic Church by my spiritual mentor, Fr. Peter Milward, shortly before that date; and third, that I contributed a listing of Hopkins-related books and articles by Japanese critics and scholars (published up to 1970) to Tom Dunne's *Gerard Manley Hopkins: A Comprehensive Bibliography*, then in preparation. These three factors combined, I may reasonably say, decided the course of my later academic career. And though I am now in an administrative position at a small college, I still embrace my longtime interest in Hopkins.

As I look back upon those early days, I see that I was then under the general influence of Louis Martz's *The Poetry of Meditation* and the more specific influence of David A. Downes's *Gerard Manley Hopkins: A Study of His Ignatian Spirit*. My debt to Fr. Milward was immense, from my post-graduate days on to my years of teaching at Keio University, during which time, living as I was in Tokyo, I was lucky enough to keep in close touch with this great master. My own contribution to Dunne's bibliography was a modest one, but the task of gathering all available Japanese materials related to Hopkins forced me to ponder what it is that sets Hopkins study by the Japanese apart from that by Westerners. The theme is still with me, and so in the rest of this article, may I briefly dwell on what particular aspect of Hopkins is so much of a concern to the Japanese?

Perhaps I may best start with a mention of the existence of

two centers of Hopkins study in Japan. One is in the ancient capital of Kyoto, and the other in the modern metropolis of Tokyo. Together, they form the two branches of the Hopkins Society of Japan, each publishing its own journal annually.

Not all of the members of that Society are academics, but even those who are not academics share with their academic friends a keen interest in Hopkins as a poet. Academics, or non-academics, they all love to read, and study, his poetry. Most of them, however, are not Catholics—not even Christians. That may be the reason why their understanding of Hopkins' poetry has to remain *partial*. I say *partial* because Hopkins' poetry—at least that part of it which Hopkins wrote after he became a Jesuit—is deeply infused with his Christian—or more specifically—his Ignatian vision.

Despite certain handicaps that non-Christian Japanese readers inevitably have when they set out to understand Hopkins' avowedly Christian poetry, they find at least some portions of it satisfying to their poetic taste. Take, for instance, stanza 4 in "Part the first" of "The Wreck of the Deutschland":

> I am soft sift
> In an hourglass—at the wall
> Fast, but mined with a motion, a drift,
> And it crowds and it combs to the fall;
> I steady as a water in a well, to a poise, to a pane,
> But roped with, always, all the way down from the tall
> Fells or flanks of the voel, a vein
> Of the gospel proffer, a pressure, a principle, Christ's gift.

There should be no trouble, even for non-Christian readers, in appreciating the two images—one of the sand falling in an hourglass, symbolizing man (specifically the poet) disintegrating both physically and spiritually—and the other of the water in a well fed continually by streams running down the sides of the hill. The Japanese love these lines for the beauty of those images—and well may they. But then comes the Christian image of man (or the poet) "roped with . . . a vein / Of the gospel proffer, a pressure, a principle, Christ's gift." Biblical implications of the last line may well be a puzzle to non-

Christian Japanese. As Catherine Phillips suggests in her note to this line, it would be necessary for them to refer to John 4.14, and to Peter Milward's *Commentary* if they were to gain a proper understanding of the line in question.

What I want to suggest is that in order to appreciate Christian aspects of Hopkins' poetry, non-Christian readers do need really good guides, such as Philip M. Martin's *Mastery and Mercy* and Peter Milward's above-mentioned *Commentary*, along with the same author's wonderful exposition in *Landscape and Inscape*.

I am a Catholic layman, and as such, I may be allowed to think that perhaps I am in a slightly better position to appreciate Hopkins' religious poetry than most of my non-Christian compatriots. Being a fellow countryman, however, I naturally share with them much of their Japanese sensibility. What in Hopkins appeals most to us Japanese is his power, above all, of describing details in what he saw in the natural world, in his fellow humans (particularly those under his pastoral care), and in his own inner world (particularly during his spiritual crisis in Dublin). This is not the place to deal extensively with such matters. So let me merely name some of the poems or parts thereof, which may reasonably be supposed to appeal to all Japanese lovers of Hopkins—myself included.

As to the great Christian ode "The Wreck of the Deutschland," the descriptions of the scene of the snow-storm in stanzas 13 to 17 must be felt by most Japanese to be quite impressive. Witness, for example:

> And the sea flint-flake, black-backed in the regular blow,
> Sitting Eastnortheast, in cursed quarter, the wind;
> Wiry and white-fiery and whírlwind-swivellèd snow
> Spins to the widow-making unchilding unfathering deeps.

Among other poems of Hopkins, there are some whose descriptions of beauty in nature may well appeal to the imagination of Japanese poetry readers. Witness, for instance, the exquisite scene of the "dapple-dawn-drawn Falcon" in the morning sky, in "The Windhover":

> High there, how he rung upon the rein of a wimpling wing
> In his ecstacy! then, off, off forth on swing,
>   As a skate's heel sweeps smooth on a bow-bend: the
>   hurl and gliding
>   Rebuffed the big wind.

Or the slow movement of clouds above the fields in harvest time, in "Hurrahing in Harvest":

> Summer ends now; now, barbarous in beauty, the stooks rise
> Around; up above, what wind-walks! what lovely behaviour
> Of silk-sack clouds!

No poems that Hopkins wrote when he was caring for parish people would impress the minds of Japanese poetry readers more than the sonnet "Felix Randal." This belongs to the category of poetry which deals not with the natural world but with human relationships, especially that between the priest and his parishioners. If "The Windhover" stands highest in the group of sonnets of "nature" as viewed sacramentally by the priest-to-be, "Felix Randal" should rank highest in the group of poems of "human relationships," as penned by the priest-at-work.

Even religious people such as the Catholic priest, in so far as he is a human being, cannot escape being struck, from time to time, with melancholia, or doubt. Sometimes it may go as far as "despair." To the Japanese-Christians or non-Christians, such an experience is not beyond understanding. It is exactly for this reason that they can appreciate what are called Hopkins' sonnets of desolation. Particularly impressive to them would be lines such as:

> I am gall, I am heartburn. God's most deep decree
> Bitter would have me taste: my taste was me;
> Bones built in me, flesh filled, blood brimmed the curse.

Or lines such as:

> O the mind, mind has mountains; cliffs of fall
> Frightful, sheer, no-man-fathomed. Hold them cheap
> May who ne'er hung there.

It is true that non-Christian Japanese who brave unfamiliar paths through Hopkins' poetry may sometimes stumble on one theological block or another, but that may be cleared for them by some helpful professional guide. Even in cases where no such guides are available, there is always a chance that they may come upon some unexpected spot from which to gain access to the core of Hopkins' poetic art. Hopkins, even to us Japanese, is by no means an inaccessible poet. *Deo gratias.*

READING HOPKINS

Reading Gerard Manley Hopkins has been the best thing to happen to me as a poet, scholar, and person.

I feel fortunate to have discovered his poetry, and later his letters, journals, and sermons, because they put me in touch with someone I could admire and love. I first read Hopkins' poems when I began seriously to write poetry in my early twenties, and for a time I imitated his style and sprung rhythm. My muse and music still echo his influence.

Graduate school led me into the Renaissance and to a doctoral dissertation on the sonnets of Sir Philip Sidney, but Hopkins always remained close to my heart. In Sidney, too, I found the self-awareness, concise choice of words, intelligence, and humanity that Hopkins possessed.

My first publication on Hopkins was provoked by a footnote reference to "The Slaughter of the Innocents" in my well-worn Penguin edition of the selected poetry and prose. The note was vague (it has since been corrected), but my Sherlock Holmes instincts told me that the phrase referred to the burning of his early poems before Hopkins decided on a religious vocation. I was convinced that the episode in the opening stanzas of "The Wreck of the Deutschland," which describe the harried poet's "altar and hour" as a place and moment of critical spiritual decision, recalled the May night of his retreat at Roehampton when he renounced the role of poet in favor of the call to the priesthood. In these lines, Hopkins honors his past resolution and declares, like Sidney, he has assumed the psalmist and prophetic role of *vates*, the poet who speaks with divine witness to his fellow human beings.

That article led to another monograph on the "Wreck" as a proclamation of Christ's mastery of souls, an inscape of his presence which can be instressed through stars and storms, a cry to Christ as God that echoes through the nun's call from the first to the last lines of this great ode.

On the basis of these publications, I applied for a summer stipend to the National Endowment of the Humanities with a proposal to continue my studies with two more articles on the sonnets. In that memorable summer of 1968 I found myself writing a book. *Inscape: The Christology and Poetry of Gerard Manley Hopkins* grew out of my many years of Jesuit classical training from high school and college to the seminary which I had left before ordination in 1960. I felt that the tradition of Christian Gnosticism developed by Clement of Alexandria and Origen and revived by John Henry Newman and the Tractarians provided the key to the poet's focus of knowledge as a source of poetry and love of God. I had high hopes that literary criticism and theology would meet on common ground through Hopkins. Unfortunately, Gnosticism, literary criticism, and theology have gone their own separate ways since 1972 when *Inscape* was published after many revisions and a fruitful summer at Oxford's Campion Hall researching original manuscripts.

After finishing the book, I felt I had little more to say on the subject, and so I turned to other authors, particularly Dante. On reflecting on several reviews of my book, however, I realized that there were depths of the poetry and thought that I had hardly touched on, both in the ode and sonnets. "Spelt from Sibyl's Leaves" and "That Nature is a Heraclitean Fire and of the comfort of the Resurrection" fascinated me with their layers of allusion, complexity and unity. I still remember the epiphany of delight I experienced when I saw that "This Jack, joke" was also John of the Apocalypse being himself transformed by the "immortal diamond" of Being's I AM.

In the past decade, Hopkins has led me back to reading the Bible, the psalms, the Book of Job, the Song of Songs, to Augustine's *Confessions* and *City of God*. Since I regularly teach a course on Mythology, I have also been led to new insights of his fusing of classical (especially Homeric) imagery and Christian meaning. I am especially pleased with two recent studies, Daniel Brown's *Hopkins' Idealism* and Justus George Lawler's *Re-*

Constructing Hopkins because they open for us fresh approaches to Hopkins' immense learning. Hopkins is a genius who left his thoughts in prose fragments but who gave us poems of whole vision and inspiration, of inscape and instress.

One stimulus for me in the study of Hopkins has been the friends I have met through him. Robert Boyle, a Jesuit with a love of James Joyce that equaled his enthusiasm for Hopkins, was an early contact, and over the years Norman MacKenzie has always been generous and gracious in replying to my inquiries. Michael Allsopp has been another faithful correspondent, and Joseph Feeney an untiring supporter of all things Hopkinsian. I have enjoyed meeting Nathan Cervo each spring at the Medieval Forum in Plymouth, New Hampshire, where we agree to disagree. My wife and I have managed to attend only one summer session of the Hopkins Society in Ireland, but it was a memorable occasion.

In sum, reading Hopkins has exposed me to the beauty of mind that is genius and the beauty of character that he himself expressed so eloquently and embodied so earnestly. For that I am eternally grateful.

A Memoir about Hopkins

My first meaningful knowledge of Hopkins came in the 1960s from my brother Clarence, who was teaching English at Wake Forest College, though he soon transferred to Calvin College. I may have read a poem or two—"God's Grandeur," "Pied Beauty"—in college (Adrian), but with no lasting effect. Clare explained to me (a philosopher) the stylistic elements in Hopkins and pointed out how significant he was in influencing some of the innovations in modern poetry.

Soon afterwards I purchased a copy of *Selected Poems of Gerard Manley Hopkins*, edited by James Reeves, mostly because it was the only book on Hopkins I could find in braille. The book had just been published by the Royal National Institute for the Blind in London in 1966. The day the book arrived in Rockford from overseas was a great day for me. I still own the book and look at it occasionally, both from nostalgia and for Reeves's notes. In a few years, however, I had the famous fourth edition of Hopkins by Gardner and MacKenzie turned into braille for me privately. The transcription was done by Doris M. Frazier of the Volunteer Services for the Blind in Philadelphia. This book, in five braille volumes, has been my principal primary source ever since, though I have sent many a student reader to the library on scouting expeditions for secondary items.

Being in philosophy, I could never teach Hopkins in a regular way, as people in English can. As I told everyone, Hopkins was a hobby for me. But from the late 60s to the early 80s Rockford College had, as many colleges did, a three-week Interim session tucked away between two ordinary semesters. The Interim did not carry regular credit but had to be taken for "Interim credit." One proviso was that standard catalogue courses could not be taught during the Interim, and another was that the courses could be outside one's normal field. This arrangement gave me the possibility of doing something with Hopkins—a possibility I actualized on two occasions.

The first of these occasions was in January of 1968 in an Interim course devoted to the study of religious experience from various perspectives—psychological, literary, mystical, and so on. I chose Hopkins for a literary perspective because very early he struck me as a poet who gave profound expression to religious experience in life, particularly the Christian experience. The students took charge of some of the topics, but I assigned myself to handle the Hopkins presentation. Already the outlines of my later book were incipient in that course presentation.

But I had no thought of a book at that time. I would have to collect and read many more books on Hopkins before that became an option. So for the next decade, as I had time, I absorbed as much Hopkins scholarship as I could while teaching full-time.

In August of 1975 I spent a week studying materials in the Hopkins Room of the Crosby Library at Gonzaga University. One of my readers for that week was my nine-year-old daughter Lynne (now a graduate student in English at Notre Dame). She got an early introduction to Hopkins. I think Ruth Seelhammer was quite impressed, as were we all.

Around this time the form of the book began to take shape. I wanted to articulate the pattern of religious experience which I found exhibited in the poetry, even though Hopkins himself did not articulate those specific themes (encagement, naturation, grace). I am far from saying that this account is the only or the standard reading to be found, for there is much more in Hopkins than can be extracted by one rendering. And yet at the same time I wanted to avoid the subjectivism or deconstructionism which holds that reader response counts for everything in criticism, the author for nothing, and even the poetry itself for little. The poetry itself must always be the central point of departure, and yet the richness of it invites more than one exploration.

I made inquiry about my manuscript to many publishers who declined to look at it on grounds of overstocked lists, sales questions, and what not. So I was gratified that the first publisher who actually perused the manuscript accepted it. This publisher was the Ohio University Press. The reviewer who recommended its acceptance was, as I learned later, Jerome Bump. I did not learn his identity in time to thank him in the preface for his suggestions, but perhaps it would not be amiss here, belatedly, to thank Professor Bump for his endorsement and to acknowledge his own outstanding contributions to Hopkins scholarship.

The second Interim course respecting Hopkins which I gave was in January of 1980. By then I was much more conversant with Hopkins and Hopkins criticism. So I was able, through readings, recordings, presentations, and discussion to simply relish in the sheer joy of a brief Hopkins absorption.

My second book on Hopkins, *Selected Poems of Gerard Manley Hopkins with Modern English Paraphrases*, originally included paraphrases of all the main poems. But the publisher, Edwin Mellen, wanted to do only twenty. So I tried to pick twenty of the hardest poems, i.e., ones that beginning readers seem to find hard to read with understanding. One former student, an English major, told me that despite knowing Hopkins for a long time she never could read "The Wreck of the Deutschland" with much understanding. The idea of opposite paging of poems and paraphrases seemed to me to be a way of making Hopkins more accessible to more people.

I continue to be interested in the biographical, historical, textual, linguistic, and cultural studies of Hopkins that come out. I have great admiration for the scholars engaged in this work. I know that these areas are not areas in which I can make a contribution. My own interest in Hopkins continues to be in his work seen as religious poetry. I have not felt the depth of encagement which he apparently felt, and I have not undergone the conversion type of experience he underwent. But I find many elements of a more general religious significance in his poems, i.e., a significance that is lasting because he expresses in strikingly novel ways the experiences of many other persons besides himself. To those elements I respond with sympathetic identification. Like other great writers, he speaks for us with words we have not found ourselves.

I do not read the poems daily or regularly as a kind of Biblical norm. But when I do return to them, I usually find nuances of meaning and significance that I had not fully grasped before. Such ongoing discoverability is, I believe, another tribute to Hopkins' poetic stature.

I was once asked which is my favorite Hopkins poem. In reply I mumbled something like, "It is difficult, and unfair to the other poems, to select just one poem for that designation." But after further reflection, and in retirement, it might be safe in a personal memoir to confess (but with an apology for a subjectivist lapse) that I have always been fond of "The Caged Skylark."

JOHN FERNS

WHY HOPKINS MATTERS TO ME

Hopkins matters because he is demonstrably a major English poet. In *New Bearings in English Poetry* (1932), F. R. Leavis wrote,

> No one can come from studying his work without an extended notion of the resources of English. And a technique so much concerned with inner division, friction, and psychological complexities in general has a special bearing on the problems of contemporary poetry. He is likely to prove, for our time and the future, the only influential poet of the Victorian age, and he seems to me the greatest.

Nearly forty years later in the Second Annual Hopkins Lecture (1971) Leavis concluded,

> Hopkins, in a wholly unpejorative sense, was simple. There is nothing equivocal in his verse, and in the letters we see the simplicity as that of a man of high intelligence, fine human perception, irresistible charm and complete integrity.

Leavis, of course, thought that Hopkins' finest achievements lay in his poetry of "inner division, friction, and psychological complexities," in poems like the Sonnets of Desolation. Leavis' biographer Ian MacKillop offers a possible explanation for this:

> [I]t is hard not to associate his [Leavis'] knowledge of twenty-one months in France [1916-18] with his later respect for the literature of devastation, like Gerard Manley Hopkins' "The Wreck of the Deutschland" which he read aloud as memorably as [Isaac Rosenberg's] "Dead Man's Dump."

For me, however, the centre of Hopkins' poetic achievement lies not so much in the Sonnets of Desolation (impressive and influential as those late poems are) or even in "The Wreck of the Deutschland" (astonishing and original as that poem is) but rather in the sonnets of the spring and summer of 1877. These sonnets constitute a poetic achievement that rivals that of Keats's sonnet-like Odes of the spring and summer of 1819. Hopkins matters to me, and matters generally, because not only did he write poems of the kind and quality that Leavis admires but also because at the core of his *œuvre* we find poems like "God's Grandeur," "The Starlight Night," "Spring," "The Windhover," "Pied Beauty" and "Hurrahing in Harvest" all written between February and September 1877, which was for Hopkins surely as much a "living year" as 1819 was for Keats. There is besides, as Leavis notes, the matter of influence, and Hopkins has, as Richard F. Giles's volume *Hopkins Among the Poets: Studies in Modern Responses to Gerard Manley Hopkins* (1985) so amply demonstrates, exerted an extensive and significant influence on twentieth-century poetry.

But to return to that critical year (1877) in which Hopkins approached ordination, we find that with the achievement of "The Wreck of the Deutschland" behind him, Hopkins produced poetry that while often transcending "inner division, friction and psychological complexities" certainly extends our "notion of the resources of English." Besides, in these poems (as in many others) Hopkins transcends the limiting assessment of "devotional" or "nature" poet made by T. S. Eliot. From the Sonnets of 1877 Hopkins emerges as one of the great poets of Christian affirmation. Nowhere is this more fully felt than in the sestet of "God's Grandeur":

> And, for all this, nature is never spent;
>   There lives the dearest freshness deep down things;
> And though the last lights off the black West went
>   Oh, morning, at the brown brink eastwards, springs—
> Because the Holy Ghost over the bent
>   World broods with warm breast and with ah! bright wings.

We are not seeing here a permission for ecological irresponsibility but rather a realisation that our world is ultimately in God's hands. Hopkins experiences the presence of the Holy Ghost in the breaking of the day. The beauties of Langland and the Old English canon are strikingly recalled in the alliteration of the last line.

The opening of "The Starlight Night" is almost equally impressive. Here the night sky, rather than the dawn, draws Hopkins' awed response. He evokes a sense of wonder as readily as Blake:

> Look at the stars! Look, look up at the skies!
>   O look at all the fire-folk sitting in the air!
>   The bright boroughs, the circle-citadels there!
> Down in dim woods the diamond delves! The elves'-eyes!
> The grey lawns cold where gold, where quickgold lies!

Hopkins' nature is animated, in "God's Grandeur" by the Holy Ghost, here by fairy presences that recall in language and image the magic of Shakespeare's *A Midsummer Night's Dream*, yet by the close of the poem we receive a sense of divine in-dwelling, of "Christ home, Christ and his mother and all his hallows."

That Hopkins is a poet of deep Christian affirmation and inspiration is confirmed again in "Spring" in which he asks and answers, "What is all this juice and all this joy? / A strain of the earth's sweet being in the beginning / In Eden garden." Hopkins' genius as a poet is revealed in his capacity to realize "juice" and "joy" in a way that places him in a direct line from Shakespeare and Keats:

> Nothing is so beautiful as Spring—
>   When weeds, in wheels, shoot long and lovely and lush;
>   Thrush's eggs look little low heavens, and thrush
> Through the echoing timber does so rinse and wring
> The ear, it strikes like lightnings to hear him sing;
>   The glassy peartree leaves and blooms, they brush
>   The descending blue; that blue is all in a rush
> With richness; the racing lambs too have fair their fling.

"The Windhover" immediately reveals its Christian intention in its dedication, "To Christ our Lord." Christian meaning and significance flow beneath the surface of the poem adding to its depth and power. "Pied Beauty," on the other hand, is a quite simple poem in praise of God:

Glory be to God for dappled things—
  For skies of couple-colour as a brinded cow;
    For rose-moles all in stipple upon trout that swim;
Fresh-firecoal chestnut-falls; finches' wings;
  Landscape plotted and pieced—fold, fallow, and plough;
    And áll trádes, their gear and tackle and trim.

All things counter, original, spare, strange;
  Whatever is fickle, frecklèd (who knows how?)
    With swift, slow; sweet, sour; adazzle, dim;
He fathers-forth whose beauty is past change:
                    Praise him.

Leavis' references to "simplicity" and "irresistible charm" apply fully here.

If "God's Grandeur" is Hopkins' Nightingale Ode with a magnificent concluding difference and "The Windhover" his Grecian Urn, then "Hurrahing in Harvest" is Hopkins' "To Autumn." Like Shakespeare, both Keats and Hopkins have a wonderful command of sensuous detail and particularity. But where Keats's "To Autumn" is a poem of repose, "Hurrahing in Harvest" is full of energy and movement. The opening is dramatic: "Summer ends now." Alliteration, consonance and enjambement work together in "barbarous in beauty, the stooks rise / Around" to present a vital picture of the harvest, though by the close of the quatrain we have a subtle reminiscence of Keats's ode in "Meal-drift moulded ever and melted across skies."

However, the main endeavour through the poems of 1877 for the poet-priest approaching ordination is "to glean our Saviour." And Hopkins meets him in God's created world whether it be the natural world of these poems or later in the human world of art and labour of "Henry Purcell" and "Felix Randal."

Hopkins matters to me because of poems like these, and because he dedicated his art as well as his life to God and to our saviour, Jesus Christ. "If we care for fine verses, how much more for a noble life"—didn't Hopkins put it something like that?

FRANCIS X. MCALOON, S.J.

PRAYING WITH HOPKINS

Let him easter in us, be a dayspring to the dimness of us . . .

One snowy January morning some twenty years ago, these words from the last stanza of "The Wreck of the Deutschland" were posted on the Jesuit novitiate bulletin board at Wernersville, Pennsylvania. We first-year Jesuit novices were approaching the end of our thirty-day "Long Retreat" (the *Spiritual Exercises* of St. Ignatius of Loyola). Throughout the retreat, one of the retreat directors would frequently post poetic fragments for the delight of any novice who wanted to read them. Each day, I would make my own pilgrimage to this poetic bulletin board, not so much because I loved poetry (at the time, I didn't), but because I appreciated both the momentary distraction it provided and (more importantly) the delight, inspiration, or challenge offered in each day's installment. On more than one occasion, I transcribed the poetic fragments into my retreat journal and oftentimes prayed with them. While the verses typically were not from sacred scripture, they always spoke to some aspect of the sacred. In my own journey into the fourth week of the *Spiritual Exercises*, with its focus upon Christ's Resurrection, this verse from "The Wreck" was a source of surprise, confusion, and consolation. I had never before encountered the verb form "to easter." That day, I received two gifts. First, I gained a special insight into the mystery of Christ's Resurrection. Second, Hopkins' words opened up within me a new appreciation for the power of poetry.

Such was my first memorable exposure to the poetry of Gerard Manley Hopkins. As an undergraduate English major, I had encountered Hopkins in the requisite survey course on British literature, but at the time, I was unwilling and unable to open myself to the glorious voice of his poetry. Even after becoming a Jesuit, I was not particularly taken with Hopkins, although I certainly heard enough about him from older Jesuits. Indeed, any extended and serious engagement with Hopkins' poetry occurred only after I was fifteen years a Jesuit and even then only because I was in doctoral studies in the academic discipline of Christian Spirituality.

In the autumn of 1997, I was at the comprehensive-examination stage of my Ph.D. program at the Graduate Theological Union, Berkeley, California. One of the five required comprehensive exams in my program was in a non-theological discipline. I selected literary theory and studied with a member of the English department at the nearby University of California. In my research, I eventually settled upon new-historicist literary criticism, also known as cultural poetics. Among other things, this poststructuralist approach to literary studies asserts the fundamental historicity of all texts and the textuality of all history. New historicists are concerned with the circulation and exchange of social power within and around literary texts, their creation and reception. When the time came to focus my research upon a single author, a Jesuit theologian friend suggested Hopkins. Initially, I resisted the idea because I had never particularly enjoyed poetry, let alone Victorian poetry. However, upon further reflection, I took the risk. My Cal professor was delighted. "Oh, yes," she said, "I think Hopkins is ripe for a new-historicist investigation." I was on my way.

My purpose here is not to share the fruits of my research, but to describe how my initial hesitancy in studying Hopkins evolved into an ardent appreciation for the man and his poetry. In addition to the usual research and study that went into the preparation for the exam, I began each day with an extended meditation upon a Hopkins poem. This meditation was modeled upon the Christian monastic prayer form known as *lectio divina*. Briefly described, after an initial period of quieting prayer, deep breathing exercises, and other methods for clearing one's mind of distracting thoughts, I slowly read the day's poem, first quietly and then aloud. I initially focused my attention upon the poem's sound, rhythm, and rhyme. Next, I would return to words or images within the poem that invited my attention—or reached out and grabbed me by the collar. For example, I would linger with language that struck me as curious, provocative, confusing, beautiful or painful. These invitations to attentiveness created a space within my consciousness for resting, listening, and attending to whatever the poem invited me to hear, perceive and feel. This sort of encounter with the poetic text typically gave rise to one or more points of connection to my own life experience. Oftentimes, I was able to correlate aspects of my own faith journey with elements of the poem's text. The underlying presupposition of this sort of prayer within the Christian tradition is that through the gifts of the Holy Spirit, God may address the person praying through the words and images projected by the poetic text. This is not to suggest that Hopkins' intentions or experiences, let alone his supposed spiritual insights, controlled or determined my prayerful encounter with the poem. Rather, the creative product itself, the poem as text, facilitated an open communication between the divine and me. This prayer experience could be affirming and challenging, consoling or upsetting. Towards the end of the prayer period, I addressed God using my own words of praise, petition, or expressions of ongoing concern. This prayer-with-poetry concluded with a final reading of the poem and time spent journaling about the experience. This prayer lasted anywhere from twenty to fifty minutes.

This experience of *lectio divina* with Hopkins' poetry was consoling, confirming, and challenging. Not only did I gain an intimate knowledge of the poetry, I also enjoyed a deeply rich prayer practice. Indeed, much to my surprise, I discovered that God could and would address, invite, encourage and challenge me through praying with these poetic texts. The usual markers of a fruitful Christian prayer experience were in evidence. My sense of self and relationship with God were deepened and enriched. I was more centered, focused, and grounded in my spiritual life. This crossed over into my relationships with friends and family, studies and pastoral activities. Overall, it was a time of spiritual consolation; however, even during intermittent periods of spiritual desolation or anxiety, the prayer with Hopkins' poetry was enriching.

Following the successful completion of my comprehensive examinations, I reflected upon my prayer-with-poetry experience. Before this time, poetry for me was not a significant source of enjoyment or spiritual insight. Nevertheless, I recognized that something important had occurred. Hopkins' poetry—its rhyme and rhythm, sound and sense, metaphor and meter, power and presence—challenged, provoked, soothed, and delighted me. Not only did I gain a renewed appreciation for poetry as a literary genre, I grew to love Hopkins' poetry in itself and as a vehicle for deepening my relationship with God. The question arose in my mind as to what were the possibilities for investigating this experience from the perspective of the academic discipline of Christian Spirituality. From this experience was born a dissertation entitled "A Christian Spirituality Theory of Interpretation for Praying with Poetry."

Much has changed over the past twenty years of my life, but one thing remains constant: My hope and prayer is to "*let him easter in us, be a dayspring to the dimness of us . . .*"

DRAWN IN BY HOPKINS

" . . . O thou my friend . . ."

MY HOPKINS APPRENTICESHIP

I recently celebrated an anniversary, my thirtieth since my "first looking into" Hopkins' poems. I remember that a few had to be read and prepared for my third-year exam from Hayward's *Oxford Book of Nineteenth Century Verse*. There was then only one, very bad Italian anthology of translations with facing texts, which is still available, though no one, after several reprints, ever seems to have noticed and corrected a curious, preposterous blunder in "'To seem the stranger'"—where "This to hoard unheeded" was, and still is, rendered as "Inudita dalle orde," completely confusing "hoard" (verb) with "horde" (noun). Hopkins bordered on the legendary in our academic world and for the reading public in general, and the first reactions that I can recall are those of a fascinating vernacular. I asked myself which was the relationship with poetry, or Poetry, of words and phrases such as "the midriff astrain," "His mystery must be instressed, stressed," "the flange and the rail," which sounded to me either as non-poetry or poetry of the future, or to belong to the language of medical science or railway engineering. I unconsciously became a Bridgesian reader of Hopkins long before I could fully tackle, and come to reject, Bridges' purism and his indirect vision of Hopkins as a bold iconoclast (a vision it would take me a few years to radically upset). The Italian—one would say the international—approach to Hopkins was then through modernism, i.e., still saw him largely as a forerunner of the poetry of the 1930s, or directly as a contemporary of Cecil Day Lewis and Auden (and, among the Italian poets, of the "ermetismo" and of Eugenio Montale, who gave some unsurpassed translations). No one made much at the time of Hopkins' religion and theology, while very much was made of his alleged capacity to render verbally the subtlest operations of the mind. Significantly, the only pioneering essay written in Italian before the seventies dealt with Hopkins' sonnets, both joyous and terrible, in terms of Victor Šklovskij's *ostrannenija*. This interest in technique also accounts for the singular neutrality towards Hopkins of the Marxist *intelligentsia* which then controlled the Italian academic world; no critic chose to reopen, as I have argued elsewhere, the stale debate over the confessional and oratorical, rather than truly artistic and poetic value of Hopkins' poetry—a debate that had fiercely divided our critics of the novel *The Betrothed* by Alessandro Manzoni until only a few decades earlier. Not even Croce, far from tender towards confessional literature, had found fault with Hopkins' Catholicism in 1937, in the first historical presentation of our poet to Italian readers.

My serious study of Hopkins began in the Seventies, after I wrote my first book (on Dylan Thomas). I remember I was particularly struck by superficial and to a certain extent genuine similarities in the two poets, especially in the straining of syntax, in the use of compound words and in the coining of new words. Dylan Thomas fired in me a curiosity and then an absorbing interest when I found in his correspondence a couple of passages in which he flatly declared—telling of course a brazen lie—that he had never read, let alone imitated, Hopkins (he and other left-wing poets felt somewhat ashamed to admit to being influenced by a Catholic poet who was also a Jesuit priest). Structuralism, semiotics and the new rhetoric were gaining ground in Europe in the late seventies, and Hopkins, to whom scholars and linguists of the calibre of Roman Jakobson had acknowledged the status of a pioneer of the *science* of verse and of rhythm, seemed to provide an inexhaustible mine for investigations aiming to show the several functions of poetic discourse and in particular the ways in which sound, rhythm, syntax and meaning cohere in the most ingenious parallelistic patterns. Subsequently I became completely absorbed, while not certainly repudiating my first formalistic and structural approaches, in the attempt to probe into the complex relationship between Hopkins and his time, which gave as a result a bewildering graph of acceptances and rejections of the most widely shared cultural codes.

Having now devoted several years to the study of Hopkins' poetry, produced three books and half a dozen essays, and translated thirty-seven of his best poems into Italian—and though I do not plan to write extensively on him any more—I have no doubt that to study him has been a unique formative experience. I have acquired a "professional bias" of which I am not at all ashamed. I know colleagues who having become experts, say, of Swift or Conrad, tend to discuss everything from the point of view of those writers and always to bring grist to their own mill. Similarly, I see English literature as B.H. (before Hopkins) and A.H. (after Hopkins), especially now, when I have ceased to be and to consider myself a Hopkins scholar and would find this label limiting. To a student of general Victorian literature, and a historian of English literature, as I would now define myself, Hopkins has become, as he said all poets should be, a touchstone, or the linchpin not only of Victorian but also of English literature: I interpret it in its development as converging to and diverging from Hopkins. I am now completing a history of Victorian literature, and I frequently catch myself almost unconsciously making comparisons or finding contrasts between Hopkins and the other writers I write about. Hopkins seems to me the most shaped of all English poets, while at the same time he is the poet who most shaped those who came after him. Scarcely a day passes that I do not discover new links, echoes and associations between him and figures of the past, and between him and poets who, after reading him, were indelibly branded.

WHY HOPKINS AND ME?

I have already described elsewhere my very personal lifetime companionship with the writings of G.M. Hopkins. In that essay I tried to express how powerfully shaping has been that mysterious relationship that sometimes occurs between an author who speaks so directly as the daimon of his reader. In this essay, I wish to discuss another aspect of my encounter with Hopkins, my scholarly engagement with him.

One of my frustrations as a student of literature has been uncovering the intellectual fundament on which the writings of great authors rest. That the human imagination is so facile in representing all kinds of experience without understanding it very much has always been a fascination for me, but also a nettling wonder. While, of course, serious writers, certainly great ones, do offer some points of view about the human and ontic reality they depict, at best the thinking reader is left to try to reconstruct how each author understands how the universe of self and reality works. Thus as a graduate student and later as a beginning scholar, I found the mystery of mind in the authors I read to be intriguing but often baffling. At this level of reader response, so much deep analysis is disenabled by the sheer absence of anything said or written that can be construed with any true accuracy as to an author's understanding of things as they are lying beneath their productions of things as they can be imagined. For some time, this attitude of mine seemed to preclude any sustained readership and study of one author beyond the necessities of the classroom and that occasional article which might be described as "How about this angle of depose?"

When I was given a serious introduction to the writings of G.M. Hopkins by John Pick at Marquette University, I thought his deep enthusiasm a bit overdone, a kind of literary fetish that I was beginning to see in other instructors and some students, the perennial "ooh and ah" contingent whose tastes change as each moved from one class to another. I knew this kind of engagement would not produce much of a long lasting endeavor in the way of serious scholarship (for students often crashing early on the shoals of trying to write a dissertation). I doubted that I would find any writer who would sustain over a lifetime both my personal selving and my professional career.

This disenchantment nearly deterred me from going on to doctoral study. Of course, accounting for the ways of the incredible richness of the human imagination offers much satisfaction both personally and professionally. While reading literature in general provides ample opportunity to understand the ways of the world, as a branch of knowledge literature offers much less in the way of informing one's mind as to the deep nature and ordering of what is called by frontier thinkers the reality of real being. In a word, literary authors are not ordinarily thinkers.

This attitude was, of course, the prideful ambition of a young man looking for answers. What I yearned for was a complete poet, one who offered profound analysis of the self selving reality as the ground of his imagination and who possessed the artistic capacities to capture this intellective imaginative vision in powerful redescriptive language. The "greats," of course, proffer such virtues, at times abundantly, though so often their sense of reality and ultimate reality in their writing is out of the immediacy of a reader's time frame, is fragmentary, frequently incoherent, downright obscure, even sometimes inane, W.B. Yeats's spiritualism for example.

When I took my first teaching job at Gonzaga University, I considered it a test of my resolve to enter fully the teaching profession. I soon discovered the challenges of authentic teaching, the immense opportunities to provoke human development; at the same time I valued the chance to spend a life perusing the rich productions of the literary imagination, past and present. Attractive as this prospect was, it offered less than I aspired to accomplish, which was to spend my intellective and spiritual life in trying to understand the mystery of my selving personality encountering the mystery of appearance and reality, a personal soul journey. Moreover, my first taste of graduate school gave me a desire to somehow express this journey in some written form.

My personal and professional aspirations received an intense recognitive reversal shock when I met Fr. Anthony Bischoff, the English Chair who hired me. A young Jesuit (finished with his basic training and completing his Yale doctorate), now beginning his university career in earnest, Father Bischoff, using his charming capacities for initiating personal friendships, soon became my mentor. Slowly but with continuing progress, he introduced me to the full literary corpus of Hopkins with a love and dedication I first glimpsed in John Pick. Father Bischoff put before me all the copies of Hopkins MSS and materials he had gleaned in a colossal research pilgrimage he had made in the late 1940s in England and Ireland. I saw Hopkins in the original as few mature scholars had seen him up until that time, certainly not a young, green, aspiring one like myself.

Looking back I now see how I gradually became hooked on Hopkins. As I walked through the materials under Fr. Bischoff's guidance, I was becoming interested in Hopkins' literary story, and I began to uncover some of his deeper intellective strains. But my motives still were blurred, partly because I felt the need to hold at a distance Father Bischoff's huge dedicatory spirit and, of course, he was also my academic superior. But then one day he said to me that I now knew enough about Hopkins to think about enlisting in his endeavor to put Hopkins on the literary map. Knowing I had to complete a doctorate to reach full status in the academic profession, and that I was seriously contemplating doing just this, he suggested that I consider doing a dissertation on Hopkins, not just as an academic exercise of basic scholarly proficiency, but a dissertation that would be on the scholarly frontier of a new major author. Why not become a Hopkins scholar?

Against protests of my personal scholarly insufficiency and still limited knowledge of Hopkins, in addition to determining my dissertation topic before I entered a university to complete my course work and come to the selection of a dissertation topic with all of the academic politics that such an activity involves, Fr. Bischoff persisted. Clinching his proposal, he suggested a dissertation topic, a study of Hopkins' Ignatian qualities by using many of his prose writings, specially his Commentary on The Spiritual Exercises of St. Ignatius. He would put in my hands all the pertinent materials from Hopkins' canon and suggest many helpful books and commentaries to give me a Jesuit insight into the history, character, and uses of *The Spiritual Exercises.*

Afraid and anxious, I was also intrigued. Seeing my hesitation, particularly my undertaking a project that seemed better suited to a member of the Society of Jesus, he countered by saying that every Jesuit personalizes the Exercises, thus often making their approach to studying the historical and literary uses of the Exercises subject to bias; morever, he asserted that he agreed that an "insider" would be required to catch the spiritual character of the Exercises, by "insider" meaning that in his opinion a Catholic Christian would be more in religious touch with the spiritual, doctrinal, and methodological character of the Exercises.

As the bromide goes, "The rest is history." I did go on to doctoral study at the University of Washington with a nearly completed dissertation in hand. And thanks to the academic integrity and generosity of Professor Robert B. Heilman, then Chair of English, my dissertation Chair, Professor James Hall, and surprisingly the encouragement and understanding of the notable poet Theodore Roethke, a powerful advocate on my dissertation committee (so far as I know the only dissertation committee he ever sat on), I completed my doctorate in two years and published my dissertation in 1960.

I also changed my academic and scholarly focus from sixteenth and seventeenth-century British literature to that of the nineteenth century, and the writings of G.M. Hopkins became my central focus. I determined that I would not seek employment in a major research university where scholarship is often forced, overly competitive, and politicized. In making this choice, I knew that if I ever did much scholarship, I would have to do it during semester breaks, summers, and amid carrying full loads of teaching. I also had to carry it on with unstable eyesight. Whatever I might do in the way of writing about my study of Hopkins would arise less from any academic necessity than from the quandaries and questions that arose from my private reading and study of Hopkins, essentially an avocational effort being carried on under the auspices of my personal spiritual and literary pursuits, outside of any driving professional aspirations. Should there be no professional crossover, so be it.

In the beginning, I wondered whether reading Hopkins would remain a central focus of my continuing literary education. After some intense activity engaging Hopkins, I knew there would be lapses and disengagements. Over the years this did happen. But a stimulating letter from Father Bischoff, who followed my career throughout his lifetime, or provocative letters or essays from other Hopkins scholars would jump-start my interest again. Fresh readings would suggest new perspectives and culminate in my attempting to redescribe them in written form.

Looking back over the work I have done, I realize that the one constant in my scholarship has been an effort to sort out a holistic understanding of selving an intelligible life. Over a lifetime I have been constantly engaged in trying to comprehend what is truly real on both the natural and supernatural levels, how we know what is real, and what are the implications of this knowledge in trying to live a truly human life. I saw and see in Hopkins' life and literary works a prodigious effort to achieve the same goal. More and more his poetry becomes for me a dramatization, not just about selving reality, but an enactment of the self in the act of selving the real. Hopkins' poetry for me is essentially about how the consciousness grasps real being, how we take being in, and how we re-express our assimilations in powerfully discrete, extremely accurate, articulated modes, catching the excitement and energy of personal apprehension itself, while truly "seeing" the real nature of the thing seen. This ground-breaking search led me to study Hopkins' esthetic temper (which I compared to that of Walter Pater and later sought sources of influence in John Ruskin); I became interested in putting his uses of the religious imagination in the context of his time by studying fictional accounts of faith happening and not happening (using some Victorian religious novels), and finally I went on to explore Hopkins' own queries into the nature of the self, the selving phenomenology of belief and the role of poetic language in sponsoring transcendent awarenesses of ultimate reality.

Such has been the professional overlay of my journey reading and contemplating Hopkins' life and writings. The path has been an awesome one of discovery and self-discovery. Scholarship and selving have become united in the enriching literary heuristic of the poet-priest. While the published record of this personal selving diary and professional progress does detail the sights and insights, I doubt that it does capture the elation and the satisfaction of this longtime literary companionship. Now, nearly at the end, I have returned to where I began. I am back to a kind of personalization of *The Spiritual Exercises*, that is, to reflect again on the foundational mysteries of the selving self, the mystery of Creation, and the "great sacrifice," which in Hopkins' poetry is to ponder ever more the polysemy of his lines in his ode, "The Wreck of the Deutschland," so splendidly symphonized throughout all his great poetic canon: "His mystery must be instressed, stressed; / For I greet him the days I meet him, and bless when I understand."

COMING TO HOPKINS

Memory is a deceitful jade, but as far as I can remember, I first met Hopkins—poetically—through "Inversnaid" during my secondary school days fifty years ago in South Wales. It must have impressed me because it is still a favourite of mine with its sense of mystery and powerful rhythm, but curiously enough I have no memory of doing Hopkins at university in the 50s: I was not a Catholic at the time and the university itself was non-denominational. I know many readers of Hopkins have been inspired by the Catholic element, and although I myself did become a convert a few years later, I cannot say that his poetry was any part of the motivation. In my later writing on him, I have always been wary of the purely religious approach and its dangers of turning a poet into a religious icon.

Again, relying on unreliable memory I would say that I did not become fully *aware* of Hopkins until after my post-graduate years (my research was not even concerned with the nineteenth century) and after the beginning of my working life. The time and place for this "conversion" was, not surprisingly, when I went to teach at St Mary's Hall, the Junior School to Stonyhurst College, with all the (now) well-known associations with the poet. No great importance seemed to be attached to the name there, in the early 60s—no plaques, portraits, folders for visitors, exhibition cases, &c. Now it's very different.

Perhaps I may take the liberty of reminding readers that St Mary's Hall was the Jesuit seminary for students of Philosophy in Hopkins' time, although since the Second World War it had been turned into a "prep," i.e., junior school, and when I arrived the only Jesuits were the Headmaster and one or two assistants—most of the staff were lay.

"SMH," as its past and present pupils know it, is a plain but neatly symmetrical stone building, with room for about 150 boys and adults, looking south towards the great whale-back of Pendle Hill, a few miles distant. The latter's presence can always be felt, great cloud-shadows floating across it in summer, frost or snow outlining its long ridge in winter, and a swirling outline in cloud and rain. Hopkins found it impressive, so did I (and so do I now, in my mind's eye, although far removed from those Lancashire landscapes).

Students of Hopkins' journal for the period will appreciate how reading it, which I naturally did, lent an extra resonance to the landscapes in which I lived and worked—the almost Alpine ridge of Longridge Fell to the north, the deceptively placid River Hodder to the east, and the dim chimneys of industry in the distance—shadows of later Bedford Leigh and Liverpool. All this, coupled with a visit to St Beuno's and a meeting with the now-deceased but memorable (and voluble!) Fr Alfred Thomas, took me further into the reading of Hopkins' prose and poetry . . . and, patient reader, nearer to the time at which I felt I had something to write on the subject.

However, I was too busy with schoolmasterly things to think of writing at SMH, and it was only when I moved to join the staff of the College in 1969, that the more intellectual atmosphere, the stimulating companionship of staff and students, together with better facilities for research, led me, after completing an M.Phil. at the University of Leeds in 1972, to penning my first article. The piece in question was a humble beginning, "A Reference to Hopkins in the *Stonyhurst Magazine*," and it was directly due to my residence in the College, where, both in the Community and Boys' Libraries, with complete runs of the *Stonyhurst Magazine* from its inception in 1881, I came across the relevant material. In a copy of the magazine for 1883 I had noted under "Items of Local History" a description of a catechizing expedition from St Mary's Hall into the local neighbourhood by a writer describing an incident of earlier date. Recalling from the journal that Hopkins had been on such an expedition, I discovered by comparing the details that the two occasions were the same. Although my hopes that Hopkins himself might have penned this later account were dashed when I was given access to the editor's copy on which the contributor's name was written, at least I merited a small page in Fr. Thomas' *Hopkins Research Bulletin*, that modest but excellent predecessor to *HQ*.

This was also a period when, granted access to both printed and MS sources at Stonyhurst, my interest in Hopkins expanded to things Victorian in general. Fr Frederick Turner, S.J., archivist at the College, must take some responsibility for my later writing, for his help and interest were never wanting. A highly respected classics teacher himself in his heyday, he also had, after a lifetime in the Society, a great knowledge of Jesuit matters, and of Stonyhurst in particular, but without the narrowness that sometimes comes with specialisation.

So with his help I plundered the wonderful and surprising collections of the College, strong in Victorian biography and in Victoriana of all sorts, including runs of nineteenth-century magazines that supplied valuable background material to anyone interested in Victorian Catholicism, for example *The Month*, the Society of Jesus' own periodical, and *The Tablet*, which was from its inception in 1840 a remarkable compendium of Catholic news and views of the time. I still remember that it was so cold in the area of the library where I studied these and other volumes that Fr. Turner was kind enough to allow me to remove them to study in my own rooms!

As I have suggested, an interest that began with Hopkins at St. Mary's Hall had now extended, fruitfully I think, to the man and his time. The Victorian massiveness of much of the College building, the mill towns of roundabout, Clitheroe, Preston, and Blackburn, the local galleries and churches with their notable Victorian characteristics all contributed to my increasing preoccupation with the nineteenth century—which was to be expressed in some semi-historical essays for Dublin *Studies* and provide essential background for my later *Hopkins* in the Macmillan Literary Lives series.

In another direction I have been led into looking more curiously at some of the unique poetic and temperamental voices of modern English writing, Edward Thomas, Ivor Gurney, Alun Lewis, whom, in an article in *HQ*, I placed together with Hopkins in the pantheon of modern melancholics. In the context of twentieth-century culture, philosophic as well as aesthetic, I think there is still more to be quarried here. All in all, my involvement with the study of Hopkins has certainly given focus to my own scholarship though never, I hope, limited my interests in such a way that the poet becomes a dead end and I a seeker after scraps!

PETER MILWARD, S.J.

HOPKINS AND I

"It is hard for thee to kick against the goad." And it has been hard for me to struggle against my fate. That fate was in no small measure determined by the circumstances of my birth and upbringing. I was born on the South Bank of the Thames, at Barnes, and shortly afterwards my parents moved to Wimbledon, to provide me and my two brothers with a Catholic education at the Jesuit school there. South London isn't quite the same as North London; but Wimbledon may claim to be quite as countrified for a suburb of London as Hampstead. My parents were both Catholic; but my father had been Anglican till the time he met my Irish mother. Moreover, my education at school was thoroughly classical, in the Victorian no less than the Jesuit tradition. Then, instead of going up to Oxford to read the classics, I went and joined the Society of Jesus in 1943. And of all places my noviceship was spent at St Beuno's College—two years of it besides my first year of juniorate, making three years.

So it was inevitable! Nor did it help matters when for our summer vacation as juniors in 1946, we went for a couple of weeks to Hodder Place, near Stonyhurst. Even when I left St Beuno's behind me for three years of philosophy at the more recently acquired college of Heythrop in Oxfordshire, we went for our summer vacation three years running to Barmouth—including the customary row up the estuary of the Mawddach to the George Inn and Penmaen Pool. At Heythrop College, while having my nose rubbed in the muddled philosophy of Suarez, I made the delighted discovery of Scotus, without realizing I wasn't altogether alone. Then from Heythrop I went up to Oxford to follow my destined course of the classics. Only, at classical "mods," I was obliged—owing to my destination for Japan—to turn aside and read English instead. And so, in 1954, I became an exile, "at a third remove" from England, destined to teach literature at a foreign university.

And for all this—believe it or not—Hopkins was for me little more than a name, the name of an odd Jesuit poet of the old Victorian era: I had hardly dipped into his poems, except to confirm me in the conviction that they were quite incomprehensible. During my studies I had come across two young American Jesuit priests who struck us as crazy about Hopkins. One came all the way to Barmouth with us, just because Hopkins had written a poem on "Penmaen Pool," while the other wanted to take photos of all the places associated with Hopkins and his poems, including the very spot where the Deutschland had been wrecked off the Essex coast. A third, who seemed just as crazy along a different line (the logic of Ramus), later made his name as a Hopkins scholar. Somehow, it occurred to me, Hopkins had a knack of evoking in people what Shakespeare has appropriately termed "fine frenzy."

So it wasn't till I came all the way to Japan and could view myself and my native country as well as English literature from a distance, that I thought the time had come for me to speak not just of "cabbages and kings" but even of Hopkins and his poems. After all, here I was, an English Jesuit in exile, professing to teach English literature to Japanese university students. And so, what more natural a subject was there for me to teach them, by way of second string to the plays of Shakespeare, than the poems of Hopkins? I therefore made a beginning by taking one of the last and most difficult of his poems, "That Nature is a Heraclitean Fire and of the comfort of the Resurrection." I was on vacation with other Jesuit students beside a lake; and one day I went out with an American who had studied Hopkins under one of the crazy Jesuits mentioned above, the photographer. So he knew more of Hopkins than I did, though it wasn't much. Along the lake there was a headland, and there we sat down facing Mount Fuji on the opposite shore with the text of the poem in our hands. And together we pieced out the possible meaning of the poem word by word and line by line—albeit finding more questions than answers. Yet by the time we came to an end, for all the gaps in meaning that still remained, we found everything growing (as Shakespeare puts it) "to something of great constancy."

"Well begun is half done." So when I came to teach Hopkins in a more formal fashion to my students at Sophia University—when I was no longer a Jesuit student but a fully fledged priest—I still followed the same method as when I had been sitting "beside the lake, beneath the trees." That is to say, I went through the poems, this time beginning with "The Wreck of the Deutschland," teasing out the meaning with my students word by word and line by line. Hopkins, I found, is an admirable poet for such piecemeal treatment. There is so much meaning and feeling he packs into every word and line. His every poem is like a Christmas pudding, so rich in substance as well as the brandy that has gone into its making. One can't take too much of it at once without getting intoxicated. In any case, for Japanese students it is dangerous to concentrate too much on the meaning of the words. One has to pay no less—or even more—attention to the feeling conveyed by the sounds, the rhythm, the assonance and alliteration, the incantation of the whole poem. The detailed reading of the poem is perhaps necessary as a preliminary to the "ah!" of wonder, when one steps back and surveys it as a whole—just as in "God's Grandeur" one comes at the end of the sestet to the poet's vision of the Holy Ghost at sunrise with his "ah! bright wings."

It was in this way, progressing now no longer just from word to word and line to line within one poem, but from poem to poem, at least the mature poems from "The Wreck" onwards, that I came to compose my two commentaries on "The Wreck" itself and then on the sonnets. I went on to collaborate with the "crazy photographer," whose worth I could now appreciate—as well as that of those other "crazy" Americans—in two further books on Hopkins, one entitled *Landscape and Inscape*, utilizing as many of his Hopkinsian photos as possible, and the other an edition of centenary essays called *Readings from the Wreck*. It was an appropriate means of atoning for my previous imputation of craziness to my American colleagues, or at least of associating myself with that imputation. Studying Hopkins may well be compared to playing with fire. Before one realizes it, one is on fire with the "fine frenzy" of Hopkins oneself. So beware!

Yes, I have not only followed, all unconsciously, in the footsteps of Hopkins, from school in London to college at Oxford, then in the Society of Jesus to St. Beuno's and Stonyhurst, to St. Aloysius Oxford and Farm Street London, to Mount St. Mary's and Liverpool and Leigh and even Glasgow with Inversnaid, not to mention Dublin and Clongowes and Monasterevin. But now in this land of exile, teaching Japanese students the classics of English, I confess that I too have composed what may be termed "terrible sonnets." Few of them have yet been published, and only in obscure places; nor do I anticipate their future publication. Amazed as I am at the similarities between myself and Hopkins, I have also to confess "that we two must be twain." We remain two different individuals—and he is the poet.

HOWARD W. FULWEILER

POSTMODERN INDETERMINACY
AND THE SEARCH FOR MEANING:
WHY HOPKINS MATTERS TO ME

"I think I like English, but I hate poetry" is one of the most common and most depressing locutions to be heard on the lips of contemporary undergraduates. Along with this widespread prejudice is a knee-jerk adverse judgment of anything Victorian (Victorians are conceived to be not only stuffy and sentimental but also misogynist). Often added to the list is a suspicion of anything thought to be religious, especially if it is dogmatic. The handicaps in teaching Hopkins are daunting. He is guilty on all counts: a Victorian Roman Catholic who has recently been accused of male chauvinism and who writes difficult poetry. Yet for many of us—not only older readers like myself who started to write about him over thirty years ago, but younger readers as well—Hopkins is one of the essential writers of our literature. He seems as fresh and challenging today as he did to the Kenyon critics of the forties.

Why? How can a writer who bears such a load of late twentieth-century negatives still "matter"? The answer—for me at any rate—lies in the near paradox that Hopkins, the poet of uncompromising faith in a definite "something," nonetheless writes poems as conflicted and as problematic as could be desired by the most committed New Critic of the past or Poststructuralist of today. His intellectual honesty is as uncompromising as his faith:

> Why do sinners' ways prosper? and why must
> Disappointment all I endeavour end?
>
> Wert thou my enemy, O thou my friend,
> How wouldst thou worse, I wonder, than thou dost
> Defeat, thwart me?

Although Hopkins' poetry is notorious for its powerful feeling, there is always a penetrating intellectual substance. When Hopkins writes a nature poem like "God's Grandeur," with its Wordsworthian sensitivity to the divine spirit within nature, the result is not simply an overflow of emotion recollected in tranquility, but a theological precision and intellectual ingenuity worthy of Donne or Herbert. There is always the surprise of the unexpected.

He is very much a man of his age, of course, as he writes his poems about saintly females, some of which are more than a little sentimental—the St. Dorothea poems, "St. Thecla," "Ad Mariam," "Rosa Mystica." Hopkins' obsession was shared by other nineteenth-century writers both in real life and in fiction: Dickens' Mary Hogarth and Little Nell, James's Minny Temple, Browning's Elizabeth Barrett and Pompilia, Mill's Harriet Taylor, Mark Twain's Susy, to name only a few. And yet his masterpiece, "The Wreck of the Deutschland," seems far from sentimentality. The poem, growing out of a particular nineteenth-century political struggle, Bismarck's *Kulturkampf* against the Church, as well as a spiritual crisis in the life of its author, is far from the saccharine treatment of other Victorian heroines. Despite an occasional touch of melodrama, "The Wreck" is not only the greatest experimental poem of the nineteenth century, but offers a moving and beautiful account of an historical event and its spiritual significance.

Hopkins' idiosyncratic unpredictability carried over into his personal life and opinions. Although he held generally conservative views, he was quite capable of sending his "red letter" to Bridges and quick to condemn Coventry Patmore's antisemitic attack on Disraeli. Hopkins reminded his friend that Disraeli was a Christian and, further, if his attack was "for race," his race could be "no reproach but a glory, for Christ was a Jew." Similarly, there is something touching in the lonely but courageous spirit who has given up family, friends, and worldly prospects for Roman Catholicism, but paradoxically feels isolated in Catholic Ireland where he can only rail at the Irish bishops who seem to behave as traitors to Queen Victoria and the British Empire.

Yet the important site of Hopkins' unpredictability is always in the poetry itself. Here we find a devoted priest who in his best known poem emphasizes not the loving, redeeming Christ, but Christ as a "dangerous" bird of prey. In the nearly suicidal "'No worst, there is none,'" we are left not only with the sickeningly vertiginous mountains of the mind but with a grammatically undecidable conclusion: "all / Life death does end and each day dies with sleep." Is the subject of the sentence "Life" or "death"? The terrifying vision of a world finally reduced only to "right" and "wrong" in "Spelt from Sibyl's Leaves" is open to suggesting on the one hand the need for simple moral rectitude, but on the other the shocking realization that such a reduced world is hell itself:

> reckon but, reck but, mind
> But thése two; wáre of a wórld where bút these | twó tell,
>   each off the óther; of a rack
> Where, selfwrung, selfstrung, sheathe- and shelterless, |
>   thóughts agáinst thoughts ín groans grínd.

Finally, in "(Carrion Comfort)," one of the darkest of the terrible sonnets, the speaker's struggle with God appears as one not only without a clear winner, but even without clear identities on either side:

> Cheer whom though? The hero whose heaven-handling
>   flung me, foot tród
> Me? or me that fought him? O which one? Is it each one?

It is small wonder that this sort of apparent indeterminacy has attracted interest from poststructuralist criticism, from J. Hillis Miller's deconstructionist emphasis on Hopkins' "overthought" and "underthought" to Michael Sprinker's bleak picture of a failed poet, betrayed by language itself.

Although the appearance of indeterminacy and the primacy of the problematic in Hopkins' poetry has in fact served as an attraction for some postmodern critics despite his heavy load of twentieth-century transgressions, these qualities are not, in my view, a sign of his ultimate concurrence in the worldview of Derrida, de Man, or Foucault. They reflect his intellectual complexity, but not conscious or unconscious sympathy with the nihilism implicit in some Postmodernist language theory. On the contrary, the clash of opposing forces in Hopkins results in the power described by Coleridge as polarity. As Owen Barfield explains it in *What Coleridge Thought*, polarity is a vital and generative interpenetration: "Where logical opposites are contradictory, polar opposites are generative of each other—and together generative of new product. Polar opposites exist by virtue of each other *as well as* at the expense of each other."

What is so rewarding then in the poetry of Hopkins in the present postmodern environment of disconnection, loss of language reference, even of the older certainties of personal identity, is a persistent honesty and courage, coupled with a penetrating intelligence and understanding of these problems. For Hopkins the difficult dilemmas of his poetry are "problematic" not because they are ultimately undecidable, but because of the determination, focused intellect, and committed spiritual energy required to solve them. Even in the depths of what now appears to have been a clinical depression, Hopkins cries out that "the lost are like this," but their condition is "worse." Hopkins matters because he was able to recognize the modern maze in which we seem to be lost, but refused to give up seeking the way out.

HOPKINS' POETRY: I CANNOT CHOOSE BUT HEAR

Personal mileposts, signs of the times:

1. Prematurely warm spring afternoon, March 1960. Through open windows the crack of bats, a coach's growl—baseball practice. Inside, a half dozen high-school seniors listen with half-concealed impatience to the Advanced Placement English teacher. (In 1960 all Advanced Placement courses met after regular school hours, like some kind of club.) The first poem for study today, he says, is by a Jesuit priest. Groans: we've already had "the poet-priest of the South," a Civil War-era poetaster blessedly forgotten, and Evelyn Waugh, and Joyce Kilmer (funny name for a guy), and T.S. (an even funnier name) Eliot, a poet so "Catholic" you could just about drop the "Anglo-." Intro to lit seems to mean, insofar as possible, an introduction to literature written by Catholics, and for restive eighteen-year-old males who already sense that there is a larger world awaiting us, the *reductio* is now almost *ad absurdum.*

And yet, as we unfold "God's Grandeur" together, and then "The Windhover," I have to admit, of course only to myself, that the intricacies of these poems tease my intellect, and their rhythm and sound begin to haunt my ear. Reluctant admiration, a feeling that there is something here that would repay future study. . . .

2. Winter 1963, a college Brit lit survey. After class I ask the teacher, in connection with finding a paper topic, if she can recommend a poet not on our syllabus who would appeal to someone who had liked the Metaphysicals two months earlier. Well, she says, there is this Victorian fellow Hopkins, said to be very baroque, not that she knows much about him, but what little she's read she has liked, even if he is a Catholic priest.

So then it becomes a matter of tasting the bitter fruit of the terrible sonnets, and working out a thesis on Augustinian elements in Hopkins' poetry, and finding again, in myself and in my instructor, that strange fascination with a poet who (in 1963) may not yet be fully canonical yet whom everybody seems to admire.

3. Spring 1967, a graduate course in Victorian poetry. The one day in the syllabus apportioned to Hopkins, a poet who I conclude must now be safely canonical because he is being taught by a person who despises him. Clever fellow, this Hopkins, the professor says, but a pitiable victim both of his own folly and the bungling of his Jesuit superiors.

Well, one doesn't have to accept all the verdicts of one's future dissertation director. But clearly there's not going to be any acceptable research project here either. So put a bracket around Hopkins, at least for now—come back to him later, after graduate school, maybe, sometime. . .

So the years pass, and other research projects intervene, take root, control one's agenda. One publishing project leads to another, and it's always easier to accept that next suggested or commissioned book or article than it is to start *de novo* with a project of one's own devising. Also, administrative tasks take their own toll, at times making any scholarly work impossible. Still, one does get to teach Hopkins in survey courses—just for a day or two, but that seems quite enough. . . .

4. Summer 1988. Leaving an administrative position with feelings akin to the young Wordsworth's: "Long months of ease and undisturbed delight / Are mine in prospect." A research leave has been granted for the following spring, to begin new work in a by-now-familiar area, the Pre-Raphaelites. But as I try to plan for the spring a recurrent thought keeps breaking in, disturbing concentration. I don't know where the thought comes from, but its message is insistent: "You don't really want to work on the Pre-Raphaelites any more," it says; "you've come to find them jejune, almost trivial. You really want to work on Hopkins." It's almost like the supernal voice which spoke to Augustine: "Take and read."

Why, now in 1988, take and read Hopkins?

Actually it's easier to say why *not* Hopkins. Based just on the first three mileposts—and here's where these mileposts also become signs of the times, otherwise they would not be worth recording—it is clear that Hopkins has now become a canonical poet. But it is equally clear that his poetry and the response to his poetry are both linked inextricably with his religious beliefs. Whether the reader's attitude toward these beliefs is admiring, like my high school teacher's, or amusedly detached, like my college instructor's, or overtly hostile, like my dissertation director's, the first thing anyone seems to notice and say about Hopkins has something to do with religion.

Understandable enough—after all, just about every poem has a connection to religious belief, and Hopkins himself said to Alexander Baillie, "Religion, you know enters very deep; in reality it is the deepest impression I have in speaking to people." But that makes for dangerous waters, first because you cannot evade Hopkins' religious questions, and therefore cannot evade asking your own either, and second because—no matter how you answer the questions—others will judge what you say publicly about Hopkins in terms of their own answers and the assumptions they make about yours. Americans claim that politics and religion are the two forbidden topics in public conversation because we cannot discuss them civilly, but the stricture really applies now only to religion.

Dangerous waters or not, the voice remains insistent, and in January 1989 I begin the semester's leave studying, not the familiar Pre-Raphaelites, but Hopkins. And Hopkins has been the principal focus of my scholarly work and my scholarly happiness since.

I say "happiness" because regarding Hopkins I hold firmly to what T.S. Eliot said of another poet: "His grave needs neither rose nor rue nor laurel; there is no imaginary justice to be done; we may think about him, if there be need for thinking, for our own benefit, not his." If we read poets for our own benefit, not theirs, we must constantly ask questions, if only of ourselves, about why we do what we do. What benefits *do* we gain, what pleasures can we experience? Unfashionable questions these days, but without satisfactory answers for them our work is aimless, our motives suspect.

Speaking only for myself, what keeps me motivated is Hopkins' singularity—that voice like no other voice, that startlingly original way of speaking which I recognize as clearly as I recognize the voice of a dear friend. There is no other voice quite like it. Hopkins himself spoke of the "bidding" quality of good verse, including his own, and when I read him I find that indeed I am bidden, I am engaged. Like Coleridge's mariner, "I cannot choose but hear"; I find the secret power of the poems lodged, like Yeats's Innisfree, in my deep heart's core. No catalog of the qualities of this voice—its alliterativeness, for example, or its inventiveness—could ever capture this singularity.

Along with Hopkins' originality I place special value on the declamatory power of his verse. No poetry more insistently demands to be heard rather than read. In fact Denis Donoghue has argued that the very function of a poem is to prolong our contemplation of its words: if there is truth in what he claims, then Hopkins is a canonical poet *par excellence*, for the very sound of his words demands and rewards the attention of his readers/listeners. I have occasionally had the experience of hearing a poet read in a language I do not speak or understand, yet still feeling the sound and the rhetorical power of the poetry coming through nonetheless (Russia's Andrei Voznesenski comes to mind): Hopkins strikes me as one of the few English poets who might pass the same test. Rhythm and sound combine in Hopkins' poetry to engrave certain phrases and lines on the tablet of the mind, so that for me his poems, or rather parts of his poems, are quite literally unforgettable.

And what of that second sign of the times, Hopkins' obsession with matters religious? Here is where other readers of Hopkins—such as the many contributors over the years to *The Hopkins Quarterly*—have had a deep impact on my reading of him. With the help of many readers whose angles of approach are so markedly different one from another, I have come to understand that, while religious themes may predominate (students see this right away), they function in Hopkins' poetry no differently than Pope's preoccupation with political and social life or even Arnold's preoccupation with personal loss and change. In other words, what speaks to my heart (Newman's *cor ad cor loquitur*) is the heart of another, of a friend. For and from our friends we try to understand and learn and accept, even where they most differ from us or where their values are not our values. What we do not try to do is judge, because we know the limits of our own wisdom and the passionate nature of our own preoccupations.

Why does Hopkins matter to me, the editors of the *Quarterly* are so good as to ask. No better answer than Dryden's: "Words are my stock, and wanting to commend / So great a poet, so good a friend."

TOM ZANIELLO

CATCHING UP WITH HOPKINS

> It was easy to see the cross-hatched lines of flow in the
> glaciers below the Gornergrat: they—or it, one should say—
> make a table or stage from which the mountains spring. . . .
> In this great glacier the water in the holes was really of
> Prussian, that is green blue.
> —Hopkins in Switzerland, Journals, July 24, 1868

I was an undergraduate biology major at Tufts University
when I first encountered Hopkins' poetry. Stalking planaria at
ponds in the Boston suburbs or digging up sea worms on North
Shore beaches were typical moments for those of us seduced by
invertebrate zoology. I read Hopkins' nature poetry in literature
classes, taken (at first) mainly to satisfy general studies
requirements. For reasons outside the scope of this essay I
became an English major, after briefly flirting with the idea of
double-majoring in biology and English, encouraged by the
example of one of my professors, Martin Green, who had himself
tried to bridge the "two cultures" gap then popularly associated
with C.P. Snow. Green's book *Science and the Shabby Curate of
Poetry* took its title from W.H. Auden: "Whenever I find myself in
a roomful of scientists I feel like a shabby curate." There was
never much doubt which group I identified with at first: I didn't
even want to be an unshabby curate.

Reading Hopkins became mildly obsessional, especially
when I turned to the *Journals*. I remember being especially taken
by his wide learning and dexterity in many different fields.
Studying Hopkins in the morning and tracing the evolution of
the lungfish in the afternoon seemed to be worth doing.

But I could not quite pull off a double major—those long
afternoons in the field and in the labs!—and I became a hardcore
lit major, treating my organic chemistry professor with a brief
apoplectic experience when he signed my drop-add slip

(Shakespeare in, organic chem out). A professor of animal behavior in the biology department was more sympathetic: he had always loved poetry, he told me. Years later I learned he became an expert in whale-songs.

The next year I developed an interest in James Joyce and Benedetto Croce and formulated a senior honors thesis on Hopkins' inscape, Joyce's epiphany, and Croce's "aesthetic fact" or moment of expression. When I added Virginia Woolf's moment of vision and Ezra Pound's ideogram, I developed the topic which eventually became the doctoral dissertation I completed at Stanford University in 1972, "The Moment of Perception in Nineteenth and Twentieth Century Literature."

It may have been because of my undergraduate training in science (and two years teaching science in the public schools), but it was primarily Hopkins the naturalist and journal-writer who appealed to me in the long run. I have written about Hopkins in the context of Victorian science and philosophy (*Hopkins in the Age of Darwin*) and almost always (but not exclusively) about his prose rather than his poetry.

Hopkins has remained one of the continuities of my life as a reader, scholar, and traveler. He has provided my family and myself with numerous opportunities to explore the vestiges of his Victorian world, his Roman Catholic milieu, and of course the British countryside. I had dedicated *Hopkins in the Age of Darwin* to members of my family who, as we travelled, took turns to ask, "Does this place have anything to do with Hopkins?" I have more recently undertaken an extensive study of his favorite architect, William Butterfield. Now I hear, "Does this church have anything to do with Butterfield?" And, "Isn't Virginia Woolf's house in Sussex too?"

Last year I followed the energetic Hopkins to numerous Swiss peaks, glaciers, lakes, waterfalls, museums, and shrines, impressed as ever with his curiosity about nature, art, and religion. For example, one day (July 6, 1868) he was admiring "The Crucified Christ in the Tomb," an amazing painting by Holbein the Younger in Basel's Kunstmuseum; two days later he climbed the Rigi (almost 6,000 feet) and noted the color of the

Vierwaldstättersee as "egg-blue, blue strongly modulated to green"; and the next day he visited the "stations [of the cross] painted all the way down" from the summit. And he still had twenty-four more days to go in Switzerland!

Over a hundred years later I'm still trying to catch up. And while the stations of the cross are gone from the slopes of the Rigi, I can attest that "in the glaciers below the Gornergrat" the "water in the holes" is still "really of Prussian, that is green blue."

PI   W.H. Gardner and N.H. MacKenzie, eds., *The Poems of Gerard Manley Hopkins*, 4th ed. rev. (London: Oxford University Press, 1970).

PII   Catherine Phillips, ed., *Gerard Manley Hopkins*. The Oxford Authors. (Oxford: Oxford University Press, 1986). This is the text used for quotations from Hopkins' poems in the present collection of essays.

PIII   Norman H. MacKenzie, ed., *The Poetical Works of Gerard Manley Hopkins* (Oxford: Clarendon Press, 1990).

J   Humphry House and Graham Storey, eds., *The Journals and Papers of Gerard Manley Hopkins* (London: Oxford University Press, 1959).

S   Christopher Devlin, S.J., ed., *The Sermons and Devotional Writings of Gerard Manley Hopkins* (London: Oxford University Press, 1959).

LI   C.C. Abbott, ed., *The Letters of Gerard Manley Hopkins to Robert Bridges*, 2nd imp. rev. (London: Oxford University Press, 1955).

LII   C.C. Abbott, ed., *The Correspondence of Gerard Manley Hopkins and Richard Watson Dixon*, 2nd imp. rev. (London: Oxford University Press, 1955).

LIII   C.C. Abbott, ed., *Further Letters of Gerard Manley Hopkins including his Correspondence with Coventry Patmore*, 2nd ed., rev. and enlarged (London: Oxford University Press, 1956).

EPM   Norman H. MacKenzie, ed., *The Early Poetic Manuscripts and Note-books of Gerard Manley Hopkins in Facsimile* (New York: Garland Publishing, 1989).

LPM   Norman H. MacKenzie, ed., *The Later Poetic Manuscripts of Gerard Manley Hopkins in Facsimile* (New York: Garland Publishing, 1991).

NOTES

[*The notes are keyed to page number and line number in the text of this volume.*]

4. 14. "Keel: red ochre stain used for marking sheep, cattle, timber, etc." [Author's note.]

12. 11. "Spring and Fall" (composed 1946, published 1947); "Spring" (1947/1953); "Three Motets on Poems of Gerard Manley Hopkins" (1973/1974) ("O Deus, ego amo te," "Oratorio [*sic*] Patris Condren," and "Thee, God, I come from"); "Prayer to Jesus" (1974/[n.d.]); and "Peace," in "Serenade on Five English Poems" (1975/1979).

16. 17. J, July 12, 1874.

38. 19. (Oxford: Blackwell, 1934), 52.

41. 8. 64.

43. 19. LI, 246.

44. 1. Notably the opening of "It is a beauteous evening, calm and free, / The holy time is quiet as a nun, / Breathless with adoration."

44. 9. Wordsworth, *Prelude* (1850), VI, 617-40.

45. 24. See my "Inscapes of Insomnia in Hopkins, Thomson and Lowell," in John S. North and Michael D. Moore, eds., *Vital Candle: Victorian and Modern Bearings in Gerard Manley Hopkins* (Waterloo: U of Waterloo P, 1984), 79-98.

46. 6. C.S. Lewis, *Letters to an American Lady*, ed. Clyde S. Kilby (Grand Rapids: Eerdmans, 1967), 11.

54. 7. J, 289.

54. 19. LI, 46.

54. 30. J, 86.

55. 20. J, 229.

56. 4. LI, 28.

74. 15. "Gravity and Grace in the Poetry of Gerard Manley Hopkins," forthcoming in *The Hopkins Quarterly*.

74. 18. Geoffrey Hartman accounted for this constricting notion in his reading a *horror vacui* as underlying the windhover's controlled flight. Cf. "The Dialectic of Perception," in *Hopkins: A Collection of Critical Essays*, ed. Geoffrey Hartman (Englewood Cliffs, NJ: Prentice-Hall, 1966), 117.

76. 17. *The Poetics of Space*, tr. Maria Jolas (Boston: Beacon P, 1969), ch. 8, "Intimate Immensity," 183-210.

76. 21. Bachelard, 104, 190, 184.

76. 24. *L'oiseau* (4th edition, 1858), 208 ff., cited by Bachelard, 100.

76. 33. Bachelard, 100-01, 101, 104.

77. 37. 211.

78. 15. I am grateful to Richard Austin and Cary Plotkin for pointing out to me that "my boughs" also suggests a configuration of the speaker as a tree—in addition to a bird (the call for the bird to "*under* be my boughs" expresses the speaker's wish to perch and nest on these boughs). This condensation of a bird and its perching/nesting place aligns with the prevalent metonymical connection between subjects and their spaces in Hopkins (birds and their actual as well as their aerial nests, for example), which this essay is about.

82. 25. LIII, 200-01.

82. 26. LIII, 117.

82. 29. J, 221, 235.

82. 30. J, 256.

82. 35. LI, 278; LIII, 177.

87. 5. This is from the poem "Love at First Sight," in Wislawa Szymborska's *Poems New and Collected: 1957-1997*, tr. Stanislaw Baranczak and Claire Cavanagh (New York: Harcourt Brace, 1998).

95. 3. The collection was published in 1996 by Deutsche Verlags-Anstalt, Stuttgart.

95. 10. J, 211; there is a German translation by Peter Waterhouse: *Journal (1866-1875) und fruehe Tagebuecher (1863-1866)* (Salzburg: Residenz-Verlag, 1997).

95. 27. I have written a short article on Hopkins in Uwe Böker, Horst Breuer and Rolf Breuer, eds., *Die Klassiker der englischen Literatur: Von Geoffrey Chaucer bis Samuel Beckett* (Düsseldorf: Econ, 1985), 104-07.

96. 12. Cf. Uwe Böker, "Hopkins in German Culture and Literature," *Studies* [Dublin] 87 (1998): 146-55.

96. 26. J, 133.

96. 33. J, 345.

97. 16. J, 164; Gardner, 110.

98. 4. Norman White, *Hopkins: A Literary Biography* (Oxford: Clarendon P, 1992), 152.

98. 13. J, 179, 181; Gardner, 116, 117.

98. 22. J, 230; Gardner, 128.

98. 29. J, 230; Gardner, 128.

99. 2. J, 233; Gardner, 129.

99. 6. For similarities between current nineteenth-century theories of language and Hopkins' poetic methods, cf. Michael Sprinker, "*A Counterpoint of Dissonance*": *The Aesthetics and Poetry of Gerard Manley Hopkins* (Baltimore: Johns Hopkins UP, 1980), ch. 2.

99. 18. Margaret Johnson, *Gerard Manley Hopkins and Tractarian Poetry* (Aldershot: Ashgate, 1997), 45.

99. 24. Cf. Linda Hutcheon, *A Poetics of Postmodernism: History, Theory, Fiction* (New York: Routledge, 1988), 59; Catherine Belsey, *Critical Practice* (London: Methuen, 1980), 4.

99. 33. Cf. Belsey, 44-46.

100. 13. Hugo von Hofmannsthal, "Ein Brief," in *Sämtliche Werke*, vol. 31: *Erfundene Gespräche und Briefe*, ed. Ellen Ritter (Frankfurt: S. Fischer, 1991), 48-49 (my translation). Cf. Walter Jens, *Statt einer Literatur-geschichte* (Düsseldorf: Artemis und Winkler, 1998, first pub. 1956), ch. 5, who sees in Hofmannsthal's "Brief" the classical statement of modernism (111ff.); cf. also Rolf Grimminger, "Der Sturz der alten Ideale: Sprachkrise, Sprachkritik um die Jahrhundertwende," in *Literarische Moderne: Europäische Literatur im 19. und 20. Jahrhundert*, ed. R. Grimminger, J. Murasov and J. Stückrath (Reinbek: Rowohlt, 1995), 169-200.

100. 16. Cf. Theodore Ziolkowski, "James Joyces Epiphanie und die Überwindung der empirischen Welt in der modernen Prosa," *Deutsche Vierteljahresschrift für Literatur und Geistesgeschichte* 35 (1961): 594-616.

101. 21. Kirsch, *Bodenlos*, 61 (my translation).

123. 15. 3 (1997), 458-72.

123. 24. This paper was published in full in *Rivista di Studi Vittoriani* 2 (1997), 51-71, and, in abbreviated form, in *Studies* 86 (1997): 135-44.

123. 29. This paper is unpublished.

123. 31: Forthcoming in *Rivista di Studi Vittoriani*.

125. 6. References to this book, abbreviated to *HSG*, along with citation of relevant pages, will serve to guide the reader to secondary sources not fully documented in this essay.

126. 18. *HSG*, 7.

126. 20. *HSG*, 7.

127. 3. Kathleen Welch has exhaustively detailed this in her *Electric Rhetoric: Classical Rhetoric, Oralism, and a New Literacy* (Cambridge: MIT P 1999).

127. 30. *HSG* 27.

128. 5. *HSG* 27.

128. 11. *HSG*, 8-11, 15.

128. 37. *HSG*, 9-10.

129. 3. *HSG*, 22.

129. 7. *HSG*, 22.

129. 16. *HSG*, 22.

173. 24. J, March 1871.

181. 16. *Hopkins Research Bulletin* 4 (1973): 6.

181. 22. LI, 92.

181. 26. LI, 46.

181. 28. LII, 23.

182. 29. These two examples are from the author's *The Uttermost Mark* (New York: University P of America, 1990), 143-44, 147.

183. 35. PIII, 380.

184. 4. Jayantha, *The Literary Criterion*, II.2 (1974): 26.

184. 7. Jayantha, 26.

184. 10. PIII, 383; *The Dragon in the Gate: Studies in the Poetry of G.M. Hopkins* (Berkeley: U of California P, 1968), 151.

184. 15. Peter Milward, S.J., *A Commentary on the Sonnets of G.M. Hopkins* (Chicago: Loyola UP, 1969), 37.

192. 15. 67.

192. 25. 167.

196. 7. I, 202-03, in John Morely, *The Life of William Ewart Gladstone* (New York: Macmillan, 1903).

197. 2. See my "Teaching Emotional Literacy," in *Writing and Healing: Toward an Informed Practice*, C. Anderson and M. MacCurdy, eds. (Urbana: NCTE, 2000), 314-15.

197. 20. "Victorian Religious Discourse as Palimpsest: Hopkins, Pusey, and Mueller," *Religion and the Arts* 5 (2001).

197. 32. "Centenary Celebrations of *The Wreck of the Deutschland*," *HQ* 4 (1977): 69-80; "Gerard Manley Hopkins," *Victorian Poetry* 23 (1985): 322-35.

198. 35. 67-78 in "Reader-Centered Criticism and Bibliotherapy: Hopkins and Selving," *Renascence* 41 (1989-90): 65-86.

199. 11. J, 26, 33.

213. 13. Peter Milward, S.J., and Raymond Schoder, S.J., *Landscape and Inscape* (London: Elek, 1975).

214. 25. George Steiner, *Real Presences* (Chicago: U of Chicago P, 1991), 9.

214. 28. William E. Buckler, ed., *Walter Pater: Three Major Texts: The Renaissance, Appreciations and Imaginary Portraits* (New York UP, 1986), 158.

219. 28. LI, 281.

219. 34. LIII, 63.

219. 37. LII, 20.

234. 23. S, 197; PII, 288-9.

234. 33. Karl Barth, *Church Dogmatics*, II/2, "The Doctrine of God" (Edinburgh: T.& T. Clark, 1957), 94ff.

235. 25. The point in the history of theology where a mystical exploration of the Trinitarian life and Christ's sacrifice comes to explicit and rich expression is in French 17th-century spiritual writings: Condren, Bérulle and their followers explore this with great rhetorical cogency. Was Hopkins familiar with this tradition? Again, to my knowledge, there is no evidence of it and I do not see it coming through in Marie Lataste's writings that Hopkins transcribed. In her account of the Annunciation, Lataste has Christ say, "Mon incarnation était le chef-d'oeuvre des manifestations extérieures de Dieu au ciel et sur la terre. Toute l'éternité Dieu a préparé cette oeuvre." (S, 330). But there is no explicit reference to sacrifice.

235. 30. "God, three-numberèd form" ("Deutschland"); "the Immortals of the eternal ring, / the Utterer, Utterèd, Uttering" ("Margaret Clitheroe").

258. 9. 156.

258. 15. Reprinted in G. Singh, ed., *The Critic as Anti-Philosopher* (London: Chatto and Windus, 1982), 97.

258. 24. *F. R. Leavis: A Life in Criticism*, (London: Allen Lane, 1995), 46.

259. 23. See Ronald Bush, "Eliot and Hopkins," in Richard Giles, ed., *Hopkins Among the Poets* (International Hopkins Association Monograph #3, 1985), 32-35.

272. 2. "A Reader's Life: Selving Through Reading Hopkins," *Saving Beauty* (New York: Garland, 1994).

287. 29. LI, 27-28.

287. 32. LIII, 342-43.

288. 29. J. Hillis Miller, *The Linguistic Moment: From Wordsworth to Stevens.* (Princeton: Princeton UP, 1985); Michael Sprinker, *"A Counterpoint of Dissonance": The Aesthetics and Poetry of Gerard Manley Hopkins* (Baltimore: Johns Hopkins UP, 1980).

289. 9. Owen Barfield, *What Coleridge Thought* (Middletown, CT: Wesleyan UP, 1971), 3.

Lionel Adey fell in love with Hopkins' poems during his war service, between spells at Birmingham University, and taught them in English high schools (1950-67) and at the University of Victoria, British Columbia. He wrote on them for *Vital Candle* (1984), *The Hopkins Quarterly*, and other journals, and since 1981 has served on *The Hopkins Quarterly*'s Board of Scholars.

Michael E. Allsopp, Academic Dean at Presentation College in Aberdeen, South Dakota, co-edited (with Michael Sundermeier) *Gerard Manley Hopkins: New Essays on His Life, Writing, and Place in English Literature* (1989) and (with David A. Downes) *Saving Beauty: Further Studies in Hopkins* (1994). He has written essays and reviews for *Chicago Studies*, *Christianity and Literature*, and other journals.

Brian Arkins is Associate Professor of Classics at the National University of Ireland, Galway. His six books of criticism include *Sexuality in Catullus* and *Builders of My Soul: Greek and Roman Themes in Yeats*, and he has published over one hundred journal articles.

Richard Austin trained for three years and spent ten years working in England as an actor, on stage and in television. After a series of life-altering events, he became a healer and teacher, primarily using massage and aromatherapy. He has now integrated the creative with the therapeutic, and divides his time between writing/performing and healing. He is married, with three children.

Uwe Böker, born in northern Germany in 1940, studied English and German at the University of Regensburg. A Visiting Professor at Tübingen, Siegen, Munich, Mainz, Freiburg, Passau, Göttingen, and Northern Iowa, he has been since 1993 Full Professor at the Technical University of Dresden. He has written, co-written, and co-edited books and monographs, as well as over sixty essays on English, American, French, and German authors.

Ewa Borkowska is Professor of English literature and literary theory at the Institute of British and American Culture and Literature at the University of Silesia in Poland. She has published two books—*Philosophy and Rhetoric: A Phenomenological Study of G.M. Hopkins' Poetry* and *From Donne to Celan: Logo(theo)logical Patterns in Poetry*—and articles on Hopkins, European modernism, cultural studies, and other writers.

Jerome Bump, of the University of Texas at Austin, is the author of *Gerard Manley Hopkins* (1982) and over fifty articles and chapters, primarily on Hopkins. He edited *Gerard Manley Hopkins: A Centenary Celebration* (1989) and *Texas Studies in Language and Literature* (1986-92), and serves on the advisory boards of *Victorian Poetry* and *The Hopkins Quarterly*.

Mariaconcetta Costantini is Associate Professor at the University "G. d'Annunzio" of Pescara, Italy. She is the author of *Poesia e sovversione: Christina Rossetti, Gerard Manley Hopkins* (2000) and has published articles on Edith Wharton, Elizabeth Gaskell, G.M. Hopkins, Christina Rossetti, Thomas Hardy, Angela Carter, Raymond Carver, Chinua Achebe, and Ben Okri.

James Finn Cotter, Professor of English at Mount Saint Mary College in Newburgh, New York, is the author of *Inscape: The Christology and Poetry of Gerard Manley Hopkins* (1972) and articles on Hopkins, Chaucer, Sidney, Salinger, and modern poetry. President of the International Hopkins Association, he has also published poetry and translated *The Divine Comedy* (2000).

Renzo D'Agnillo teaches English language and literature at the University "G. d'Annunzio" of Pescara, and translation at the Translators and Interpreters School in Vasto. The author of *Bruce Chatwin: Settlers, Exiles and Nomads* (2001), he has done articles on D.H. Lawrence, Woolf, Hardy, Yeats, Hopkins, Shelley, Dante, Christina Rossetti, and Desmond Egan. He co-authored a volume of essays on Irish poetry, and translated two books of literature.

Sean Davidson is a doctoral candidate at McMaster University, currently studying 17th-century English literature. He has forthcoming articles in *The Hopkins Quarterly* and *Victorian Poetry* on "Reading 'the unshapeable shock night': Symbolic Action and The Wreck of G.M. Hopkins" and "Towards a Pragmatic Poetics: The Convergence of Form, Act, and Ontology in G.M. Hopkins' 'The Leaden Echo and the Golden Echo.'"

David Anthony Downes is Professor Emeritus of English at California State University, Chico. Among his books are *Victorian Portraits: Hopkins and Pater* (1965), *The Great Sacrifice: Studies in Hopkins* (1983), *Hopkins' Sanctifying Imagination* (1985), *The Ignatian Personality of Gerard Manley Hopkins* (1990), and *Hopkins' Achieved Self* (1996), and he has published articles and reviews in *Victorian Poetry*, *Studies in the Literary Imagination*, and other journals.

Desmond Egan is a full-time writer who has published fifteen books of poems, one of prose, and two translations of Greek plays. His books have appeared in fifteen languages, and Hugh Kenner and Brian Arkins have edited critical studies of his work. He is Artistic Director of the G.M. Hopkins Summer School in Ireland, and the subject of a documentary video published in the United States.

Kazuyoshi Enozawa is deputy president of Honan College in Japan and Professor Emeritus of English at Keio University. He has degrees from Tokyo Kyoiku University (B.A., 1959; M.A., 1962), taught at Keio University from 1969-99, and co-authored books and published articles on Thomas More, Shakespeare, Milton, and G.M. Hopkins.

Joseph J. Feeney, S.J., is Professor of English at Saint Joseph's University in Philadelphia and Co-Editor of *The Hopkins Quarterly*. He has discovered one poem, one fragment, four letters, and one short story by Hopkins, publishing them in *TLS: The Times Literary Supplement* and (in critical editions, some forthcoming) *The Hopkins Quarterly*. He has done over one hundred essays on Hopkins, British and American authors, and Jesuit education.

Francis L. Fennell is Professor of English at Loyola University Chicago. A specialist in Victorian literature and rhetorical theory, he has written several articles on Hopkins and edited two volumes, *The Fine Delight: Centenary Essays on Gerard Manley Hopkins* (1989) and *Rereading Hopkins: Selected New Essays* (1996). His latest project is a book on the reception of Hopkins' poetry by non-academic readers.

Ernest J. Ferlita, S.J., Professor of Drama at Loyola University New Orleans, is the author of *The Uttermost Mark* (1990), a book about the dramatic criticism and dramatic works of Gerard Manley Hopkins. His play *Ma-Fa* was the second-place winner of The International Competition of Religious Drama for the year 2000.

John Ferns, Professor of English at McMaster University, Hamilton, Ontario, has published books on A.J.M. Smith (1979), Lytton Strachey (1988), and F.R. Leavis (2000). He has also published five books of poetry, and co-edited *The Essays of George Whalley* (1985) and *The Poetry of Lucy Maud Montgomery* (1987).

Howard W. Fulweiler, Professor Emeritus of English at the University of Missouri–Columbia, is the author of *Letters from the Darkling Plain: Language and the Grounds of Knowledge in the Poetry of Arnold and Hopkins* (1972), *Here a Captive Heart Busted: The Sentimental Journey of Modern Literature* (1993), and numerous essays on 19th-century fiction, poetry, culture, and scientific history.

Peter Gale is a British actor, singer, writer, and director, recently seen in the London premieres of Athol Fugard's *The Captain's Tiger* and Gershwin's *Of Thee I Sing*. He played Mr. Victor in the Spielberg film *The Empire of the Sun* and has acted in many TV productions such as *Hamlet*, *Sense and Sensibility*, and *The Darling Buds of May*.

Bruno Gaurier has been for 35 years involved in the French and European disability movement. Once a musician and singer, he was always close to poetry and literature. He has published a book on semiotics (1971), two novels (1996, 1999), two "Carnets de voyage" (1992, 1993), a book of essays (1998), collections of poetry, and diverse articles, and has translated G.M. Hopkins (1998), Thomas Bernhard (1993), A.E. Housman (1999), and Desmond Egan (2000).

Ron Hansen is the author most recently of the novels *Mariette in Ecstasy*, *Atticus*, and *Hitler's Niece*, and of the non-fiction collection *A Stay Against Confusion: Essays on Faith and Fiction*. He is the Gerard Manley Hopkins, S.J., Professor in the Arts and Humanities at Santa Clara Univesity.

Seamus Heaney was born in County Derry in Northern Ireland. *Death of a Naturalist*, his first book, appeared in 1966, and since then he has published poetry, criticism, and translations which have established him as one of the leading poets of his generation. He has twice won the Whitbread Book of the Year, for *The Spirit Level* in 1996 and *Beowulf* in 1999. In 1995 he was awarded the Nobel Prize for Literature.

Alan Heuser, born in Montreal and educated at McGill (M.A., 1949) and Harvard (Ph.D., 1953), taught at Princeton (1952-54) and McGill (1954-92). Retired as Professor of English, he now lives in Vancouver. He wrote *The Shaping Vision of Gerard Manley Hopkins* (1958) and later edited three selections of Louis MacNeice for the Clarendon Press, Oxford (1987, 1990, 1993).

Lesley Higgins, Associate Professor of English at York University, Toronto, has published numerous essays on Hopkins and Walter Pater. Her teaching and research interests include modernism and gender studies, poetry, and textual studies. *The "Cult of Ugliness": Gendered Politics in Modernist Aesthetics* is forthcoming from St. Martin's Press.

Tomiko Hirata, S.P.C., was born in Fukuoka, near Nagasaki, and belongs to the Sisters of St. Paul de Chartres (France). A professor in the English Department at Shirayuri College in Tokyo, she teaches The Bible and English and American Literature. She is also involved in The Hopkins Society of Japan, Tokyo Area, as part of her ongoing studies of Hopkins and his poetry.

Margaret Johnson studied in the United States and New Zealand before receiving her doctorate from The University of Western Australia. She has published books and articles on various Victorian topics, including Hopkins and his circle of friends.

Joaquin Kuhn teaches English at St. Michael's College, University of Toronto. He has composed games and a book of palindrome puzzles, *Rats Live on No Evil Star* (1981), written on Hopkins and founded a writers' group. He co-edits *HQ* and promotes knowledge of Hans Paasche and his Germany of 1910-20 by translating Paasche's anti-militarist, reform works and satiric-ironic travel and war narratives. He owes Irish philately an account of his discovery of the rarest ever Irish stamp at the post office.

Maria Lichtmann is the author of *The Contemplative Poetry of Gerard Manley Hopkins* (1989) as well as numerous articles on the mystics and on Hopkins. She has just completed a book on poetry and prayer in Hopkins. She and her husband reside in Boone, North Carolina.

Jeffrey B. Loomis is Professor of English at Northwest Missouri State University and the author of *Dayspring in Darkness: Sacrament in Hopkins*. He has also written articles on dramatists ranging from Shakespeare, Goethe, and Strindberg to Albee, Zindel, Sondheim, and Howe.

Norman H. MacKenzie, Professor Emeritus of English at Queen's University in Kingston, Ontario, edited *The Poetical Works of Gerard Manley Hopkins* for the Clarendon Press (1990), complemented by *The Early Poetic Manuscripts and Note-books of Gerard Manley in Facsimile* and *The Later Poetic Manuscripts of Gerard Manley*

Hopkins in Facsimile (Garland, 1989, 1991). He also published *Hopkins* and *A Reader's Guide to Gerard Manley Hopkins.*

Paul Mariani, who taught at the University of Massachusetts/Amherst over thirty years, now holds a Chair in English at Boston College. He published biographies of William Carlos Williams, John Berryman, Robert Lowell, and Hart Crane; five books of poetry; and book-length studies of Hopkins and others. Viking has recently published his *Thirty Days*, a daybook on his experience of the *Spiritual Exercises* of St. Ignatius. He is now writing a biography of Hopkins.

Franco Marucci taught English at the University of Siena and, since 1987, at the University of Venice "Ca' Foscari," where he has headed the Department of English and German Studies and the Institute of English. He has organized international conferences, lectured widely, and served on four editorial boards. He published books on Dylan Thomas and on Hopkins, and is currently working on a history of Victorian literature from 1830 to 1870.

Francis X. McAloon, S.J., has recently completed a doctorate at the Graduate Theological Union, Berkeley, California, in the academic discipline of Christian Spirituality, with an interdisciplinary dissertation on Hopkins' poetry from the perspective of Ricoeurian hermeneutics, theological aesthetics, and new-historicist literary criticism. He now teaches at Santa Clara University.

John McDade, S.J., studied French literature at Oxford and theology at London and Edinburgh. He was Editor of *The Month* from 1986 to 1995, and has been teaching Systematic Theology at Heythrop College, University of London, since 1985, becoming Principal in 1999.

Robert F. McGovern is Professor Emeritus at the University of the Arts in Philadelphia, where he studied and taught. He is active in painting, printmaking, and sculpting, and has executed numerous commissions for churches, schools, and hospitals throughout the United States. Additionally, his works are in many private and public collections.

Peter Milward, S.J., an English Jesuit, came to Japan from Oxford in 1954, taught at Sophia University, Tokyo, from 1962 to 1996, and is now Professor Emeritus at Sophia. He has published widely on Shakespeare, Hopkins, etc., and edits *Hopkins Research*.

Jude V. Nixon, Associate Professor at Oakland University, is the author of *Gerard Manley Hopkins and His Contemporaries: Liddon, Newman, Darwin, and Pater*. He has written many book chapters, and his essays appear in major Victorian journals. He serves on the editorial board of *Victorian Poetry*, has guest-edited *Religion and the Arts* on Victorian Religious Discourse, and since 1995 has reviewed Victorian poetry for *The Year's Work in English Studies*.

Leonora Rita V. Obed, a specialist in Anglo-Irish and Victorian literature, wrote a dissertation on Gerard Manley Hopkins and Oscar Wilde at the University of Edinburgh. Born in Manila, raised in New Jersey, and educated at the Universities of Saint Joseph's, Toronto, and Edinburgh, she was shortlisted for the David Wong Fellowship, and is currently working on a novel about the English occupation of Manila and on a play about Philadelphia.

Walter J. Ong, S.J., University Professor Emeritus at Saint Louis University, was twice a Guggenheim fellow, a frequent visiting professor and lecturer in America, Europe, East Asia, and Africa, and president of the Modern Language Association. He is known throughout the world for his many books (*Orality and Literacy* has been translated into twelve languages), and has contributed to scores of other books and to both learned and popular periodicals.

Catherine Phillips is a Fellow of Downing College and a Newton Trust Lecturer in the Faculty of English, University of Cambridge. Her work on Hopkins includes the Oxford Authors *Gerard Manley Hopkins*, his *Selected Letters*, and *Selected Poetry* in the Oxford World's Classics series. She has also written *Robert Bridges: A Biography*, done an edition of W.B. Yeats for the Cornell Yeats series, and co-edited, with A.J. Smith, a book on John Donne.

Cary Plotkin received his early education about 75 miles northeast of Inversnaid, and took his B.A. at Yale and his Ph.D. at Columbia. A former Woodrow Wilson Fellow, Fellow at the Ludwig-Maximilians University (Munich), and guest professor at the University of Caen (Normandy), he now teaches at Barnard College. He is the author of *The Tenth Muse: Victorian Philology and the Genesis of the Poetic Language of Gerard Manley Hopkins* and essays on Victorian poetry.

Gerald Roberts was born in South Wales, educated locally at the University of Wales, and has a teaching diploma from Oxford. He taught at Stonyhurst College from 1963 to 1985. Now semi-retired in East Sussex, he still examines "A" level English students. His last book is *Gerard Manley Hopkins* in Macmillan's Literary Lives series (1994).

Ned Rorem, born in Richmond, Indiana, and now living in New York City, won the Pulitzer Prize in 1976 for his orchestral suite "Air Music." In 1998 he completed "Evidence of Things Not Seen," a 36-song cycle based on the work of 24 poets that prompted *Time Magazine* to call him the world's greatest living composer of song. He has written fifteen books and diaries, and in January 2000 was elected president of the American Academy of Arts and Letters.

Rachel Salmon Deshen teaches English literature and literary theory at Bar-Ilan University in Israel. Her main research interest is religious poetry. She has published on Henry James, Jewish hermeneutics, and the poetry of Gerard Manley Hopkins. At present she is co-authoring a book with Kinereth Meyer on the contribution of a Jewish hermeneutic approach to the reading of the poetry of Hopkins.

Kunio Shimane, Professor of English Literature at Nagoya City University in Japan, is a reader for *The Hopkins Quarterly*, a contributor to *Readings of the Wreck* (1976), and author of *The Poetry of G.M. Hopkins: The Fusing Point of Sound and Sense* (1984). He writes also on Shakespeare, Milton, Keats, Tennyson, and others, and is currently collaborating with Desmond Egan on a book about his poems.

Alison G. Sulloway, Professor Emerita at the Virginia Polytechnic Institute and State University, received the Ansley award for her dissertation at Columbia University, and has published *Gerard Manley Hopkins and the Victorian Temper*, *Jane Austen and the Province of Womanhood*, and various essays on Hopkins. Now in her eighties, she is currently at work on "Hopkins and the Four Elements," a short essay.

R.K.R. Thornton, recently retired from Professorship at Birmingham University, had published books on Hopkins and on the Decadents, and edited the work of Clare, Hilliard, and Ivor Gurney. He is currently working on editions of Ernest Dowson. Instead of a list of works, he adds, "I usually prefer the verse,

'How curious to know Kelsey Thornton;
He is so exceedingly tall.
His life is of interest to no one
And he has no achievements at all.'"

Donald Walhout was born in Muskegon, Michigan, and earned a B.A. from Adrian College. His advanced degrees are from Yale. He taught philosophy at Rockford College from 1953 to 1992, and is now emeritus. He has done two books on Hopkins, plus articles in several anthologies and in *The Hopkins Quarterly*.

Eynel Wardi is a lecturer in the English Department of the Hebrew University of Jerusalem. She is the author of *Once below a Time: Dylan Thomas, Julia Kristeva, and Other Speaking Subjects*. She has written on "Gravity and Grace in the Poetry of G.M. Hopkins," and on Dickens, Borges, and Marguerite Duras, and pubished a Hebrew translation of *The Europeans* by Henry James.

Nick Weber, an American actor, had theater and the performing arts as his first loves in college, but was early drawn to the richness of Hopkins' language. Now a professional actor and sometime teacher, he has developed a one-man recital/lecture on the poetry of Hopkins, "Earth, Sweet Earth," which he performs throughout the United States.

Norman White wrote M.Phil. and Ph.D. theses on Hopkins, lived in associated places (Highgate, Liverpool, North Wales, Dublin), co-founded the Hopkins Society in London, was the first editor of the *Hopkins Research Bulletin*, and published many articles and three books on him: the award-winning *Hopkins: A Literary Biography* (Oxford), *Hopkins in Wales* (Poetry Wales Press), and the forthcoming *Hopkins in Ireland* (University College Dublin Press).

Tom Zaniello is Professor of English and Director of the Honors Program at Northern Kentucky University. He has published *Hopkins in the Age of Darwin* (Iowa), and his current research interests include Hopkins' favorite architect, William Butterfield, about whom an essay will appear in a book-in-progress titled "The Divided Victorian Church."

Sjaak Zonneveld was born in The Hague, Holland, where he lectures at the Institute of Higher European Studies. He wrote *The Random Grim Forge: A Study of Social Ideas in the Work of Gerard Manley Hopkins*, and with a colleague has recently published a book entitled *Europeans in The Hague*. Besides his work on Hopkins, he has written seventeen books for children, and numerous articles on educational psychology, history, and the visual arts.